Predicting the Next President

Predicting the Next President

The Keys to the White House

2012 EDITION

Allan J. Lichtman

ROWMAN & LITTLEFIELD PUBLISHERS, INC.
Lanham • Boulder • New York • Toronto • Plymouth, UK

Published by Rowman & Littlefield Publishers, Inc.
A wholly owned subsidiary of The Rowman & Littlefield Publishing
Group, Inc.
4501 Forbes Boulevard, Suite 200, Lanham, Maryland 20706
http://www.rowmanlittlefield.com

Estover Road, Plymouth PL6 7PY, United Kingdom

British Library Cataloguing in Publication Information Available

Library of Congress Control Number: 2007941760

ISBN: 978-1-4422-1211-4 (pbk. alk. paper)
ISBN: 978-1-4422-1212-1 (electronic)

♾ ™ The paper used in this publication meets the minimum requirements of
American National Standard for Information Sciences—Permanence of Paper
for Printed Library Materials, ANSI/NISO Z39.48-1992.

Printed in the United States of America

Contents

Introduction

Since the disputed American presidential contest of 2000, citizens of the world's oldest ongoing democracy have keenly focused on assuring that their votes are fully and fairly counted in elections. In 2000, for the first time since Benjamin Harrison defeated Grover Cleveland in 1888, the winner of the popular vote lost the Electoral College tally that decides presidential elections in the United States. Vice President Al Gore, the Democratic nominee, prevailed in the popular vote over his Republican opponent, Texas Governor George W. Bush, by some 544,000 votes, exceeding the nationwide margin of victory for John F. Kennedy over Richard Nixon in 1960 or Richard Nixon over Hubert Humphrey in 1968. Yet George W. Bush carried the Electoral College and became president-elect when the United States Supreme Court halted a vote recount in Florida, with Bush leading Gore by 537 votes out of nearly 6 million votes cast in the state. Bush earned all twenty-five of Florida's Electoral College votes and a narrow Electoral College majority of 271 votes to 266 votes for Gore.

The circumstances of Bush's eyelash victory in Florida raised serious questions about whether the state's election had accurately reflected the intent of Florida's voters. In an election decided by fewer than 600 votes, election officials in Florida rejected some 180,000 ballots as invalid—nearly 3 percent of all votes cast in the presidential election. Most rejected ballots were not under-votes in which no apparent vote was tallied for president, but over-votes in which more than one vote for president appeared to have been recorded on the ballot. Ballot rejection fell with special force on African-American voters. Election officials discarded more than one out of every ten votes cast by African-

Americans, compared to less than one out of every fifty votes cast by whites. If the rate of ballot rejection had been equal for blacks and whites, more than 50,000 additional ballots cast by blacks would have been counted in the election.[1]

In the wake of the 2000 election, Florida upgraded its voting system by replacing outmoded punch card technology with the new electronic voting machines. But punch cards remain in use in other states, including the crucial swing state of Ohio, and computer scientists have raised questions about the security and verifiability of votes cast using electronic technology. Congress recognized the importance of protecting the integrity of American democracy when it passed the Help America Vote Act of 2002, which set up a new Electoral Assistance Commission to help the states reform their electoral systems. The work of the Commission is ongoing and will continue for many years, especially given the limited funding available and America's decentralized electoral system, where procedures differ across states and among localities within states. In 2005, former President Jimmy Carter and Republican James S. Baker III formed the independent Commission on Electoral Reform organized under the auspices of American University's Center for Democracy and Electoral Management. In Carter's words, "We will try to define an electoral system for the twenty-first century that will make Americans proud again."[2]

This renewed focus on the American democratic process highlights the importance of understanding—not just mechanically, but also substantively—how elections really work in the United States, especially America's crucial quadrennial contests for its president, the most powerful leader in today's world. A properly functioning democracy demands not only fair and accurate systems for voting, but also a candid and wide-ranging exploration of crucial issues and ideas by the presidential candidates and their parties. Yet every four years Americans are subjected to shallow and even offensive campaigns for president. Nothing changes from one election to the next, because the media, the candidates, the pollsters, and the consultants are complicit in the idea that elections are exercises in manipulating voters and in giving us negative campaigns, bland and scripted lines, and meaningless debates. We will not reform our politics and get meaningful participation by the American people until we realize that presidential elections turn on how well an administration has governed the country, not on how well candidates have performed in the campaign.

If candidates and the media could come to understand that governing, not campaigning, counts in presidential elections, we could have a new kind of presidential politics. Presidential aspirants could abandon attack ads and instead articulate forthrightly and concretely what Americans should be accomplishing during the next four years. Candidates could bring the public back into presidential elections by using campaigns to build grassroots support for the policy agenda they would follow if elected president. And incumbent presidents could prepare for upcoming elections by focusing on the stewardship of the country, not the politics of campaigns.

The study of history shows that a pragmatic American electorate chooses a president according to the performance of the party holding the White House, as measured by the consequential events and episodes of a term—economic boom and bust, foreign policy successes and failures, social unrest, scandal, and policy innovation. If the nation fares well during the term of the incumbent party, that party wins another four years in office; otherwise, the challenging party prevails. Nothing that a candidate has said or done during a campaign, when the public discounts everything as political, has changed his prospects at the polls. Debates, advertising, television appearances, news coverage, and campaign strategies—the usual grist for the punditry mills—count for virtually nothing on Election Day. The only issues that matter are the ones for which the results are already in before the campaign begins. Thus, the fate of an incumbent party is largely in its own hands; there is little that the challenging party can do through politics as usual to influence the outcome of a presidential election

This new vision of American politics is based on The Keys to the White House, a prediction system based on the study of every presidential election from 1860 to 2008. This system also provides insight into party prospects for the 2012 election at a time when polls forecast upcoming election results about as accurately as the flipping of coins. I first developed the Keys system in 1981, in collaboration with Vladimir Keilis-Borok, a world renowned authority on the mathematics of prediction models. The system shows that it is possible to predict well in advance the outcomes of presidential elections from indicators that primarily track the performance and strength of the party holding the White House.

The Keys are thirteen diagnostic questions that are stated as propositions favoring re-election of the incumbent party. When five or fewer of these propositions are false, or turned against the party holding the White House, that party wins another term in office. When six or more are false, the challenging party wins. The Keys indicate incumbent party success or failure long before the polls or any other forecasting models are of any value. Unlike many models developed by political scientists, the Keys include no polling data, but are based on the big picture of how well the party in power and the country are faring prior to an upcoming election. In addition, the Keys do not presume that voters are driven by economic concerns alone. Voters are less narrow-minded and more sophisticated than that; they decide presidential elections on a wide-ranging assessment of the performance of incumbent parties, all of which are reflected in one or more Keys.

Retrospectively, the Keys account for the results of every presidential election from 1860 through 1980, much longer than any other prediction system. Prospectively, the Keys predicted well ahead of time the popular-vote winners of every presidential election from 1984 through 2008. They called Vice President George H. W. Bush's victory in the spring of 1988 when he trailed Mike Dukakis by nearly twenty points in the polls and was being written off by the pundits. The Vice President defied the polls and the pundits, not because he discovered negative ads or refurbished his image, but because voters ratified the performance of the Reagan administration—four years of prosperity, the defusing of the Cold War, and a scandal that faded away. In 1992, George H. W. Bush lost his chance for a second term, as the Keys predicted, when a sour economy and a lack of domestic accomplishment tarnished his record as president. The Keys predicted President George W. Bush's 2004 re-election in April of 2003, a year and a half before a contest that pollsters found too close to call right up to election eve. As a sitting president with no prospective challenger in his own party or a serious third-party competitor, Bush's mixed record of accomplishment at home and abroad was sufficient to anticipate in his victory in 2004.[3]

Although President Bush was not on the ticket in 2008, the fate of his would-be successor in the Republican Party, Arizona Senator John McCain, depended upon the president's performance in his second term. As early as February 2006, the Keys to the White House correctly forecast that voters would dismiss the incumbent Republicans. The forecast pointed to the failed responses of the Bush administration to the domestic and foreign policy challenges of the times. It also noted the structural disadvantages facing the incumbent Republicans in 2008, including the lack of a sitting president running for reelection and likely major losses in the midterm elections. In the 2012 presidential election, as the Keys first indicated in a forecast published at the beginning of 2010, the Democrats should retain enough positive indicators to secure President Barack Obama's reelection, regardless of the identity of the opposition nominee. The 2012 forecast poses an especially stern challenge to the Keys to the White House. The Keys are predicting Obama's reelection even in the midst of one of the worst sustained economic disasters in the United States since the Great Depression of the 1930s. Even if Obama loses both the short-term economy key 5 and the long-term economy key 6, he would still be a predicted winner in 2012, according to the Keys.[4]

The Keys to the White House focus on national concerns such as economic performance, policy initiatives, social unrest, presidential scandal, and successes and failures in foreign affairs. Thus, they predict only the national popular vote and not the vote within individual states. Indeed, no system could have predicted the 537 vote margin for George Bush in Florida that decided the 2000 election. In three elections since 1860, where the popular vote diverged from the Electoral College tally—1876 (when Democrat Samuel J. Tilden won the popular vote, but lost in the Electoral College to Republican Rutherford B. Hayes), 1888, and 2000—the Keys accurately predicted the popular vote winner. Based on the historical odds since 1860, the chances are better than twelve to one that the popular and Electoral College vote will converge in any given election. However, these odds presume continuity over time in the relationship between popular and Electoral College votes. Some analysts have suggested, however, that this relationship may have changed given the sharp division in America between Republican "red states" and Democratic "blue states."

To the tables in Chapter 2, based on 34 elections from 1860 to 1992, we can now add four additional elections—1996 through 2008—for a larger sample of 38 elections, including 7 (1984–2008) in which I reported advance forecasts based on the Keys to the White House. These predictions, all of which correctly anticipated the popular vote results, ratify the logic of the keys as drawn from the prior analysis of American presidential elections. The Table below, reports the turning of the keys for all 7 elections in which the Keys forecast results, not retrospectively, but prior to an upcoming election.

Although the Keys system as developed for American elections cannot be mechanically applied to other political systems, the Keys' big lessons have worldwide implications as democracy spreads to previously autocratic societies. As demonstrated by the uprisings that spread across the autocratic Arab world in 2011, ordinary people are ready and willing to risk their lives and safety to shape the political destiny of their lands. Electoral experience in the United States, as gauged by the Keys, suggests that leaders who gain power in democratic societies, whether established or developing, would be well advised to focus on governance, not politics. As democracy inevitably spreads across the globe in the twenty-first century, world leaders should take heed that those who serve their people well will likely succeed politically in free and fair elections. Those who fail the people will likely fail at the polls as well, no matter how brilliant their consultants or how clever their campaigns.

TABLE I.1
How the Keys Turned: 1996–2008
The Incumbent Party Won the Popular Vote, 1996–2004
The Challenging Party Won the Popular Vote, 2008

	1	2	3	4	5	6	7	8	9	10	11	12	13	Total
1996	X	O	O	X	O	O	X	O	O	O	X	X	O	5
2000	O	O	X	O	O	O	X	O	X	O	X	X	O	5*
2004	O	O	O	O	O	X	X	O	O	X	O	X	O	4
2008	X	O	X	O	X	X	X	O	O	X	X	X	X	9

*Electoral vote did not coincide with popular-vote results.

Chapter 1

Logic of the Keys

How Presidential Elections Really Work

How is it possible to predict the winners of presidential elections without recourse to the polls—sometimes in direct contradiction of them—and without knowing how the campaign would be conducted, what the salient issues would be, or how candidates would fare in televised debates?

The answer is that presidential elections do not work the way most people think they do. Contrary to assumptions made by pollsters, pundits, and political experts who track presidential campaigns, our quadrennial contests for executive power are not contests at all. They do not pit one candidate's popularity, leadership ability, positions on the issues, or vision against another's. They do not turn on the party loyalties of voters, their devotion to liberal or conservative ideologies, or their perception of which candidate is closer to the center of the political spectrum. The electorate does not simply vote its pocketbook, retaining the party in power in good times and throwing the rascals out in bad. Elections certainly are not horse races in which candidates surge ahead or fall behind as they sprint toward Election Day.

Presidential elections are primarily referenda on the performance of the incumbent administration during the previous four years. That is the verdict disclosed by the Keys to the White House, a diagnostic prediction system developed through the application of mathematical procedures to the study of presidential elections since 1860. This unique method of historical inquiry reveals what events past and present really have in common, freeing forecasters from ad hoc and often erroneous lessons of history. Embodying a broad-based ''performance'' theory of

1

presidential elections, this prediction system identifies thirteen historical conditions, or keys, that gauge the political strength and performance of the executive party as a presidential term progresses. The
keys measure an incumbent party's reelection prospects long before
polls, pundits, or political scientists have anything meaningful to say.

Each of the thirteen keys (see page 3) asks a question that can be
answered yes or no before an upcoming election. To avoid the confusion
of double negatives, the keys are stated as threshold conditions that
favor reelection of the incumbent party. When five or fewer keys are
false, the incumbent party wins the popular vote; when six or more are
false, the challenging party prevails.

The principal historical lesson to be drawn from the keys is that the
fate of an incumbent administration rests largely in its own hands; there
is little that the challenging party can do to affect the outcome of an
election. If the nation has fared well during the term, the executive party
is reelected; if not, the White House changes hands. But such simple
notions as "peace and prosperity" do not adequately measure an administration's success or failure. The Keys to the White House gauge
the multiple dimensions of incumbent strength and performance that
together identify the point at which the party in power crosses the line
separating victory from defeat.

Nothing either party has said or done during the fall campaign has
ever changed its prospects at the polls. Debates, television appearances,
fund-raising, advertising, news coverage, and campaign strategies—the
usual grist for the punditry mills—count for virtually nothing on Election Day. The only issues that matter are the ones for which the results
are already in.

Because the Keys to the White House diagnose the national political
environment, they correlate with the popular balloting, not with the
votes of individual states in the electoral college. Only three times since
1860, however, has the electoral college not ratified the popular vote: the
"stolen" election of 1876, when Democrat Samuel J. Tilden outpolled
Republican Rutherford B. Hayes 51 to 48 percent but lost a disputed
contest for the electoral vote; the election of 1888, when electoral college votes overrode President Grover Cleveland's narrow popular-vote
margin over Benjamin Harrison; and the 2000 election described above.

Each of the keys expresses a condition associated with incumbent-
party success, but only in combination do they accurately predict the
outcome of an election. The first four keys—the political keys—
primarily gauge the strength and unity of the incumbent party. Keys 5
through 11—the seven performance keys—measure its perceived

THIRTEEN KEYS TO THE WHITE HOUSE

The Keys to the White House are stated as conditions that favor reelection of the incumbent party. When five or fewer statements are false, the incumbent party wins. When six or more are false, the incumbent party loses.

KEY 1   Incumbent-party mandate: After the midterm elections, the incumbent party holds more seats in the U.S. House of Representatives than it did after the previous midterm elections.

KEY 2   Nomination-contest: There is no serious contest for the incumbent-party nomination.

KEY 3   Incumbency: The incumbent-party candidate is the sitting president.

KEY 4   Third party: There is no significant third-party or independent campaign.

KEY 5   Short-term economy: The economy is not in recession during the election campaign.

KEY 6   Long-term economy: Real annual per-capita economic growth during the term equals or exceeds mean growth during the two previous terms.

KEY 7   Policy change: The incumbent administration effects major changes in national policy.

KEY 8   Social unrest: There is no sustained social unrest during the term.

KEY 9   Scandal: The incumbent administration is untainted by major scandal.

KEY 10   Foreign or military failure: The incumbent administration suffers no major failure in foreign or military affairs.

KEY 11   Foreign or military success: The incumbent administration achieves a major success in foreign or military affairs.

KEY 12   Incumbent charisma: The incumbent-party candidate is charismatic or a national hero.

KEY 13   Challenger charisma: The challenging-party candidate is not charismatic or a national hero.

achievements and failures across a broad range of concerns. The final two keys—the charisma keys—recognize that personality makes a difference in presidential politics, but the difference is critical only when a candidate is either unusually compelling or of heroic stature.

Armed with the keys and knowledge of how they have been turned in the past (see chapter 2), anyone can analyze the electoral prospects of an incumbent party throughout a presidential term. The individual keys begin lining up the day after an election; although most cannot be turned with certainty until the election year, many can be reasonably anticipated much earlier. The keys provide a long-range outlook on the incumbent party's reelection prospects and indicate precisely how those prospects would change in response to specific circumstances and events. They are an electoral road map to the four years of a presidential term.

After Ronald Reagan had been in office only a year, for example, the keys already disclosed his "superior prospects for reelection" in 1984. In the spring of 1988, eight months before the election, the Republican administration had enough keys in place to make George Bush a shoo-in for reelection. In 1990, when most commentators were bullish about George Bush's reelection prospects, the keys indicated that "Bush looks more like a Carter than a Reagan."[1]

The keys correctly anticipated even the closest elections in American history. James A. Garfield faced a deficit of four keys when he beat Winfield Scott Hancock by only two thousand votes in 1880—a margin of victory of less than one-tenth of 1 percent, by far the narrowest in history. Four years later, James G. Blaine, the nominee of the incumbent Republican party, lost seven keys in his 26,000-vote loss to Grover Cleveland. More recently, John F. Kennedy's eyelash win—by less than two-tenths of a percentage point—over Richard Nixon in 1960 was clearly anticipated by the GOP's nine-key deficit.

From the standpoint of the keys, there is no such thing as a surprise victory. Just as the outcome of the 1988 election was predictable when the pollsters were burying George Bush, so too was Harry Truman's supposed come-from-behind victory in 1948. Despite the nearly universal opinion that Thomas Dewey would swamp the beleaguered incumbent on Election Day, Truman had the minimum eight keys locked in his favor by the time the nominating conventions had adjourned. Truman did not come from behind in 1948 any more than George Bush did in 1988. As the keys to 1948 show, Truman had the election wrapped up before his "Give 'em hell, Harry" whistle-stop campaign ever began.

In the history of our modern, two-party system, only one presidential candidate can be said to have come from behind to win. During the Civil War, Sherman's capture of Atlanta in early September and other triumphs of Union arms, turned a likely negative forecast for the incumbent party back in President Abraham Lincoln's favor. In every other election since 1860, enough indicators of incumbent-party strength and performance have been set to predict the outcome by the time the general election campaign began. Keys have changed after that—John Kennedy and Ronald Reagan emerged as charismatic during the course of their campaigns—but never yet have enough keys changed during the fall campaign to alter a prior verdict.

The lesson? Despite the hundreds of millions of dollars and months of media attention lavished on them, general-election campaigns don't count. The critics have it backwards when they complain that candidates and their handlers deceive the public with sound bites, negative ads, dirty tricks, and stage-managed events. Rather, the candidates deceive themselves into thinking that such machinations can get them elected. Robert Strauss, Jimmy Carter's campaign manager in 1980, understood—in retrospect at least—the futility of battling adverse conditions with the pols' usual weaponry: "With all the politics in the world . . . I think I could have stayed in bed the last ninety days and he would have got exactly the same number of votes he had, give or take two. . . . The real world is all around us."[2]

What losing candidate has ever run a brilliant campaign? Such judgments always follow perceptions of how a candidate is doing or the election result itself. Had George Bush been trailing Michael Dukakis in the polls on election eve, commentators would have blamed Bush's difficulties on his relentlessly negative campaign—the same campaign that supposedly fueled his "come-from-behind" win. Would John F. Kennedy be remembered today for having run one of the best campaigns in history if a few thousand votes had shifted in Illinois and Texas, and Theodore White's best-seller, *The Making of the President, 1960,* had been devoted to explaining a Nixon triumph?

The lessons of the keys go far beyond recent history to disclose an underlying logic of presidential elections that has prevailed through vast changes in American political, social, and economic life. By showing how a pragmatic people respond to the major successes and failures of a presidency, the keys reinterpret American political history, connecting the actual governing of America to the selection of its leader.

No approach to tracking and analyzing elections can fully explain why elections turn out the way they do. But the unique ability of the Keys to the White House to account for the popular vote in every election since 1860, as well as to predict well ahead of time the outcomes of 1984 through 1992, strongly suggests that U.S. presidential elections turn on certain factors and not on others. The fact that the outcome of every election is predictable without reference to issues, ideology, party loyalties, or campaign events allows us reasonably to conclude that many of the factors most commonly cited in explaining election results count for very little on Election Day.

Handicapping the Horse Race

Most of what we hear about presidential politics comes out of the horse-race approach to politics taken by the media, pollsters, campaign consultants, and many politicians. Although the horse-race crowd appropriates ideas as needed from more formal political theories, campaign dynamics are its preeminent concern; every twist and turn of the campaign trail is chronicled in minute detail and dissected for its alleged electoral impact. In this view, presidential politics is primarily a matter of electoral strategy and tactics, a contest in which the candidates battle for the lead position, and the pollsters keep score until Election Day. The problem with this approach is that there is no way to determine what, in the final analysis, really matters. In the horse race, everything potentially counts: personality, image, advertising, issues, ideology, the economy, eloquence, agility, organization, fund-raising, stamina, whatever. Every analyst has his or her own way of counting, and these accounts are continually revised to fit the latest polls and ultimately the election itself.

Polls have become the driving force behind campaign strategy, coverage, and analysis. As polls have become ubiquitous, the media have tilted away from covering campaign speeches and events in their own right and toward reporting how the speeches and events played in the polls—or how the polls shaped the speeches and events in the first place. Polls are perfect for fostering the impression of a race that doesn't exist because they continuously simulate elections that don't take place. The truth is that no one understands the relationship between polls and subsequent elections—that is, when respondents' impressions stop and their intentions begin.

The premise behind polls seems reasonable enough: "If the election were held today, would you vote for candidate X, Y, or Z?" But the election is not being held today. In answering the question, interviewees may respond to developments that later will be forgotten; they may not have yet focused on the election but feel pressure to answer anyway; or they may react differently to an artificial contest than they would to an actual election. They may reply in accord with their perceptions of prevailing opinion, and they may simply lie. None of this takes into account the methodological problems of adjusting for subjects who do not respond, are genuinely undecided, or subsequently don't vote. Finally, as a result of sampling error, the percentages for each candidate are usually only accurate within plus or minus 3 percent—assuming that all responses are valid and the methodology perfect.

However imperfect polls may be, in practice they are irrefutable. No preelection poll can ever be independently replicated or confirmed because there is no "reality" against which results can be checked. Each simulation is a unique event that evaporates when the interviewing ends. If the polls are right, they're right. If they're wrong, they're still right—at least "at the time they were taken." Not even the election itself can prove or disprove a poll, because opinion can change between the time the polling stops and the balloting begins. This raises an obvious question: What use is an instrument that is accurate only when it virtually coincides with the event it is supposed to presage?

In 1980, for example, pollsters and commentators concocted a "Big Bang" theory to explain away the polls' "dead heat" call on the eve of Ronald Reagan's lopsided win: "In our best judgment," rationalized George Gallup, Jr., "Reagan's lead grew steadily" after the Gallup organization ceased polling on Saturday.[3] What will never be known is whether a gigantic shift to Reagan actually occurred in the last two days of the election, or whether the polls had simply failed to detect true voter intentions all along.

The polls are notoriously unreliable election predictors, especially at long range. Eight months before Election Day 1980, the Gallup Poll had Carter leading Reagan 58 to 33 percent, missing the final result by thirty-five percentage points. Swings of twenty points or more are common in the last ten to fifteen weeks of the campaign. A Roper survey released 9 September 1948 showed Thomas Dewey fifteen points ahead of Harry Truman, who won by four percentage points. In 1976, a 1 August Gallup Poll showed Jimmy Carter with a remarkable thirty-three-point lead over President Gerald Ford, thirty-one points off the final mark. Several polls showed Michael Dukakis seventeen points ahead of George Bush in late July of 1988. The twenty-five-point gap between the summer 1988 polls and the final result was wider than the gap between any preelection poll taken in 1948 and Truman's actual margin of victory.

The polls correlate better with election results as Election Day nears. But when it comes to picking winners, the pollsters' record is hit-or-miss even at point-blank range. So sure were they that Thomas Dewey would defeat Harry Truman in 1948 that they quit polling ten days before Election Day. They never again would stop this early. Still, they dubbed "too close to call" Dwight Eisenhower's eleven-point victory over Adlai Stevenson in 1952 and Ronald Reagan's ten-point defeat of Jimmy Carter in 1980. Likewise too close to call, even in the final polls, were the elections of 1960, 1968, and 1976. On the day before the 1988 election, the nation's two preeminent polling organizations, Gallup and Harris, could not agree on whether Bush was an easy winner or Dukakis had pulled within striking distance. Gallup's final survey gave Bush a safe, twelve-point lead, while Harris's had him only four points ahead— leaving a Dukakis victory within the survey's margin of error. Although election-eve polls were accurate in 1992, a Gallup Poll taken just a few days earlier had shown Bush pulling within one point of Clinton, a statistical dead heat. The final polls taken on the eve of the 2004 election ranged from a two point win for John Kerry to a six point win for George W. Bush.

Surveys can be useful in political analysis. Used with due caution, they can shed light on current, though often transient, attitudes regarding issues, personalities, and parties. After an election they can probe individuals' perceptions of why they voted as they did. But as a means of forecasting election results, polls that simulate elections—as distinct from attitudinal surveys—are of limited use.

The pollsters and the political analysts who rely on polls acknowledge that a poll is a snapshot of the electorate that does not actually predict an upcoming election. But polls still drive and validate horse-race commentary and analysis. Consequently, like the polls themselves, the horse-race commentators can never be wrong. Any interpretations or predictions they make are valid only until the polls reveal the next shift in the race. In reality, horse-race commentators can never be right, either, because no independent criteria exist against which to measure their assessments. Commentary is continually adjusted to fit changing circumstances—including the outcome of an election itself. The classic example comes again from 1948, when the pundits scoffed at Harry Truman's whistle-stop campaign as the death rattle of a doomed candidate—until his unexpected victory transformed futility into post hoc genius.

Since then, almost every snippet of horse-race commentary has included an escape hatch. When Dukakis was riding high in the polls in the spring of 1988—and was clearly the touts' odds-on favorite to win—the race was described as the Democrats' to lose. No matter which candidate finished first in November, the pundits were sure to hold a winning ticket. In the end, the countless television images and reams of print devoted to the horse race tell us plenty about campaigns, but very little about elections—what really matters and why. Because nothing that is said can be tested, and because everything can be explained ex post facto, no enduring lessons are learned. Election history becomes a grab bag of anecdotes and analogies rather than a reliable guide to understanding the most consequential decision made by the American people.

Theory versus Reality

Social and political scientists offer specific electoral theories designed to explain and predict election results. These theories cover a broad range of conflicting and competing ways to understand presidential elections.

One major school of political thought focuses on the enduring loyalties of voters to political parties. In this view, the party identification of voters is the primary determinant of election results. Most party-voting theorists divide American history into political eras dominated by one party or the other. The balance of party power, according to this theory, should shift every generation or so as new voters enter the electorate, new issues arise, and new political leaders emerge. With the electorate thus periodically ripe for change, some national crisis—such as the struggle over slavery that led to the Civil War or the Great Depression of the 1930s—triggers a realignment of the political system. This realignment occurs in the course of one or more critical elections that mark the transition from one political era to another.[4]

There are two serious problems with this approach. First, presidential-election results have not followed such purported shifts in the balance of party power. Although most people who identify themselves with one party or another do vote the party ticket, the dominant party of an era often loses the White House. Party-voting theorists attribute such exceptions as Woodrow Wilson's two terms in the midst of Republican dominance and Dwight Eisenhower's presidency during a Democratic era to the effects of short-term factors, but these factors can neither be explained nor anticipated by the general theory. Moreover, American political history has not been characterized by regular, periodic realignments of voter loyalties. The last clear realignment took place more than sixty years ago, when the Democrats came to power during the Great Depression.

Another school of thought holds that the winning candidate is the one whose positions on critical issues coincide most closely with the weight of public opinion. This principle is said to operate as well over the longer term, with public sentiment on such enduring issues as civil rights, welfare, taxation, and national security tending to favor one party or another over a span of elections.[5] But it is very difficult to identify in advance the salient issues on which an election will turn, and often just as difficult to ascertain the candidates' positions on them. Voters may adjust their perceptions of candidates' positions to fit preferences based on other factors, such as party, performance, and personality. Finally, the electorate sometimes chooses candidates whose specific positions on major issues do not represent prevailing opinion. In 1984, for example, while Ronald Reagan was sweeping forty-nine states, surveys showed that the public favored Walter Mondale's positions on many major issues, including defense and social spending, the Equal Rights Amendment, the nuclear freeze, and the environment. Democrat Bill Clinton defeated Republican George Bush in 1992, at a time when surveys showed the country moving closer to conservative views more typical of Republican than Democratic positions on national issues.[6]

A variant of issues theory suggests that the electorate simply chooses the candidate closest to the center of the ideological spectrum.[7] But a center is difficult to locate in a political system in which neither voters nor parties are ideologically consistent. Even if a center can be fixed in advance of an election, telling which candidate is closer to it can be difficult. Voters in the center of the political spectrum may also be less responsive to issues than voters holding more extreme positions. Indeed, the apparently more centrist candidate has lost on occasion. In 1860, for example, Democrat Stephen Douglas occupied the middle ground on the expansion of slavery, the overriding issue of the era, yet lost to Abraham Lincoln. In 1980, conservative Republican Ronald Reagan defeated the reelection bid of centrist Democrat Jimmy Carter.

With the decline of realignment theory, the focus of election analysis has shifted from the long term to the very short term. An influential contingent of economists and political scientists emphasizes the primacy of the election-year economy in deciding elections. These "pocketbook" theorists all use some index of economic change during the election year in explaining and forecasting election results, although they do not agree on which indices to use (gross domestic product percapita, disposable income, or net domestic product), what time period should be covered (e.g., the second or third quarters versus the entire year), or what other factors should be included (e.g., incumbency, trends in party support). Their various models demonstrate that economic conditions correlate with election results, but none shows that elections turn primarily on economic considerations. All the models include some noneconomic variables and some actually include candidate support or approval polls. The inclusion of polls may improve the accuracy of models, but such catchall surveys make it impossible to ascertain what factors are actually involved in the electorate's decision. None of the economic models include a sufficient range of noneconomic factors to avoid serious error.[8]

Yale professor Ray Fair developed in the mid-1970s the most fully tested and most celebrated economic theory of presidential election results. In its first five predictions of election results, the Fair model had a score of two correct, two in error, and one indeterminate, no better than a coin flip. He missed 1992, predicting a near-landslide for President Bush with about 56 percent of the two-party vote. He also missed 1976, when he had likewise predicted a 56 percent victory for incumbent President Ford. "I am still living this one down," Dr. Fair wrote in a 1978 article.[9] In 1980, Dr. Fair's equations produced contradictory predictions that he did not resolve until after the election. "No conclusions were drawn from the earlier results regarding this [1980] choice," Dr. Fair wrote.[10]

Dr. Fair's model and all other economic theories falsely presume that voters are driven by economic concerns alone. Voters are not that single-minded. Dr. Fair blew 1976 because his model ignored Watergate and the collapse of Vietnam. He couldn't make a call in 1980 because his equations neglected the Iran hostage crisis and President Carter's stalled domestic agenda. And he missed 1992 because he couldn't account for George Bush's failed leadership, his lack of a record of policy change, or the Perot campaign.

Recognizing the failure of single-theory models, some political scientists have devised explicitly eclectic models that do not embody particular theories of elections but rather incorporate diverse elements drawn from the major theories. Issues, ideology, party image, economic performance, and voting trends—along with such factors as incumbency, congressional election results, candidates' regional affinities, and results of the nominating process—are all considered. Like some of the economic models, some eclectic models also include poll results for catchall questions, such as approval of a president's performance or measures of what voters like and dislike about competing candidates. Professors Michael Lewis-Beck of the University of Iowa and Tom Rice of the University of Vermont, for example, developed in early 1992 a four-variable model that includes real economic growth, presidential approval ratings, the outcome of the prior congressional election, and the incumbent's performance in primary elections.

In their 1992 survey of political-science models, Lewis-Beck and Rice identified only two models that both had come reasonably close to estimating the percentage votes for candidates in elections from 1948 to 1988 and had "nontrivial lead time for prediction." These included their own model and one developed in 1988 by Alan Abramowitz of Emory University. The three-variable Abramowitz model includes presidential approval ratings, real economic growth, and incumbency. But the Abramowitz model had missed the winner in four of the eleven elections from 1948 to 1988. The Lewis-Beck model correctly identified all but one winner of these elections, but, in its first and only predictive test, the model forecast a smashing Bush victory in 1992 with 56 percent of the two-party vote.[11]

With catchall poll results included, these models have little to say about the electoral process, regardless of their track record in accounting for election results. Even models with nontrivial lead time rely upon numerical indicators that cannot be measured until well into the election year. They give little indication of how an executive party's electoral prospects rise and fall during a term, and no indication of the role played by specific events, such as Richard Nixon's China breakthrough or the riots of the late 1960s.

The Keys to the White House

The Keys to the White House differ from the abstract formulas of the election modelers as well as the lively but anarchic approach of the commentators. Like the horse-race approach, the keys are dynamic—they recognize that politics is a matter of real people and events that unfold over time. Like the academic models, the keys are conceptual—they provide a systematic guide to the electoral process. Also like these models, the Keys to the White House are diagnostic—they do not tell us explicitly *why* people vote the way they do.

Unlike the models, however, the keys identify the concrete circumstances in which the electorate retains or rejects the party in power. The keys are driven by a dominant idea: that the American electorate is pragmatic; it responds to the broad-based performance of the party in power, not just the condition of the economy. Seven of the keys (5 through 11) gauge performance directly, and four more (political keys 1 through 4) reflect executive performance indirectly. Not a single key directly measures ideology, issue positions, voters' party identification, or campaign strategy or tactics. Although these and other factors may have some influence on the decisions of individual voters, none of them improves the ability of the keys to discriminate between winning and losing candidates, and the inclusion of several—ideology (centrism) and party identification, for example—diminishes the predictive power of the system.

In picking winners and losers, the keys differ from conventional models that try to estimate each candidate's share of the popular vote. Although there is a rough correlation between the number of keys turned against the party in power and its percentage of the popular vote, the final verdict depends only on the simple, unweighted total of negative keys (the use of weighted keys does not improve the ability of the system to distinguish between incumbent and challenging-party victories). A threshold of six negative keys separates the losers from the winners of the popular vote without regard to their percentages. Although this either/or approach involves some loss of information, it achieves a stability of results that eludes more detailed analyses. The keys are able to predict the outcomes of close elections that the percentage models miss because the differences between the candidates' shares of the vote are well within their average error margins. The winners of all five elections decided by six or fewer points since 1948 (1948, 1960, 1968, 1976, and 1992) are missed by one or more of the percentage models published to date. Unlike the percentage models, which can be "right"—within an arbitrary margin of error—even when they forecast a plurality for the second-place finisher, predictions made by the keys are always either right or wrong.

The threshold principle also operates at the level of the individual keys. Rather than assigning a numerical value to each key—for example, the rate of economic growth during the election year—information is consolidated in each key as a single threshold condition favoring incumbent success; thus, a recession during the campaign counts as one unmet condition regardless of the severity of economic problems. This approach avoids the modelers' questionable assumption that each variable has the same influence in every election (for example, that every 1 percent increase in real first-quarter GNP always yields a 1.4-point increase in the incumbent-party vote) and, further, that each variable relates to every other variable in a specified way—in other words, that there is a specific formula to which all elections conform. By avoiding numerical measurements and specific formulas, the threshold approach allows the keys to combine interchangeably (if any six are discrepant, the incumbent loses) rather than requiring that each key contribute incrementally to the prediction. This results in a system that may appear to be less refined but is far more robust than the numerical models as no single variable can throw the prediction off by overwhelming others.

Subjectivity and the Keys

Upon first encountering the Keys to the White House, some observers question the subjective nature of several keys: Who's to say, for example, what constitutes "major national policy change" or "charisma"? But deciding how to turn the judgment keys merely requires the kind of informed evaluations that historians invariably rely on in drawing conclusions about past events. Three factors distinguish these assessments from the ad hoc judgments offered by conventional political commentators. First, decisions about the keys must be made consistently across elections, according to the definition of each key. For an upcoming election, the turning of each key is guided by preset criteria and the precedent set by turning the keys in previous elections. Second, once a decision is made for all thirteen keys, the system yields a definite prediction that serves to test the judgments made. Third, the keys have a successful track record. They not only consistently accounted for the outcomes of elections from 1860 to 1980, but they also correctly predicted the elections of 1984 through 2008. It is difficult enough to fine-tune judgment calls on the keys to fit the known results of thirty-one past elections. It is impossible to make such adjustments predictively, especially when a forecast runs counter to the conventional wisdom of the time.

To avoid historical judgments, as some political scientists attempt to do, is to miss much of the reality of presidential elections, as the errors made by the social science models indicate. For example, factors such as foreign-policy disasters, scandals, and policy change are not readily measurable by statistical data alone. One explanation for the widening gulf between political science and the practice of politics is the political scientists' insistence on considering only what can be quantified. The keys attempt to achieve the most valid possible model of presidential elections even if it leaves open the possibility that different analysts may reach different judgments on individual keys or, in the case of close calls, make different predictions about an upcoming election.

The judgments required in turning the keys are also not so different from those made by other modelers. Dr. Fair, for example, "corrected" his erroneous prediction of a Ford victory in 1976 by deciding, after the fact, that only elected presidents (Ford was an appointed vice president who became president on Nixon's resignation) should get the incumbency "bonus points" built into his model. The judgments made in turning the keys certainly are no less subjective than many of the decisions made in the selection and adjustment of polling samples, let alone in the wording of survey questions. Subjectivity even creeps into the forecasts generated by the megamodels that predict the economic future. Economists sometimes adjust their models subjectively to guard against counterintuitive results.[12] In the case of the keys, the decisions made in calling individual keys are forthrightly in view, and subject to analysis and debate.

The exercise of informed, independent judgment has other advantages over relying solely on quantitative factors in making historically based predictions. The judgments made in turning the keys require close attention to what really has occurred in the past and how past events actually compare to similar situations in the present. The keys are thus a source of historical analysis, discussion, and debate. The use of the keys for an upcoming election brings back to life all of American history since the days of Lincoln and Douglas. How, for example, does the Oklahoma City bombing of 1995 compare to John Brown's raid on Harper's Ferry in 1859? Does Bill Clinton's record of policy change measure up to Woodrow Wilson's? The scrutiny of close calls provides new insights into the dynamics of presidential elections and reveals possible refinements of the system itself. That equally informed analysts might disagree on a call shows simply that the system is not a fully determined one. Knowledge of the definition of each key and the circumstances under which it has been turned in the past, however, should usually, but not always, result in agreement on the calls for an upcoming election.

In 1992, for example, Ken DeCell, my coauthor on the earlier version of this work, released an early prediction of a Bush victory in 1992. In his judgment, only four keys could be counted against Bush in the midsummer of 1992. In my view, this forecast was premature. First, although at that time Ross Perot had formally withdrawn from the presidential race, he was still pursuing his campaign in the individual states. He would likely appear on all state ballots, and win much more than the 5 percent of the presidential vote needed to topple Key 4, even if he did not again pursue a national campaign. As a noncandidate, Perot was still receiving about 15 percent support in some polls. Of course, Perot returned to the race with far more support than would be necessary to turn Key 4 against Bush. Second, even though economic-growth numbers appeared to indicate the end of the recession that had begun in 1991, the National Bureau of Economic Research had not yet declared the recession over. More important, surveys consistently indicated that an extraordinary 75 to 80 percent of the public believed the economy was still in recession. My own forecast, completed in early September, counted both the third-party key and the short-term economy key against Bush, for a total of six keys, just enough to predict his defeat. As explained in the next chapter, this correct prediction in 1992 was important for clarifying the importance of public perceptions in calling the short-term economy key.[13]

Subsets of the Keys

The historical advantages of controlling the White House are such that a forecaster who simply picked the party in power to win every election would be right 61 percent of the time. All but one of the keys individually (incumbent charisma) do better than that. Contest key 2 alone predicts all but five of the past thirty-eight elections (1880, 1932, 1960, 1976, and 2008), a record unmatched by any other electoral model. The contest key and the short-term economy key together call all but one election (1880). If neither key falls, the incumbent party wins; otherwise the challenging party wins. However, this two-key system would have led to an erroneous advance forecast of the 2008 victory by the challenging Democrats. The election-year recession was established only after the election or at best shortly before Election Day. The contest key did not fall in 2008. The full thirteen key system correctly forecast the outcome of this election in early 2006.

Some larger subsets of the thirteen keys also correctly predict the outcome of all elections since 1860. Why not, then, use a smaller set of keys? First, the full set of thirteen keys provides the greatest separation between incumbent wins and losses over the entire sample of elections. Second, given the limited sample of prior elections, the thirteen-key system has the greatest capacity to capture future variations in political circumstance that smaller subsystems might miss. For example, at the time we originally developed the system in 1981, the combination of only four keys—contest key 2, third-party key 4, short-term economy key 5, and policy-change key 7—correctly predicted every election from 1860 to 1980 (the party in power wins unless two keys are turned against it). However, this four-key system would have miscalled President Clinton's reelection in 1996 (the party in power lost Keys 4 and 7), which the thirteen- key system correctly predicted. Third, the greater stability and range of the full system also provides the ability to conduct long-term forecasts of a future election. Finally, all of the thirteen keys have strong theoretical justification for their inclusion. This criterion is consistent with the dual objective of the keys system—both to predict and explain the outcome of American presidential elections.

In addition, the smaller the subsystem, the greater its reliance on the political keys, the strongest reflectors of circumstances measured by other keys. But the political keys usually are determined well in advance of the election. The possibility exists that enough keys could be turned during the latter party of the election year to affect the final outcome.

Long after the mandate question, the nominees, and any third party activity have been decided, other events—an economic downtown, a foreign triumph or disaster, or a major scandal—could still occur to influence the outcome of the election. A close approximation of this scenario occurred in 1864 as a result of late Union victories on the battlefield. Only the full set of thirteen keys has the capacity to capture future variations that smaller subsets can and already have missed.

There is no final guarantee that thirteen keys will cover all future elections, although they have done so in advance for seven consecutive elections from 1984 to 2008. But the thirteen-key system incorporates the broadest range of threshold variables that combine in a manner consistent with nearly 150 years of electoral history and are therefore likely to capture the dynamics of future elections as well. Although additional variables correlate reasonably well with electoral results, none identified so far can be added to the system without diminishing separation or creating errors. The thirteen keys enable forecasters to track electoral prospects better and to incorporate historical experience more fully than does any subsystem or any expanded system.

Chapter 2

Turning the Keys to the Presidency

The presidential elections of 1860 and 1992 barely resemble one another. The electorate of 1860 included no women and virtually no Blacks, Hispanics, Asians, or Eastern or Southern Europeans—groups that make up more than three-quarters of today's electorate. In an era before broadcast media and personal campaigning by candidates, Abraham Lincoln was neither seen nor heard on the campaign trail in 1860. In 1992, the candidates crisscrossed the country and appeared nightly on television for months on end. Lincoln, the Republican winner in 1860, and Bush, the Republican loser in 1992, hardly would be recognized as members of the same political party. In 1860, the Republicans were the party of activist national government and Black aspirations, the Democrats of states' rights and the status quo.

It is precisely because the Keys to the White House encompass the diverse experience of these elections—and the thirty-two in between— that they can predict the results of future elections, each of which will take place under yet a different set of conditions. Although no key stands alone, each one is an enduring indicator of electoral response. Every key has both a historical rationale and a specific history of its own. To turn a key for an upcoming election, a forecaster not only must apply its general criteria to current circumstances, but also must measure those circumstances against examples from previous elections. The abstract rule that a foreign failure must constitute a major setback and not just a failed initiative, for example, is clarified by the knowledge that President Bush's failure to topple Iraqi dictator Saddam Hussein did not turn the foreign-failure key against him in 1992.

Tables 2.1 and 2.2 show how I turned each of the thirteen keys for all thirty-eight elections from 1860 to 2008. A notation of ''X'' indicates that the statement expressed by a given key is false; a notation of ''O''

19

TABLE 2.1
How the Keys Turned: Chronological Record, 1860–2008

	1	2	3	4	5	6	7	8	9	10	11	12	13	Total
1860	O	X	X	X	O	O	X	X	O	O	X	X	O	7
1864	O	O	O	O	O	X	O	X	O	O	O	X	O	3
1868	O	O	X	O	O	O	O	X	O	O	O	O	O	2
1872	X	O	O	O	O	O	X	X	O	O	O	O	O	3
1876	X	X	X	O	X	X	X	O	X	O	X	X	O	9*
1880	O	X	X	O	O	O	O	O	O	O	X	X	O	4
1884	X	X	X	O	X	X	X	O	O	O	X	O	O	7
1888	X	O	O	O	O	O	X	X	O	O	X	X	O	5*
1892	X	X	O	X	O	O	O	X	O	O	X	X	O	6
1896	X	X	X	O	X	X	X	X	O	O	X	O	O	8
1900	X	O	O	O	O	O	O	O	O	O	O	X	X	3
1904	O	O	O	O	O	O	O	O	O	O	O	O	O	0
1908	O	O	X	O	O	X	O	O	O	O	O	X	O	3
1912	X	X	O	X	O	O	X	O	O	O	X	X	O	6
1916	X	O	O	O	O	X	O	O	O	O	O	X	O	3
1920	X	X	X	O	X	X	O	X	O	X	O	X	O	8
1924	X	O	O	X	O	O	O	O	X	O	O	X	O	4
1928	O	O	X	O	O	O	X	O	O	O	O	X	O	3
1932	X	O	O	O	X	X	X	X	O	O	X	X	X	8
1936	O	O	O	O	O	O	O	O	O	O	X	O	O	1
1940	X	O	O	O	O	O	O	O	O	O	X	O	O	2
1944	X	O	O	O	O	O	O	O	O	X	O	O	O	2
1948	X	O	O	X	O	X	O	O	O	X	O	X	O	5
1952	O	X	X	O	O	X	X	O	X	X	O	X	X	8
1956	O	O	O	O	O	O	X	O	O	O	O	O	O	1
1960	X	O	X	O	X	X	X	O	O	X	X	X	X	9
1964	X	O	O	O	O	O	O	O	O	X	O	X	O	3
1968	X	X	X	X	O	O	O	X	O	X	X	X	O	8
1972	X	O	O	O	O	X	X	O	O	O	O	X	O	4
1976	X	X	O	O	O	X	X	O	X	X	X	X	O	8
1980	X	X	O	X	X	O	X	O	O	X	O	X	X	8
1984	O	O	O	O	O	X	O	O	O	O	X	O	O	2
1988	O	O	X	O	O	O	X	O	O	O	O	X	O	3
1992	X	O	O	X	X	X	X	O	O	O	O	X	O	6
1996	X	O	O	X	O	O	X	O	O	O	X	X	O	5
2000	O	O	X	O	O	O	X	O	X	O	X	X	O	5
2004	O	O	O	O	O	X	X	O	O	X	O	X	O	4
2008	X	O	X	O	X	X	X	O	O	X	X	X	X	9

1. party mandate
2. nomination contest
3. incumbency
4. third party
5. short-term economy
6. long-term economy
7. policy change

8. social unrest
9. scandal
10. foreign/military failure
11. foreign/military success
12. incumbent charisma
13. challenger charisma

Note: X = False;   O = True

*Electoral vote did not coincide with popular-vote results.

TABLE 2.2
How the Keys Turned: Incumbent Wins and Losses, 1860–2008

	1	2	3	4	5	6	7	8	9	10	11	12	13	Total
Incumbent popular vote victories														
1864	O	O	O	O	O	X	O	X	O	O	O	X	O	3
1868	O	O	X	O	O	O	O	X	O	O	O	O	O	2
1872	X	O	O	O	O	O	X	X	O	O	O	O	O	3
1880	O	X	X	O	O	O	O	O	O	O	X	X	O	4
1888	X	O	O	O	O	O	X	X	O	O	X	X	O	5*
1900	X	O	O	O	O	O	O	O	O	O	O	X	X	3
1904	O	O	O	O	O	O	O	O	O	O	O	O	O	0
1908	O	O	X	O	O	X	O	O	O	O	O	X	O	3
1916	X	O	O	O	O	X	O	O	O	O	O	X	O	3
1924	X	O	O	X	O	O	O	O	X	O	O	X	O	4
1928	O	O	X	O	O	O	X	O	O	O	O	X	O	3
1936	O	O	O	O	O	O	O	O	O	O	X	O	O	1
1940	X	O	O	O	O	O	O	O	O	O	X	O	O	2
1944	X	O	O	O	O	O	O	O	O	X	O	O	O	2
1948	X	O	O	X	O	X	O	O	O	X	O	X	O	5
1956	O	O	O	O	O	O	X	O	O	O	O	O	O	1
1964	X	O	O	O	O	O	O	O	O	X	O	X	O	3
1972	X	O	O	O	O	X	X	O	O	O	O	X	O	4
1984	O	O	O	O	O	X	O	O	O	O	X	O	O	2
1988	O	O	X	O	O	O	X	O	O	O	O	X	O	3
1996	X	O	O	X	O	O	X	O	O	O	X	X	O	5
2000	O	O	X	O	O	O	X	O	X	O	X	X	O	5*
2004	O	O	O	O	O	X	X	O	O	X	O	X	O	4
Challenger popular vote victories														
1860	O	X	X	X	O	O	X	X	O	O	X	X	O	7
1876	X	X	X	O	X	X	X	O	X	O	X	X	O	9*
1884	X	X	X	O	X	X	X	O	O	O	X	O	O	7
1892	X	X	O	X	O	O	O	X	O	O	X	X	O	6
1896	X	X	X	O	X	X	X	O	O	O	X	O	O	8
1912	X	X	O	X	O	O	X	O	O	O	X	X	O	6
1920	X	X	X	O	X	X	O	X	O	X	O	X	O	8
1932	X	O	O	O	X	X	X	X	O	O	X	X	X	8
1952	O	X	X	O	O	X	X	O	X	X	O	X	X	8
1960	X	O	X	O	X	X	X	O	O	X	X	X	X	9
1968	X	X	X	X	O	O	O	X	O	X	X	X	O	8
1976	X	X	O	O	O	X	X	O	X	X	X	X	O	8
1980	X	X	O	X	X	O	X	O	O	X	O	X	X	8
1992	X	O	O	X	X	X	X	O	O	O	O	X	O	6
2008	X	O	X	O	X	X	X	O	O	X	X	X	X	9

1. party mandate
2. nomination contest
3. incumbency
4. third party
5. short-term economy
6. long-term economy
7. policy change
8. social unrest
9. scandal
10. foreign/military failure
11. foreign/military success
12. incumbent charisma
13. challenger charisma

Note: X = False;   O = True

*Electoral vote did not coincide with popular-vote results.

indicates that the statement is true. The last column reports the total number of false statements for an election. Table 2.1 lists all elections in chronological order; Table 2.2 divides elections according to whether the incumbent or challenging party prevailed in the popular vote.

The success of each key by itself in predicting election results since 1860 (correctly calling an incumbent-party victory when the key is true and a challenging-party victory when the key is false) is its prediction rate. Incumbency key 3, for example, has a prediction rate of 68 percent: Calling an election for the party in power when its nominee is the sitting president, and calling it for the challenger when a sitting president does not run, yields a correct prediction in twenty-six of thirty-eight elections, or 68 percent of the time.

A more refined way of looking at a key's record of success is through its ability to anticipate incumbent-party wins versus incumbent-party losses. A key's win rate is the percentage of incumbent-party victories when the key is turned in the incumbent party's favor; its loss rate is the percentage of incumbent-party defeats when it is turned against the incumbent party. A key would be a perfect predictor if it had a win rate and a loss rate of 100 percent. It would do no better than a coin flip if it had a win rate and a loss rate of 50 percent.

For example, Key 3 has a win rate of 74 percent and a loss rate of 60 percent. When the key has been true—the incumbent party has renominated a sitting president—the incumbent party has won seventeen of twenty-three elections, or 74 percent of the time; when a sitting president has not run, the incumbent party has lost nine of fifteen elections, giving Key 3 a loss rate of 60 percent. Thus, Key 3 is better (by fourteen percentage points) at predicting incumbent-party wins than incumbent-party losses. Short-term economy key 5, on the other hand, is a better predictor of defeat. The party in power has lost all nine elections in which the campaign began during a recession (i.e., the key was false), for a loss rate of 100 percent, while winning twenty-three of twenty-nine when there was no recession (the key was true), for a win rate of 79 percent.

Table 2.3 reports the prediction rate along with the win and loss rates for each of the thirteen keys. The predictive power of an individual key is a function of several factors. Each key potentially has a direct causal effect on the outcome of an election; a major foreign-policy success, for example, can contribute to confidence in the executive party. Some keys, particularly the political keys, not only have a direct impact but also reflect influences that may or may not be captured in other keys. The turning of one key can have triggering effects, causing other keys to turn as well: A sour economy can help trigger a nomination contest, a third-party candidacy, or the emergence of a charismatic challenger.

TABLE 2.3
Prediction Rates, Win Rates, and Loss Rates of the Thirteen Keys
(1860–2008, in percentages)

Key		Prediction rate (%)	Win rate (%)	Loss rate (%)
1	Party mandate	66	86	54
2	Nomination contest	87	85	92
3	Incumbency	68	74	60
4	Third party	68	69	67
5	Short-term economy	82	79	100
6	Long-term economy	68	76	59
7	Policy change	68	82	57
8	Social unrest	66	68	60
9	Scandal	63	64	60
10	Foreign/military failure	68	70	64
11	Foreign/military success	71	80	61
12	Incumbent charisma	55	80	46
13	Challenger charisma	71	69	83

The examination of each key across elections discloses its rationale, the criteria for judging it true or false, and the specific historical thresholds for turning the key in past contests. Such a study uniquely brings into focus how events and personalities, both ordinary and extraordinary, actually relate to the outcome of an election.

Political Keys

The first four keys (party mandate, nomination contest, incumbency, and third party) are the most reflective, gauging the strength, cohesion, and, to some extent, effectiveness of the party in power throughout the term. The political keys clearly reflect circumstances diagnosed separately by the performance keys (5 through 11) and the incumbent-charisma key (12), as evidenced by the high correlation between the number of political keys and the number of performance keys turned in any election.

To the extent that issues and ideology play a role in presidential elections, for example, that role is reflected in contest key 2 and third-party key 4. It is a very different role from what is commonly supposed. Rather than constituting the crux of the contest between the major-party nominees, ideological differences most often spark intraparty strife or insurgent campaigns. The classic example is 1912, when the split between the GOP's progressive and old-guard factions led to the nation's first primary contest and to the most successful third-party campaign to date, both instigated by former president Theodore Roosevelt. More recently, moderate incumbent presidents have been challenged from the Right and the Left within their own parties—Gerald Ford by Ronald Reagan in 1976, and Jimmy Carter by Ted Kennedy in 1980. No incumbent party has ever lost three political keys and won reelection. Only three times has the party in power lost two political keys and held on to the White House. When fewer than two political keys have been turned against it, the executive party has won every time, except in 1932, in the midst of the Great Depression.

Key 1: Incumbent-Party Mandate

After the midterm elections, the incumbent party holds more seats in the U.S. House of Representatives than it did after the previous midterm elections.

The party-mandate key provides an update on the party's momentum midway through the term. It is based on proportional changes in the U.S. House of Representatives, which is apportioned according to population and more accurately captures national trends than does the Senate. In addition, all House seats are contested every two years, when only a third of the Senate is up for grabs.

The incumbent party wins the mandate key if it achieves a net gain in House seats in the previous presidential and midterm elections combined. For example, in the 1980 election that brought Ronald Reagan to power, Republicans gained thirty-five House seats; two years later, in the 1982 midterm elections, they lost twenty-seven, for a net gain of eight seats since the previous term. Thus, the GOP held the mandate key for the 1984 election.

Congressional strength is measured on a percentage basis. Until 1913, the number of seats in the House increased as new states entered the union. Therefore, increases in the number of seats held by a party did not automatically translate into percentage increases, as was the case in 1868, when the Republicans gained six seats but saw their percentage drop from 74 percent to 70 percent, as the Democrats gained fourteen seats. Since the number of House seats was fixed at 435 in 1913, numerical gains and losses have resulted in corresponding percentage changes as well.

Whether the party in control of the White House also controls Congress obviously has a major influence on an administration's ability to enact its agenda and run the government successfully. The magnitude of shifts in executive-party congressional strength also parallels such performance indicators as economic trends and presidential approval ratings. The mandate key, then, appears to be a reflector of incumbent-party performance and an aggregate indicator of electoral trends nation-wide. In addition, the key can have a trigger effect: Even marginal changes in congressional makeup can affect the administration's ability to conduct policy effectively, which in turn can affect the economy, domestic and foreign initiatives, and whether there is a contest for the incumbent-party nomination.

The mandate key is only a fair predictor by itself: Calling elections based solely on this key correctly predicts 66 percent of the past thirty-eight elections. This is partly because the key is difficult to secure—the executive party must achieve a presidential-year gain in House seats to overcome the midterm jinx that almost invariably results in midterm losses for the party holding the White House (the only exceptions are 1934, 1998, and 2002). The incumbent party has held the mandate key in only fourteen of the thirty-eight previous elections. Of those four-teen, it has won twelve; this 86 percent win rate makes the key a pretty good harbinger of incumbent victory. The lack of a congressional man-date, however, is not a strong indicator of defeat. The incumbent party has lost thirteen of the twenty-four elections in which it did not have the mandate, giving the key a loss rate of 54 percent.

Key 2: Nomination Contest

There is no serious contest for the incumbent-party nomination.

History shows that the sentiment of the incumbent party at nomina-tion time is a remarkably accurate barometer of the mood of the elector-ate as a whole. The best single predictor of the outcome of any presi-dential election is whether the incumbent party unites early and clearly behind a consensus nominee. By itself, the contest key calls thirty-three of the thirty-eight previous elections correctly, giving it a prediction rate of 87 percent. In only four of twenty-six elections has a relatively uncontested nominee been defeated—Herbert Hoover in 1932, Richard Nixon in 1960, and George H. W. Bush in 1992, and John McCain in 2008—for a win rate of 85 percent. In only one of twelve elections has the winner of a contested incumbent-party nomination been elected president—in 1880, when Republican nominee James A. Garfield defeated Democrat Winfield Scott Hancock with the smallest popular-vote margin in history—for a loss rate of 92 percent.

An uncontested nomination is one in which the nominee wins at least two-thirds of the total delegate vote on the first ballot at the nominating convention. This two-thirds threshold is above the 60 percent level generally considered to be a landslide in American politics, but it is not so high as to make a trivial challenge seem significant. A two-to-one ratio is a reasonable measure of consensus, and it is in accord with previous experience. Senator Ted Kennedy, for example, clearly mounted a serious challenge to President Jimmy Carter for the Democratic nomination in 1980, yet Carter defeated him soundly. Measured against the two-thirds rule, Carter's 64 percent tally on the convention's first ballot reflected both circumstances. In contrast, commentator Pat Buchanan's challenge to President Bush in 1992 gained much early publicity, but little support among Republican primary voters. Buchanan won not a single primary and precious few delegates; Bush swept to a near-unanimous nomination.

One contested incumbent-party nomination does not technically meet the two-thirds guideline. In 1968, the death of Senator Robert Kennedy enabled his chief rival, Vice President Hubert Humphrey, to poll almost exactly 67 percent of the delegates on the first convention ballot. Despite Humphrey's two-thirds victory, the nomination had been clearly contested, signaling deep divisions (principally over the Vietnam War) within the incumbent party, which went on to lose the election.

Internal party contests reflect incumbent performance. On average, more than twice as many performance keys (5 through 11) are turned against the party in power when there is a contest for its nomination as when there is not.

Usually the beneficiary of executive success is the incumbent president or an heir apparent within the incumbent administration. Except for Civil War hero Ulysses S. Grant in 1868 and long-serving Republican Senator John McCain in 2008, all uncontested executive-party nominees have been either sitting presidents or high administration officials (war secretary William Howard Taft in 1908; commerce secretary and domestic-policy chief Herbert Hoover in 1928; and vice presidents Richard Nixon in 1960, George H. W. Bush in 1988, and Al Gore in 2000).

In contrast, a contested nomination is usually the legacy of a failed administration and a weak president or the lack of a strong successor candidate. Of the twenty-three times incumbent presidents have run for reelection, only five have been seriously challenged for the nomination according to the criteria used for this key: Chester A. Arthur in 1884; Benjamin Harrison in 1892; William Howard Taft in 1912; Gerald Ford in 1976; and Jimmy Carter in 1980. None of them won another term; Arthur was denied his party's nomination, and the others lost in the fall. The only high administration official selected in a contested nomination was Vice President Hubert Humphrey in 1968, who entered the race after the withdrawal of President Lyndon Johnson and became the presumptive nominee only after Robert Kennedy's assassination.

Unlike a contest for the incumbent-party mantle, a fight for the nomination of the challenging party does not appear to hurt its chances; if anything, a battle for the challenger's title seems to help somewhat. The challenging party has won eleven of the twenty-two elections (50 percent) in which there was a battle for its nomination, versus only four of the sixteen elections (25 percent) in which it fielded a relatively uncontested nominee. In other words, the challenging party is slightly more likely to win when there is a contest for its nomination than when there is not. This fact certainly dispels the conventional presumption that an internal battle always hurts either party. Although a contest for the challenger nomination may reflect (or even create) intraparty divisions, it can also put the out-of-power party into public view, giving its candidates national exposure and conferring winner status on its eventual nominee.

Key 3: Incumbency

The incumbent-party candidate is the sitting president.

The advantages of an incumbent president seeking reelection to the world's most powerful office are clear. A sitting president has run in twenty-three of the past thirty-eight general elections and has lost the popular vote only six times—Harrison in 1892, Taft in 1912, Hoover in 1932, Ford in 1976, Carter in 1980, and Bush in 1992—giving Key 3 a win rate of 74 percent. (President Grover Cleveland won the popular vote in 1888 but lost in the electoral college.) The incumbent party has lost nine of the fifteen elections in which it did not field a sitting president, for a loss rate of 60 percent. Overall, the incumbency key correctly calls twenty-six of the last thirty-eight elections, for a prediction rate of 68 percent.

Americans hold the presidency in esteem and transfer some of that regard to whoever holds the office. Beyond simple name recognition, the president has powerful tools at his disposal: the ability to set the nation's agenda, to command media attention, and to utilize the resources of government in accomplishing his ends. A president can take action—with and without Congress—not just make promises. In times of crisis, the historical tendency to rally around the president offers him some immunity from partisan criticism.

Having a president on the ticket isn't enough if his performance and luck are lacking. Incumbency, however, can turn otherwise bleak prospects into victory for the party in power. The Democrats would have lost the White House in 1948 had President Truman not run: With five keys down, the loss of incumbency key 3 would have brought the total to six negative keys, a losing situation for the executive party. Considering the probability of a contest for the nomination when a president does not run (eight out of thirteen elections), the Republican party could have been losers, rather than landslide victors in 1924 and 1972, had Presidents Calvin Coolidge and Richard Nixon not sought reelection. The toppling of the contest and incumbency keys, in addition to the four already turned against the presidential party in both elections, would have produced fatal six-key deficits.

A Republican loss to George McGovern in 1972? This may seem counterintuitive, but without Richard Nixon in the running, the dynamics of the entire election year probably would have been different. Among other things, McGovern might not have been the Democrats' choice. A sitting president in any but the most vulnerable circumstances tends to keep strong challenging-party candidates out of the race. Rarely has an occupant of the White House faced the opposition's ablest campaigner. Coolidge's Democratic opponent, for example, was John W. Davis, a first-rate lawyer but a second-rate politician. Until the onset of the Great Depression, Franklin Delano Roosevelt had planned to sit out the 1932 election and run in 1936, when President Herbert Hoover would have completed his anticipated second term.

Key 4: Third Party

There is no significant third-party or independent campaign.

Third parties have been part of American politics since the early days of the Republic, and they probably always will be. They traditionally have been centered on particular issues or unconventional political philosophies and therefore have attracted small fractions of the electorate.

A few third-party movements, however, have reflected deep divisions within the political mainstream. The Republican party arose as a third party during the 1850s, when the Whig party disintegrated over the issues of immigration and slavery. Sixty years later GOP progressives temporarily divided the Republican party by joining Theodore Roosevelt's Bull Moose campaign in 1912.

Although Democrats and Republicans have remained the nation's major parties since the 1850s, many of the positions initially promoted by third parties have found their way into major party platforms. For example, the People's party (Populists) of 1892 proposed ideas—the regulation of railroads, the adoption of a more flexible currency, and federal assistance to farmers—that became accepted features of American government. During the twentieth century, the Progressive third-party movements led by Roosevelt in 1912 and Robert M. La Follette in 1924 advanced policies later adopted during Franklin Roosevelt's New Deal.

Historically, third parties fall into two general categories. The "perennials"—the Socialists, the Prohibitionists, and the Libertarians are the major examples—draw over time from a small, relatively loyal constituency. The "insurgents"—the Greenbackers of 1880, the Progressives of 1912 and 1924, George Wallace's American Independent party of 1968, Ross Perot's independent movement of 1992—rise and fall in response to particular circumstances and personalities. From the 1880s through 1920, the perennial third parties alone consistently drew 3 to 6 percent of the popular vote. Since 1920, their combined draw has dropped to an average of less than 1 percent of the vote. The decline of the perennial third parties is related to lower voter turnout, which has fallen from an average of 70 percent of the eligible populace between 1880 and 1920 to an average of 57 percent from 1924 to 1992. It appears that people who would have supported perennial third parties a hundred years ago—largely those disaffected with major-party politics—have in recent decades dropped out of the electorate rather than participate on the partisan fringes.

In nine of the past thirty-eight elections, discontent with one or both of the traditional parties has ignited a major insurgent campaign. Except for the 1850s, when the existing party system collapsed, such third-party campaigns have not arisen in times of major national calamity. For example, the severe economic depressions of the 1890s and the 1930s produced upheavals within and between the major parties rather than notable third-party candidacies. Not since the birth of the Republican party has an insurgent presidential campaign led to an enduring party that nominates candidates, contests elections, and writes party platforms.

Insurgent campaigns usually emerge instead in periods of less-generalized discontent. For example, the Populist campaign of 1892—a year before the onset of depression—was sparked by economic distress in the farm belts of the Midwest and the South. In every other case, a charismatic leader has galvanized discontent either within the incumbent party or among groups without clear allegiance to either major party. Besides Theodore Roosevelt's 1912 insurgency, the only internal challenge to an incumbent party arose in 1948, when Henry Wallace and Strom Thurmond carved separate constituencies out of the left and right wings of the Democratic party. In contrast, Robert M. La Follette's 1924 candidacy challenged the post-Wilson conservatism of both major parties. Two generations later, George Wallace rallied discontent with the "liberal establishment" represented by the major parties of his era. In 1980, John Anderson pitched his campaign to disenchanted moderates among Republican, Democratic, and independent ranks. Likewise, in 1992, businessman Ross Perot appealed deeply to independent-minded voters who felt that neither party was addressing the nation's most compelling problems.

The Perot insurgency survived the 1992 elections in the form of his United We Stand America movement. In 1995, Perot sought to transform the movement into an Independence party. He indicated that the party would consider only nominating a candidate for president in 1996. For other positions, it would endorse candidates nominated by the major parties. It remains to be seen whether the Independence party will take root as an enduring organization that nominates and elects candidates at all levels of politics.

In part, third-party campaigns count against the party holding the White House, not through their direct influence on elections, but because they are barometers of discontent. The emergence of a significant third-party contender usually signals problems with the performance of the party in power, irrespective of what's happening with the challenging party.

Third-party campaigns also change the dynamics of an election. Typically, third-party insurgents direct their fire against the party in power, ignoring the challenging nominee. With little to lose, third-party campaigners can be especially wicked in their attacks. The result is a whipsaw of criticism that makes life difficult for the incumbent-party candidate, usually before the fall campaign even begins. Never in modern U.S. history has a third-party campaign reelected an incumbent administration by splitting the opposition vote. Coolidge in 1924 and Truman in 1948 were the only incumbent-party nominees to survive a major third-party challenge. Coolidge won an outright popular-vote majority of 54.1 percent; Truman won a near-majority of 49.5 percent, despite insurgent nominees from the Left and Right of his own party.

The proportion of the vote garnered by significant third-party candidates has varied considerably, from the 27 percent won by Roosevelt in 1912 to the combined 4.5 percent polled by Henry Wallace and Strom Thurmond in 1948—the only third-party campaigns that turned Key 4 without drawing 5 percent or more of the popular vote. Gauging whether such a challenge will meet this test prior to an upcoming election can be difficult, although, as in 1948, all major third-party candidates were widely regarded as significant factors during the campaign.

For upcoming elections, any candidate who appears likely to win 5 percent or more of the popular vote is a ''major'' third-party contender. If, however, a third-party candidacy clearly resulted from a split within the challenging party, it would not topple Key 4. Although no such candidacy has emerged in past elections, some candidates, such as George Wallace in 1968, may actually have drawn more votes from the challenging than from the incumbent party.

Key 4 is not turned against the party in power when several of the perennial third parties together have garnered more than 5 percent of the vote. This occurred in the 1904, 1908, and 1912 elections in which the Socialist party of Eugene Debs took most of the third-party vote. Only in 1912 did Debs reach the 5 percent mark, but Roosevelt's candidacy turned Key 4 against the incumbent Republicans irrespective of Debs's performance.

By itself, the third-party key correctly predicts 68 percent of all elections since 1860. The incumbent party has won twenty of twenty-nine elections in which there was no significant third-party candidate (win rate: 69 percent), and it has lost six of the nine in which a third-party candidate contended (loss rate: 67 percent).

Performance Keys

Keys 5 through 11 gauge the long- and short-term economy, policy change, social unrest, scandal, and foreign affairs. Although these seven keys can reflect other circumstances, they primarily measure conditions that galvanize the electorate and trigger the turning of other keys. Only once—in 1888—has the incumbent party prevailed in the popular vote with three or more performance keys turned against it. When fewer than three have been negative, the party in power has lost the popular vote only twice, in 1892 and 1912.

Except for the long-term economy key, turning the performance keys involves assessing actual events as well as the public's response to them. Perception clearly plays a role. A classic example is policy change under Herbert Hoover. Hoover took unprecedented steps to counter the deepening depression of the early 1930s, but his programs were adopted piecemeal and were so overwhelmed by the magnitude of the economic crisis that the public believed he was doing little to combat the hard times. In contrast, the Reagan administration largely escaped blame for the 1983 bombing of the Marine barracks in Beirut—the U.S. military's worst peacetime disaster in the late twentieth century—in part because of Reagan's popular appeal.

Although the role of public perception would seem to imply that the performance keys are subject to political manipulation, exactly the opposite may be true. Despite the efforts of candidates, party operatives, and consultants to shape voter sentiment, the public discounts partisan claims and charges, particularly in the course of a campaign, when everything takes on a partisan cast. In thirty-eight elections, not one of the seven performance keys has ever been turned by anything said or done by the candidates during a general-election campaign.

Key 5: Short-term Economy

The economy is not in recession during the election campaign.

What role does the economy play in presidential elections? The rule of thumb is that a good economy helps the incumbent party and a bad economy hurts. But the relationship between the economy and election results is not quite that simple. The clearest relationship between economic performance and election results is a negative one: No incumbent administration has won reelection in any of the nine elections in which the economy was in recession during the fall campaign (making Key 5 the only key with a loss rate of 100 percent). The correlation weakens on the other side of the ledger. The key has a win rate of 79 percent, as incumbent parties have prevailed in twenty-three of twenty-nine elections in which there was no recession. Overall, it is the system's second-best individual predictor, with a prediction rate of 82 percent.

The short-term economy key does not necessarily depend on whether an economic downturn meets a narrow, technical definition of a recession. Indeed, economists cannot agree on any simple, objective way to gauge the beginning or end points of recessions. The key depends primarily on whether there is the widespread perception of an economy mired in recession during the election campaign. For most past elections, the call is easy to make because the prevailing economic trend has been sustained throughout the election year. But the key may be difficult to call if the trend of the economy is unclear or if it appears to be changing late in the election year. In 1960, for example, the economic decline was so slight that some economists disputed whether the economy had entered a recession. Still, the unmistakable trend in the economy was downward, so Key 5 turned against the party in power. In 1980 the economy plunged sharply in the second quarter, was flat in the third, then showed signs of an upturn just prior to the election. But the indicators did not show clearly that recovery was under way. The National Bureau of Economic Research, the most authoritative organization that tracks economic trends, had declared a recession and, with continued high inflation and unemployment, that stigma lasted throughout the campaign.

The situation in 1992 was similar to that of 1980. The National Bureau of Economic Research had declared in 1991 that a recession had begun in July of 1990. The bureau did not indicate prior to the November 1992 election that the recession had ended, despite a preliminary report of a real growth rate of 2.7 percent in the third quarter of that year. Similarly, throughout the election year, opinion polls revealed that an overwhelming majority of Americans believed that the economy was still in recession. A September Gallup Poll found that 79 percent of respondents believed the economy was ''now in a recession.'' A nationwide *Los Angeles Times* Poll taken just a week before the election found that 76 percent of respondents believed the economy was in recession. Only in retrospect, seven weeks after Election Day, did the National Bureau of Economic Research announce that the recession had technically ended in 1991.

The 1992 experience, combined with 1960 and 1980, suggests a modified interpretation of Key 5. In the initial key system, the emphasis was on the last major turn of the economy, either upward or downward. However, the most recent election underscores the importance of public perceptions in assessing the short-term economy key. If the overwhelming public perception is one of an economy in recession, then the key should be turned against the party in power, even if the economic statistics might suggest a more ambiguous situation. As indicated in Chapter 1, some forecasters mistakenly judged the short-term economy in 1992 according to economic growth numbers alone and failed to turn Key 5 against the incumbent Republicans. The result was to reduce the number of negative keys from six to five, just below the threshold necessary to predict the defeat of President Bush.

That nearly half the incumbent administrations turned out of office have been rejected despite favorable economic conditions suggests that

Americans expect a growing economy as a matter of course. The public does not necessarily reward the party in power for good economic performance, but it does punish an administration for handling the economy poorly. This pattern also reinforces the conclusion that the direct influence of the economy varies significantly from election to election, depending upon other circumstances that prevail at the time.

Recent critiques have exposed flaws in the capacity of conventional economic growth measures, such as the Gross Domestic Product (GDP), to gauge economic progress accurately. The GDP ignores, for example, the household and volunteer economy, the distribution of income, resource depletion, and loss of leisure time. It counts as progress money spent on deterring and punishing crime or cleaning up the environment. These omissions and distortions of the GDP underscore the perils of relying on economic growth statistics alone to gauge the health of the short-term economy. Problems with the GDP also highlight the importance of assessing election outcomes according to a broader set of indicators than measures of economic growth alone.[1]

Key 6: Long-term Economy

Real annual per-capita economic growth during the term equals or exceeds mean growth during the previous two terms.

The short-term economy is not all that counts in presidential elections. A significant correlation exists between long-term economic trends and the electorate's evaluation of administration performance. Key 6 is the only key that relies strictly on economic growth measures (the only broad-based and long-term economic gauge available). The key has a win rate of 76 percent, with the incumbent party winning sixteen of twenty-one elections when real economic growth during the term matched or bettered that of the previous eight years. The executive party has lost ten of seventeen times that growth has fallen short of that mark, giving the long-term economy key a loss rate of 59 percent and an overall prediction rate of 68 percent.[2]

The short-term economy key alone implies that the American electorate is totally forgiving of poor economic performance early in an administration; the recession of 1974–75, by that line of reasoning, did not count at all against Gerald Ford in 1976. The long-term economy key provides a logical correction to that implication, comparing the current executive's handling of the economy overall to that of previous administrations.

Key 6 captures voters' concerns that are not always reflected in the election-year economy key. Inflation, for example, was a subject of concern in the elections of 1948, 1952, and 1976, but in none of those years did it outpace nominal growth and topple the short-term economy key. In each case, though, its effects are expressed in a negative long-term economy key. The key also reveals economic difficulties that did not result in campaign recessions in 1864, 1908, 1916, and 1972. The only campaign recession that did not push real growth below the comparative long-term threshold was the sharp but brief slump of 1980; the booming economy of 1977 and 1978—following the 1974–75 recession under Gerald Ford—was sufficient to make Key 6 one of the few turned in favor of Jimmy Carter's reelection bid.[3]

Although voters do not make elaborate economic calculations in deciding how to cast their ballots, the electorate's expectations do appear to be conditioned, consciously or not, by long-term economic trends. How long is long-term? It is impossible to say for sure. Comparing growth during the current term to that of the previous two terms yields a better correlation between economic performance and electoral results than does a comparison with only the previous term. The two-term gauge thus seems to be a logical measure of relative economic performance of a given administration.

Economic troubles early in a term may not only topple the long-term economy key, but may also trigger the loss of other keys. Twelve of seventeen times the key has been turned against it, the incumbent party has also lost the mandate key (which, because it depends on the mid-term congressional elections, is unaffected by the short-term economy key). Slow economic growth often reflects a lack of administrative strength and initiative, too: In eleven elections, a lagging long-term economy has coincided with the loss of policy-change key 7, and in six, with a contest for the incumbent-party nomination.

Key 7: Policy Change

The incumbent administration effects major changes in national policy.

In politics as in other areas, Americans have a high regard for initiative and innovation. The electorate clearly rewards dynamism and change: The executive party has won fourteen of seventeen elections when it has effected major changes in national policy during the term (win rate: 82 percent), and it has lost twelve of twenty-one in which it has been content with the status quo (loss rate: 57 percent). The key's overall prediction rate is 68 percent.

Activist administrations have an advantage over less ambitious and programmatic regimes. Implementing broad new initiatives gives the executive party an image of accomplishment and success, and the changes enacted usually address widely perceived needs. Moreover, the ability to push through controversial new measures—and major changes in national policy are almost always controversial—reflects both the underlying strength and the political skills of a president and his party. Consistent with a referendum theory of elections, this key accounts for policy change only in the current term, even for a president who serves two consecutive terms in office. For example, although Harry Truman and Ronald Reagan enacted major policy initiatives in their first terms, the failure of each to follow up with comparable successes in their second terms meant that both the Democrats in 1952 and the Republicans in 1988 campaigned without Key 7 in their favor.

Major policy change can take the form of redirecting the course of government or of innovating new policies and programs that have broad effects on the nation's commerce, welfare, or outlook. The progressive reforms initiated by Theodore Roosevelt and Woodrow Wilson, and the civil-rights and antipoverty programs enacted under Lyndon Johnson, exemplify the kinds of innovation that constitute major changes in national policy. Examples of government redirection include the prohibition of slavery under Abraham Lincoln, the ending of Reconstruction by Rutherford B. Hayes, and Warren Harding's rejection of the progressive and internationalist agenda pursued by Wilson. Significant change often involves both redirection and innovation, as when Franklin Roosevelt abandoned traditional restraints on government and launched the New Deal. Nearly fifty years later, Ronald Reagan reversed the long-standing, liberal emphasis on social-welfare programs in favor of increased military spending and introduced a new "supply-side" approach to fiscal affairs.

As these examples show, policy change favors the incumbent party regardless of its ideological cast. What counts is change itself, not whether it comes from the Right or the Left. Ideology is relevant to this extent: An administration that embraces an ideology different from that of the previous regime is more likely to win Key 7 than is a centrist administration or one that follows the bent of its predecessor. Thus, Key 7 registers every historic switch in the direction of government, from conservative to liberal and vice versa. A shift in party control of the White House, however, does not guarantee significant policy change. Although Republican Dwight Eisenhower came to power after twenty years of liberal Democratic rule, his centrist approach to government did not fundamentally alter domestic or foreign policy.

Major program changes and innovations not only must depart dramatically from established policies or break new ground, but also must be widely perceived as doing so at the time. Otherwise, even significant moves can go unrecognized. Like Herbert Hoover half a century earlier, Jimmy Carter was perceived as doing too little, too late to meet the challenges of his times. Carter actually initiated the military buildup and domestic budgetary restraint later championed by Ronald Reagan. But Carter's initiatives were incremental and undramatic; he certainly was not seen as having reshaped the nation's agenda. A charismatic Reagan pushed the budget and defense initiatives further, added deep tax cuts, presented the package as a manifesto, and became the leader of a conservative revolution. The fact that he presided over a doubling of the national debt, instead of balancing the budget as he promised, did not dim the perception that he had vastly changed the course of government during his first term.

Changes of the kind registered by Key 7 usually involve domestic policy, but foreign-policy initiatives also have altered the nation's commerce, conduct, and perspective. President William McKinley's expansionist policies, which resulted in the acquisition of the United States' first colonies after the Spanish-American War and the affirmation of an open-door trading policy in the Far East, modified America's traditional isolationism and thrust the nation onto the world stage with the leading European and Asian powers. Harry Truman also greatly expanded the nation's international role during his first term through initiatives designed to contain communism and expand opportunities for foreign trade and investment. Both McKinley's and Truman's foreign initiatives had profound effects on life and politics in the United States.

National crises, such as war and depression, often present opportunities for policy change that might otherwise be difficult to achieve. The Civil War led to the abolition of slavery; the Great Depression of the 1930s provided a mandate for a new, liberal agenda; and when further New Deal initiatives grew difficult to achieve, the advent of World War II created an opening for new kinds of policy change.

Chief executives who fail to take bold action in times of crisis not only lose Key 7, but may also forfeit other keys as well. Grover Cleveland's inflexibility in dealing with a severe economic depression, for example, resulted in social unrest, a nomination contest, and the loss of the mandate key and both economic keys for the election of 1896. George Bush's paralysis in domestic policy contributed to the advent of the Perot campaign.

Key 8: Social Unrest

There is no sustained social unrest during the term.

Social unrest, like a declining economy, generates public anxiety about the stability and well-being of society. It also can indicate that an incumbent administration is unable to cope with crisis. Although the United States has experienced numerous outbreaks of social unrest, it is not often a factor in American elections; it has figured into only ten of the thirty-eight elections since 1860. The party in power has lost six of these ten contests (loss rate: 60 percent), while winning nineteen of twenty-eight when domestic tranquillity has prevailed (win rate: 68 percent). Overall, Key 8 correctly predicts twenty-five or 66 percent, of the past thirty-eight elections.

To reach the threshold for turning Key 8, unrest must manifest itself in violent challenges to authority that either are sustained or raise concerns that remain unresolved at the time of the election campaign. Isolated incidents, such as the Miami race riot of 1980 or the 1992 Los Angeles rioting that followed the Rodney King trial, do not topple the social-unrest key. The key is turned against the incumbent party not only by such sustained disorders as the Civil War or the riots of the late 1960s, but also by galvanizing events—such as John Brown's raid against the federal arsenal at Harper's Ferry in 1859—that create a widespread fear that the nation's social fabric is coming apart.

Given that the criteria for social unrest are less specific than for the other keys, and the historical antecedents more particular, Key 8 is the most difficult to call retrospectively. In several past elections, upheaval fell just short of the threshold required to turn the key against the executive party. A recent example of civil disorder that played itself out prior to an election was the campus upheaval sparked by antiwar protests in 1969 and 1970, which culminated in the killing of students by National Guard troops at Kent State University in Ohio and police forces at Jackson State College in Mississippi. Polls taken in 1970 showed campus unrest to be the nation's leading public concern. But the demonstrations dropped off precipitously, and the issue did not register at all in the 1971 or 1972 polls. Had the election been held in 1970 rather than in 1972, Key 8 would have been turned against the party in power.

Outbreaks of civil disorder in the United States historically have resulted from racial conflict, labor strife, and economic depression. As the nation has matured and its political system grown more adept at responding to economic and social concerns, sustained unrest has become increasingly rare. Key 8 has been turned against the incumbent party only three times in this century—by the race riots, labor upheavals, and "Red Scare" that preceded the 1920 election, the depression-induced disorders of 1931 and 1932, and the urban riots sparked by the racial tensions and antiwar protests in 1968.

When social unrest does prevail at election time, the executive party usually suffers. Although the incumbent party won the popular vote in four of the ten elections marked by social unrest, three of the four— 1864, 1868, and 1872—took place in the turbulence of the Civil War and Reconstruction.

Key 9: Scandal

The incumbent administration is untainted by major scandal.

It is a truism of American politics that scandal can bring down an administration. Indeed, only one administration has ever survived a major scandal and gained reelection to a second term—the Harding/ Coolidge administration of 1921 to 1924. But major scandal is relatively rare in the history of the American presidency. With only a few exceptions, the highest officials of our national government have been remarkably free of corruption. Key 9 has been turned against the party in power only five times—in the elections of 1876, 1924, 1952, 1976, and 2000. The incumbent party lost the popular vote in all elections but 1924 and 2000, (loss rate: 60 percent) and has won twenty-one of thirty-three in which the administration has remained untarnished (win rate: 64 percent), giving the key an overall prediction rate of 63 percent.

It makes sense that revelations of wrongdoing diminish public regard for an administration and impair its ability to govern; in and of itself, scandal can increase pressure for a change of parties. To produce this effect, however—and to reach the historical threshold for major scandal—the wrongdoing has to bring discredit upon the president himself, calling into question his personal integrity, or at least his faithfulness in upholding the law. The four scandals that collectively set the standard for Key 9 have either directly touched the presidency or involved extensive patterns of illicit activity on the part of administration officials that the president badly mishandled.

The first three major scandals, the "Great Barbecue" of Grant's second administration, the "Teapot Dome" scandal of Harding's term, and the "Mess in Washington" during Truman's second term involved high government officials illicitly enriching themselves through bribery, kickbacks, gifts, and the sale of government contracts. The lone exception to this pattern of using public office for personal gain was the

Watergate scandal, when Nixon administration officials engaged in illegal acts primarily for partisan rather than private advantage. The Bill Clinton impeachment scandal was the only one that involved personal behavior, not the conduct of a president and his administration.

Self-defeating attempts at damage control escalated three of four of these major scandals. The experience of these scandals shows that attempts to conceal or cover up scandal or manipulate the investigatory process don't work; their only effect has been to associate the presidency with scandal. It's well known that President Nixon's attempt to cover up the Watergate story led to the downfall of his presidency. Less familiar is how President Grant's intervention in the corruption trial of his secretary tarnished the presidency. Similarly, administration interference in the investigation of scandals magnified perceptions of a mess in Washington during Truman's second term.

Scandal has an ironically self-correcting aspect. No president has ever sought reelection in the wake of a major scandal that tarnished his integrity or fidelity to the law. Grant declined to run in 1876 for what was then a constitutionally permissible third term. Warren Harding died in 1923 and was succeeded by Vice President Calvin Coolidge, who was not implicated in any of the Harding-era scandals. In 1952, Harry Truman passed up another White House bid even though he was exempt from the recently passed Twenty-second Amendment limiting presidents to two terms. To avoid impeachment for his role in Watergate, Richard Nixon resigned the presidency in 1974, turning the office over to appointed vice president Gerald Ford, who had been serving in Congress at the time of the Watergate break-in and cover-up.

Scandal is not usually entirely self-correcting; it has triggering effects on other keys. The unwillingness of Grant and Truman to seek reelection cost their parties incumbency key 3 and contest key 2 (and perhaps charisma/hero key 12 in 1876). Although the appointment of Gerald Ford following Nixon's Watergate resignation preserved the incumbency key, the scandal had a negative impact on other keys. Heavy Republican losses in the congressional elections of 1974—held only three months after Nixon's resignation—toppled mandate key 1 and led to stalemated government during the remainder of the term. Lingering preoccupation with the trauma may also have hampered President Ford's ability to cope with the foreign crises and economic distress that plagued his administration.

Scandals reach the threshold needed to topple Key 9 only when there is bipartisan recognition of the problems besetting an administration. The voting public heavily discounts allegations of wrongdoing that appear to be the result of partisanship by the opposition party. On several occasions, revelations of wrongdoing became lost in the partisan wrangling of election years. For example, in 1860, an investigating committee of the Republican-led House charged the Democratic administration of James Buchanan with an assortment of improper activities. The allegations may well have been true, but they quickly became part of the interparty wrangling of the campaign and remained unresolved. In 1972, investigations of the break-in at Democratic headquarters implicated White House and GOP campaign officials. But the public discounted Watergate as a partisan matter because the break-in occurred during the election year and allegations of wrongdoing became part of the Democratic presidential campaign. Not until the election was over, and new facts were uncovered that raised bipartisan concerns, did Watergate become a full-fledged scandal.

One scandal that did not reach the threshold needed to turn the key differs significantly from most historical precedents for wrongdoing within an administration. Unlike previous government miscreants who sought principally to enrich themselves or gain unfair advantage for their party, the officials involved in the Iran-Contra wrongdoing appeared to act primarily in pursuit of ideological, even "humanitarian," objectives. A main target of the Iran-Contra investigation—National Security Council official Colonel Oliver North—became a hero for some Americans and nearly defeated incumbent senator Charles Robb (D-VA) in 1994. For all the excesses committed by individuals within the Reagan administration, no clear pattern of corruption emerged to taint the presidency. The combination of Reagan's disengaged management style and his personal popularity kept his Teflon coating intact. His approval rating, in fact, approached a robust 60 percent less than a year after completion of the Iran-Contra investigation.

Scandal relating to sexual impropriety has played only a minor role in presidential politics. We cannot know what impact, if any, public revelation of the extramarital affairs of Franklin Roosevelt, Dwight Eisenhower, John Kennedy, or Lyndon Johnson might have had on their political fortunes. Would the intense media scrutiny given the private lives of public officials today have brought down some of our most revered presidents? The answer probably would depend on the timing of such revelations and on how the individuals handled them. Gary Hart was forced to withdraw from the race for the 1988 Democratic nomination after his affair with Donna Rice was made public, but voters' disapproval appeared to stem less from the fact of his philandering than from his arrogance and lack of judgment in conducting the affair after being questioned about the issue during the campaign. Four years later, Bill Clinton weathered Gennifer Flowers's allegations of an extramarital affair and went on to win both the Democratic nomination and the presidential election.

An instructive example of personal scandal comes from the election of 1884. Ten days after Grover Cleveland's nomination as the Democratic challenger, his hometown paper, the *Buffalo Evening Telegraph*, headlined the revelation that he had fathered an illegitimate child. Cleveland did not deny his patrimony—noting that he had taken financial responsibility for the child—and went on to win the election. Had the story broken before the nominating convention, Cleveland might not have been the Democratic nominee; but once he became the certified challenger to an incumbent party facing a deficit of seven keys, the scandal was insufficient to change the anticipated outcome of the contest.

Key 10: Foreign or Military Failure

The incumbent administration suffers no major failure in foreign or military affairs.

Just as Americans expect a growing economy, they also anticipate the competent management of foreign and military affairs. Because the public pays only sporadic attention to international matters, Key 10 is toppled only by a major disaster that appears to undermine America's national interests or seriously diminish its standing in the world. Failed diplomatic initiatives, such as Dwight Eisenhower's inability to gain a nuclear test-ban treaty with the Soviet Union, do not count against the party in power. A miscarried military enterprise like the Bay of Pigs invasion of 1961, which resulted in humiliating defeat for the United States, does topple Key 10. Failures in foreign and military affairs usually are linked directly to administration policy, but events largely beyond American control, such as the fall of China in 1949 and the Iran hostage crisis of 1979–80, also can be perceived as major failures.

Key 10 predicts wins and losses about equally well. The incumbent administration has lost seven of eleven elections in which it has suffered a major defeat in foreign affairs (loss rate: 64 percent), and it has won nineteen of twenty seven in which it has maintained its standing in the international arena (win rate: 70 percent), yielding an overall prediction rate of 68 percent.

The two foreign-policy keys, 10 and 11, are assessed independently. A foreign success does not cancel out a foreign disaster, or vice versa:

John Kennedy's triumph in the Cuban missile crisis secured the foreign-success key but did not reverse the earlier loss of the failure key caused by the Bay of Pigs.

A foreign-policy setback can result from a single, "splash" event that commands public attention—examples include the surprise attack on Pearl Harbor and the Soviet launching of Sputnik in 1957—or from sustained disappointment with the conduct of a high-visibility foreign-policy enterprise, such as the unsuccessful prosecution of a war. Truman's inability to conclude the Korean War and Lyndon Johnson's failure to make headway in Vietnam constituted major failures for their administrations.

It is possible, however, for events to transform a failing enterprise into a triumph, thereby winning both the failure and success keys for the party in power. This has happened only once. The long, dispiriting prosecution of the Civil War added up to military failure for Abraham Lincoln's 1864 reelection bid until a string of strategic victories late in the election year—Sherman's sacking of Atlanta, Sheridan's successful campaign in Virginia's Shenandoah Valley, and the sinking of the last Confederate ramming vessel—salvaged the failure key and gained the success key for the incumbent party. (This is the only time any of the performance keys have changed after the start of the general-election campaign.)

Avoiding foreign-policy failures has become much more difficult as the United States has expanded its involvement politically, economically, and militarily throughout the world. In the 1800s America's lack of extended international responsibilities made it relatively invulnerable to setbacks abroad. In fact, all eleven foreign and military defeats that have reached the threshold for Key 10 have occurred in the twentieth century—ten of them since 1940.

Ronald Reagan is the only multiterm president since Calvin Coolidge to avoid a major foreign defeat. The Iran-Contra affair, as it did with scandal, fell short of the threshold for major disaster; the president's failure to open a channel to the moderates in Iran or gain the return of the hostages held in the Middle East represented a failed initiative rather than a defeat for the United States. Indeed, the situation in the Persian Gulf actually improved in the year and a half following the Iran-Contra revelations.

Foreign-policy failure can have triggering effects by eroding confidence in presidential leadership and sowing public discord, particularly in protracted conflicts. In 1968, the Vietnam War sent demonstrators into the streets, created a deep division within the Democratic party that led to a contest for the nomination, and prompted President Johnson to drop out of the race—toppling foreign-failure key 10 and also contributing to the loss of social-unrest key 8, contest key 2, and incumbency key 3. Had Johnson been able to avoid the stigma of failure in Vietnam and run as the consensus nominee of his party, the Democrats might have recouped three keys, reducing their deficit from eight keys to five—just enough to predict a third consecutive Democratic term.

Key 11: Foreign or Military Success

The incumbent administration achieves a major success in foreign or military affairs.

Administrations face double jeopardy in foreign and military affairs. Not only does an international setback count against reelection, but so too does the failure to achieve a major success. As with the policy-change key, positive action is necessary to prevent Key 11 from being turned against the party in power. To meet the historical threshold for success, a foreign-policy initiative must be perceived as dramatically improving the nation's interests or prestige. The INF Treaty and the thawing of U.S.-Soviet relations during Ronald Reagan's second term fit both criteria, for example, but the first-term Grenada intervention, while a minor splash, neither involved critical American interests nor significantly advanced the nation's standing in the world.

The great majority of foreign successes have been decisive victories in war and momentous treaties. Difficult as such achievements may seem, more than half of all administrations have won Key 11. Sixteen of the twenty that have won it have also won reelection, giving the key a win rate of 80 percent. Eleven of eighteen times the executive has not achieved a major success, the party has lost (loss rate: 61 percent). The key's overall prediction rate is 71 percent, tying it with Key 13 as the system's third-best individual predictor.

Whereas no foreign failures occurred before 1920, successes are dispersed throughout the period since 1860. They are, however, relatively more frequent in the 1900s. The nation's expanded involvement in world affairs during this century has brought more frequent successes and failures. But the character of American triumphs has changed in the last half-century. The successful prosecutions of the Civil War, the Spanish-American War, World War I, and World War II all secured Key 11. Attaining purely military objectives has become more difficult in an increasingly complex and dangerous world. Except for George H. W. Bush's success in the Gulf War, George W. Bush's achievements in driving the Taliban from Afghanistan and capturing Saddam Hussein, and Barack Obama's success in killing Osama bin Laden, all other post-World War II triumphs have been diplomatic. These include the formation of NATO under Truman in 1949, Eisenhower's negotiated end to the Korean War, Nixon's rapprochement with China, Carter's Camp David Accords, and Reagan's treaty on intermediate-range missiles in Europe. Even President Kennedy's success in the Cuban missile crisis was arguably a mixed triumph of arms and diplomacy.

Judgments about foreign success in past administrations must be made in the context of the times. Several achievements that won popular acclaim—and secured Key 11 for the executive party—have proved less consequential than initially presumed. In 1928, for example, the Kellogg-Briand pact, outlawing military force as an instrument of international policy, was heralded as "the treaty to end all wars," even though fascist aggression soon demonstrated the naiveté of the accord. Twelve years before Kellogg-Briand, Woodrow Wilson won credit for keeping the United States out of the world war, an accomplishment that events reversed within a month of his second inauguration.

A majority of administrations—twenty-one of thirty-eight—have split the foreign-policy keys, with relatively mixed reelection results (eleven wins and ten losses). When Keys 10 and 11 line up together, the combination is nearly decisive. The party in power has won twelve of the thirteen elections in which both keys were turned in its favor. The lone exception is 1992, when George Bush lost exactly six keys and the election, despite securing both foreign-policy keys. Only four times has the party in power lost both foreign-affairs keys—all four since 1956—and all four times it has lost the election.

Personality Keys

Observers have long tried to link various attributes of personality to electoral success: warmth, likability, appearance, trustworthiness, optimism, eloquence, vigor, and even height are said to give one candidate the advantage over another. To some extent, this hodgepodge of personal traits may influence voters. The historical pattern indicates that personality is a significant factor only at an unusually high threshold, and even then, personal appeal never has overcome the separate verdict of the political and performance keys.

Key 12: Incumbent Charisma; Key 13: Challenger Charisma

The incumbent-party candidate is charismatic or a national hero. The challenging-party candidate is not charismatic or a national hero.

Personalities do have an independent impact on elections, but only when there is an extraordinarily persuasive or dynamic candidate, or one who has attained heroic status through achievements prior to his nomination as a presidential candidate. Few candidates have reached this threshold. The major parties have selected only seven charismatic candidates in the thirty-four elections since 1860: James G. Blaine, William Jennings Bryan, Theodore Roosevelt, Franklin D. Roosevelt, John F. Kennedy, Ronald Reagan, and Barack Obama. There have been only two clearly heroic nominees, both of whom attained this stature through vital leadership in war: Ulysses Grant and Dwight Eisenhower. Many other candidates, including William McKinley, George McGovern, and George Bush, have had impressive military records but have fallen far short of the heroic status attained by Grant and Eisenhower. Of all presidential candidates since 1860, only Theodore Roosevelt, the leader of the ''Rough Riders'' during the Spanish-American War, combined personal charisma with near-heroic accomplishment.

That voters do not simply choose the more-charismatic candidate is perhaps best illustrated by the case of William Jennings Bryan, arguably the most captivating orator in American history and one of the most tireless campaigners. Yet at the height of his powers he lost twice—first as the incumbent-party candidate and then as the challenger—to the colorless William McKinley.

Still, charisma is an advantage. With a charismatic or heroic nominee, the incumbent party has won eight of ten elections, giving Key 12 a win rate of 80 percent. The lack of charisma, however, is not a major disadvantage to the party in power at election time. The incumbent party has lost only thirteen of twenty-eight elections in which its candidate lacked unusual appeal, giving the key a loss rate of 46 percent—the lowest of any of the keys. Because it is such a weak predictor of incumbent-party losses, Key 12 predicts the winner of the popular vote only 55 percent of the time.

Key 13, regarding the charisma of the challenging-party candidate, is a better overall predictor, correctly calling the winners in twenty-seven elections, or 71 percent of the time. Picking an extraordinary nominee is more important to the challenging party. Incumbent-party candidates have won twenty-two of thirty two elections in which the challenger was neither charismatic nor heroic, giving the key a win rate of 69 percent. All six charismatic challengers have won except Bryan in his second campaign (he was the incumbent-party nominee in 1896 and was no longer charismatic in 1908), for an incumbent-loss rate of 83 percent.

For incumbent parties, the charisma key has important triggering effects. No sitting president who was charismatic or a national hero has ever been challenged within his party, faced a third-party campaign or a charismatic opponent, or been defeated for reelection. Every charismatic president has been able to achieve major policy change and foreign-policy success in at least one presidential term (although in Kennedy's case, policy innovation occurred after his assassination and the succession of Lyndon Johnson). In contrast, the heroes Grant and Eisenhower never achieved major policy change, although both of them served two terms in office. In the twentieth century, only four presidents have served two full terms—Wilson, Franklin Roosevelt, Eisenhower, and Reagan. Two of them were charismatic and one was a national hero.

Charismatic candidates have tended to hold their ambitions in check until conditions were favorable for a presidential run. Franklin Roosevelt hadn't planned to run in 1932 until the Great Depression doomed the incumbent Hoover administration. John Kennedy seized his opportunity after Eisenhower's two terms ended in 1960. In 1988 Mario Cuomo, a potentially charismatic Democrat, declined to compete against the incumbent Republicans during a period of economic expansion, accomplishments abroad, and tranquillity at home.

Of all circumstances gauged by the keys, charisma is most likely to be determined during the general-election campaign. It is not always easy to call. Although widely recognized as a brilliant orator, James G. Blaine was tarnished by accusations that he had participated in the railroad swindles of the Grant years; still, as the most magnetic personality of his era, Blaine had Key 12 turned in his favor. Woodrow Wilson, on the other hand, was also a gifted orator, but the scholarly politician lacked the common touch. The charisma of Franklin Roosevelt and Ronald Reagan—although both were known as gifted speakers and appealing personalities—was not fully tested until they faced the rigors of the presidential campaign. Unlike Bryan, Theodore Roosevelt, and Kennedy (after the 1960 debates), both FDR and Reagan would have been difficult calls in advance of their first elections.

Heroic stature is easier to identify. To meet the threshold, a candidate's achievement must be deemed critical to the nation's success in an important endeavor, and probably should be of relatively recent vintage. New Jersey senator Bill Bradley's career as a highly acclaimed professional basketball player, while appealing to a large segment of the population, does not make him a national hero. Ohio senator John Glenn's achievement as the first American astronaut to orbit the earth might have conferred that status early on, but probably would no longer have secured the key had he been nominated in 1984.

The personality keys are not necessary to predict past elections, but they correlate with election results, sensibly increase the spread between winners and losers, and account for a political dimension that could be decisive in a future election. Without them—that is, using only Keys 1 through 11 (with an incumbent-loss threshold of five negative keys)—it is easy to construct a scenario in which the subsystem's prediction would be likely to fail. History offers two hypothetical tests, the elections of 1880 and 1948. In both cases, exactly four political and performance keys were turned against the party in power. If charismatic challengers had emerged against James Garfield and Harry Truman, neither of whom was charismatic himself, the eleven-key political/performance system would still predict victories for them. Yet a charismatic candidate would almost certainly have overcome Garfield's two-thousand-vote advantage in 1880 and very probably would have beaten Truman in 1948—outcomes that would have been predictable only by the inclusion of the personality keys.

Chapter 3

Civil War and Reconstruction

The American political order and ultimately the Union itself came apart in the 1850s over the issue of slavery. From this turmoil emerged the modern political system of Republicans and Democrats.

In the early 1850s, sectional conflict erupted over whether the federal territories of Kansas and Nebraska would become slave or free states. With the Kansas-Nebraska Act of 1854, the Congress, led by Illinois Democrat Stephen A. Douglas, established the principle of "popular sovereignty," leaving the question of slavery to be decided by the people in these territories. The Kansas-Nebraska Act opened a wedge for the expansion of slavery north of the Mason-Dixon line. Throughout the North, antislavery leaders denounced Douglas as a stooge of southern interests; the Democratic party was beginning to split along sectional lines.

The real victim of failed compromise was the Whig party, which included moderate but generally proslavery Southerners and northern Protestants who were in the vanguard of the antislavery, temperance, and anti-immigrant movements. This amalgam did not hold. To many fervent Protestants, both slavery and Catholic immigrants were evils that threatened to undermine republican institutions in the United States. During the battle for popular sovereignty, southern Whigs deserted the party as northern leaders sought, in vain, to use antislavery sentiment to unite the party in the North.

From the ashes of northern Whiggery emerged a new party, the Republicans, founded on opposition to slavery in any of the western territories and drawing significant support from Protestants who feared the influence of Catholic immigrants. The Republican party, like the Whigs before them, also advocated the use of government to promote enterprise, courting the support of business interests in northern states. In

49

1854 and 1855, the Republicans vied with the extremist, but formidable, American party, a semi-secret, anti-Catholic, anti-immigrant coalition (also known as the Know-Nothings because members would respond that they "knew nothing" when asked about their party) to replace the now-defunct Whigs as the major opposition to the Democratic party.

The Republicans overtook the Know-Nothings in 1856, when they first contested for the presidency, nominating as their candidate the western explorer and adventurer John C. Fremont. During the election year, the Republicans consolidated antislavery support while themselves exploiting the anti-Catholicism that had given the Know-Nothings much of their appeal.[1]

The Democrats spurned their incumbent president, Franklin Pierce, whose vacillation over the expansion of slavery had pleased neither the North nor the South, making Pierce the first American president denied a second term by his own party. They turned instead to James Buchanan, who had been abroad as ambassador to England during the struggles over Kansas. He would be known as the "available man," acceptable to Northerners within the party despite proslavery positions favored by the Democrats' now-dominant southern wing. Former Whig president Millard Fillmore entered the race as the American party nominee.

Despite Buchanan's failing health and a lackluster Democratic campaign, he won 45 percent of the popular vote; Fremont took 33 percent, and Fillmore trailed with 22 percent. The Democrats also gained 35 seats in the 236-seat House of Representatives, moving from a 35 percent minority to a working majority of 50 percent.

James Buchanan would prove unable to contain the long-simmering sectional conflict that bubbled into rebellion by the end of his term. The presidential election of 1860 would take place with the American political system in dissolution. With Buchanan wisely retiring from public life, his party would splinter into northern and southern factions, handing the presidency to Abraham Lincoln, only the second presidential nominee of the fledgling Republican party. Buchanan would be the last Democratic president for twenty-four years.

Unlike the Whigs, the Democrats would survive their internal schism to reemerge as the opposition party of the 1860s, struggling first against Lincoln's commitment to military victory and then against Republican efforts to establish civil and political rights for the freed slaves. Partisan divisions over racial issues in the 1860s would give Republicans a sizeable advantage in northern states, create a Democratic South after the demise of Republican-controlled Reconstruction governments, and define the party loyalties of voters for another seventy years. In contrast to the later roles of the two parties, the Republicans would be the activist party of the nineteenth century, whereas Democrats would defend limited government and states' rights.

1860: The Union in Peril
Incumbent-party nominee: Stephen Douglas (Democrat)
Challenging-party nominee: Abraham Lincoln (Republican)
Negative keys: 7
Result: Lincoln, 39.8%; Douglas, 29.5%; John C. Breckinridge
(Democrat), 18.1%; John Bell (Constitutional Union), 12.6%

Key:	1	2	3	4	5	6	7	8	9	10	11	12	13
Call:	O	X	X	X	O	O	X	X	O	O	X	X	O

Abraham Lincoln, remembered for some of the most moving oratory in American history, made no speeches during the campaign of 1860. The former congressman from Illinois followed tradition and stayed home while a cadre of political professionals made the stump speeches and wrote the broadsides for the Republican campaign. With the political system disintegrating on the eve of southern secession, any candidate fielded by the Republicans in 1860 would have beaten any nominee of the incumbent Democratic party.

The economy, at least, was relatively kind to the party under James Buchanan. Although a financial panic pushed the economy into a tailspin in 1857, recovery had begun by the end of 1858, and the expansion continued for another two years. Both the short-term and long-term economic keys (Keys 5 and 6) were locked in the Democrats' favor for 1860.

The ailing Buchanan, confronted with a divided party, an opposition Congress during his last two years, and a nation increasingly out of step with his proslavery leanings, never came close to securing policy-change key 7 for his party.

The Democrats also lost social-unrest key 8, although on a much closer call. The most violent incidents of "Bleeding Kansas"—the bitter struggle for control of the territory between pro- and antislavery forces—had already occurred when Buchanan took office, but strife continued there until a settlement was reached in the summer of 1858. The turmoil that would topple social-unrest key 8 was sparked on 16 October 1859, when abolitionist John Brown and a handful of followers captured the U.S. arsenal at Harper's Ferry, West Virginia. Undertaken with the aim of instigating a slave revolt in the South, the raid heightened already considerable fears that the nation was headed for a violent confrontation over the issue of slavery; although no other comparable incidents occurred before the election of 1860, the general apprehension was sustained throughout the year.[2]

Charges that the administration awarded government contracts to serve partisan ends, mismanaged federal departments, and abused presidential powers in lobbying for a proslavery constitution in the Kansas territory also rocked the Buchanan administration. But the case against Buchanan became embroiled in the interparty wrangling of the election year. Because the charges, however accurate, became partisan accusations, Key 9 narrowly remained in the Democrats' column.[3]

In an era when foreign policy was of secondary importance, the administration suffered no major foreign-policy or military failure, thus holding Key 10 in the Democrats' favor. But Buchanan's few and modest diplomatic accomplishments failed to capture foreign-policy success key 11. The splitting of the two foreign-policy keys would be typical of late-nineteenth-century administrations.

The Democrats entered the election year with prospects of retaining only a single political key—mandate key 1. As expected, President Buchanan served out his term but did not seek reelection, forfeiting Key 3 for the incumbent Democrats. After one adjournment and two walkouts by southern delegates, the Democratic convention finally nominated Senator Stephen Douglas. The bitter convention battle had cost the party Key 2. In selecting Douglas, it also lost a seventh and final key— incumbent-charisma key 12. The "Little Giant," architect of the failed policy of popular sovereignty and perceived loser of the Lincoln-Douglas debates of 1858, had not emerged as the charismatic leader he had shown promise of becoming a decade earlier.

The internal party battle would have cost the Democrats third-party key 4 as well—the bolting Democrats nominated a proslavery ticket led by Vice President John Breckinridge at a convention of their own—but by this time Key 4 already was lost. Elements of the late Whig and American parties had formed the Constitutional Union party in hopes of uniting Northerners and Southerners by avoiding the slavery issue and focusing its campaign on support for the Union and the Constitution. The party nominated a former Know-Nothing, John Bell of Tennessee, as its presidential candidate in a bid to attract border-state voters.

With the loss of three of the four political keys, as well as policy-change key 7, social-unrest key 8, foreign-success key 11, and incumbent-charisma key 12, the Democrats had seven negative keys—one more than needed to predict the party's defeat.

The Democrats had the consolation at least of retaining Key 13 when the Republicans also failed to field a charismatic candidate. Lincoln's performance in the 1858 debates had been solid but not electrifying. In fact, the "Great Emancipator" would capture the imagination of the American people only in retrospect, achieving charisma after his martyrdom half a decade later.

The Republican platform opposed the expansion of slavery but stopped short of advocating its abolition. Consonant with the party's emphasis on activist government and economic development, the platform also called for homestead legislation to promote western settlement, protective tariffs, and internal improvements.

Democratic candidate Stephen Douglas departed from the usual practice to stump the nation in his own behalf. Otherwise, the Democratic and Republican campaigns featured the spectacular pageantry and popular participation characteristic of mid-nineteenth-century politics— mass rallies, torchlight parades, daylong rounds of oratory.

Stephen Douglas—nominee of the previously dominant Democratic party—finished last in the electoral college with only 12 electoral votes, losing out to the splinter Democratic candidate, John Breckinridge, with 72 electoral votes, and even to the former Know-Nothing John Bell, who gained 39. The Republican Lincoln won with 180 electoral votes, almost all of them from the populous northern states. Despite his overwhelming victory in the electoral college, Lincoln won the popular vote with a plurality of only 40 percent—lower than any subsequent winning presidential candidate.

Lincoln would preside, however, over a unified government. Although the Republicans dropped nine seats in the House nationwide, the southern secession of 1861 would boost the party's representation in the House from a 48 percent plurality to a 59 percent majority (placing the executive party in an excellent position to gain the mandate key in 1864) and give the Republicans an overwhelming majority in the Senate as well.

1864: The Jaws of Defeat
Incumbent-party nominee: President Abraham Lincoln (Union/
  Republican)
Challenging-party nominee: General George B. McClellan (Democrat)
Negative keys: 3
Result: Lincoln, 55%; McClellan, 45%

Key:	1	2	3	4	5	6	7	8	9	10	11	12	13
Call:	O	O	O	O	O	X	O	X	O	O	O	X	O

Abraham Lincoln's election itself led to a chain of events that put his reelection in jeopardy. The selection of a Republican president was unacceptable to many Southerners. By February of 1861—Lincoln was not inaugurated until 4 March—seven southern states would secede from the Union. About a month later, on 12 April, the Civil War would begin with the bombardment of Fort Sumter in South Carolina. In that moment, social-unrest key 8 turned against the incumbents, and the fortunes of the Republican party hung on the fate of the nation itself.

Disappointment over the government's failure to defeat quickly the southern rebels contributed to a slightly declining Republican majority in the House, from 59 percent to 55 percent. But prior to 1860, the Republicans had held only 48 percent of House seats, so mandate key 1 was secure for 1864.

The war itself forced Lincoln to make major changes in national policy, securing Key 7. To finance the war effort the federal government issued paper money that for the first time since 1789 was not secured by gold, silver, or bonds. The administration instituted a graduated income tax, established a national banking system, and began a nationwide draft. The most dramatic change, however, was Lincoln's Emancipation Proclamation declaring all slaves free, except for those in the Union slave states and in areas of the Confederacy occupied by Union forces. Although the proclamation was motivated by both strategic and political considerations, and emancipation was less than universal, for the first time the federal government had taken a decisive stand against slavery.

Economic performance during the war had been slightly poorer than that of the previous eight years, so long-term economy key 6 would be lost to the party in power. Still, the economy was growing in the election year; barring an unexpected downturn, the Republicans would split the economic keys, retaining short-term economy key 5. With long-term economy key 6, social-unrest key 8, and incumbent-charisma key 12 already down, the Republicans faced a deficit of three keys as the nominating process began. Several more keys were yet to be decided.

Despite the victories at Antietam and later at Gettysburg, the Republicans entered the election year of 1864 with no assurance that Union forces would prevail on the battlefield. The fate of the parties now hinged on foreign and military affairs. Nearly four years of stalemated war meant that Lincoln still lacked a major foreign/military victory

(Key 11) and might even lose failure key 10 as well. (Lincoln had succeeded in keeping the European powers out of the war, but this merely staved off a foreign-policy and, perhaps, a military defeat.) Although Lincoln faced no strong opponent for the nomination of his own party, he was confronting the loss of third-party key 4 as Republicans disaffected with the course of the war promoted the candidacy of John C. Fremont, the Republican standard-bearer in the presidential election of 1856. The loss of all three of these keys would result in a six-key deficit and a predicted defeat for the party of Lincoln, regardless of whom the Democrats nominated in 1864.

Given this perilous situation, Lincoln's supporters reorganized their forces as a "Union" party to try to unite all those dedicated to the war effort. To broaden his coalition, Lincoln dumped his vice president, Hannibal Hamlin, a former senator from Maine, in favor of Andrew Johnson, a War Democrat from Tennessee.

But it was victory on the battlefield, rather than these base-building efforts that proved decisive for Lincoln and the Republicans. On 3 September, news came from the front that General Sherman had taken Atlanta; it was the first major Union victory of 1864. By 19 October, General Sheridan had driven rebel forces from Virginia's Shenandoah Valley—a major supply source for the Confederates—and was laying waste to the area. Nine days later, Union gunners sank the last Confederate ramming vessel, the *Albemarle*, in the Roanoke River. At last, a Union victory appeared to be at hand; the military successes secured Keys 10 and 11 and led to the abandonment of the Fremont campaign, securing Key 4.

To oppose Lincoln, the opposition Democrat chose George B. McClellan, the former general-in-chief of the Union armies whom Lincoln fired for inaction in 1862. The lackluster McClellan was a compromise candidate within the Democratic party, sympathetic to antiwar sentiment yet unwilling to endorse the pro-southern "Copperheads" who called for peace at any price. The incumbents retained challenger-charisma key 13.

Lincoln crushed McClellan 55 percent to 45 percent at the polls. The president and his Republican-based Union party increased their House majority to an extraordinary 78 percent, the largest margin for any party since the 1820s. The election virtually guaranteed Republicans the mandate key for 1868 and seemed to guarantee that the party would dominate the process of reconstructing the Union after the guns fell silent.

1868: Challenger in the White House
Incumbent-party nominee: Ulysses S. Grant (Republican)
Challenging-party nominee: Horatio Seymour (Democrat)
Negative keys: 2
Result: Grant, 52.7%; Seymour, 47.3%

Key:	1	2	3	4	5	6	7	8	9	10	11	12	13
Call:	O	O	X	O	O	O	O	X	O	O	O	O	O

Confederate commander Robert E. Lee surrendered within a month of Lincoln's second inauguration, giving the administration the military triumph needed to secure Key 11. But President Lincoln would not lead the nation through the process of restoring the rebel states to the Union, dealing with Confederate officials and soldiers, recovering from the destruction of war, and assimilating millions of freed slaves. An assassin's bullet, fired by Confederate loyalist John Wilkes Booth just a week after Appomattox, determined that Vice President Andrew Johnson, the Tennessee Democrat added to the ticket in the Republicans' Union party campaign, would preside over postwar reconstruction.

Johnson's ascent to the presidency was at first hailed by the Republican Congress, particularly the Radicals, who had always questioned Lincoln's antislavery commitment and feared that he would be too lenient in his treatment of the southern states. They assumed that Johnson, a Southerner who had courageously defended the Union in his own land, would be less conciliatory. That assumption was incorrect. President Johnson was soon in open conflict with Congress as he set about quickly restoring the secessionist states to the Union and providing only minimal federal involvement in southern race relations.

By 1866 the break between Congress and the new president was complete. With Johnson acting more like a Democrat than a Unionist, the Republican administration was now operating with a president who was, in effect, the leader of the opposition. By passing legislation and overriding Johnson's vetoes, Congress established its own version of Reconstruction. It refused to recognize southern governments organized under Johnson's plan, enacted a civil-rights bill, and passed the Fourteenth Amendment to the Constitution.

In the midterm elections of 1866, President Johnson attempted to form a new party of Democrats and conservative Republicans, but moderate and radical Republicans easily retained better than two-thirds majorities in both houses of Congress. Because their 74 percent majority in the House exceeded their 55 percent at the end of the previous term, the Republicans locked in mandate key 1.

Congress, with a firm hold on government in 1867, passed a series of Reconstruction laws that divided the South into military districts, each under the control of a commander given broad powers to use troops and military courts to keep the peace and enforce the law.

Conflict over the Reconstruction laws and Congress's attempts to limit presidential appointment powers sparked the final clash between President Johnson and the Congress. For the first ~~and only~~ time in American history, the House of Representatives voted articles of impeachment against a president of the United States. Johnson's presidency barely survived, as the Senate failed by one vote to convict him of charges brought by the House.

Despite the presence of a Democrat in the White House, the technically incumbent Republicans entered the campaign of 1868 with excellent prospects for reelection. Mandate key 1 had been in place since the 1866 elections, and the defeat of the Confederate forces had secured Key 11. The Reconstruction initiatives put Key 7 in the Republicans' column. Although a mild postwar recession had begun in 1865, recovery had gotten under way in 1867, and the election year was a good one for the economy, so the party in power counted both economic keys (5 and 6) in its favor. Incumbency key 3 was turned against the Republicans, who certainly would not nominate their enemy, President Johnson.

Nor could the party quiet the upheavals of Reconstruction. By 1866, White Southerners had begun to resist violently the prospect of Black political and civil equality. The result was sustained and widespread disorder that cost the Republicans Key 8.

Divided as it was, the administration remained untainted by major scandal, thus holding Key 9. It also suffered no military or foreign defeat, thereby securing Key 10 as well. At a nominating convention held shortly after the impeachment trial of President Johnson, the Radical-led Republicans secured two additional keys—contest key 2 and incumbent-charisma key 12—by unanimously nominating the Civil War hero General Ulysses S. Grant.

President Johnson sought the Democratic nomination in July, but the Democrats, wary of his unpopularity and struggling for survival, rejected his bid. The delegates suffered through twenty-two ballots before settling on New York governor Horatio Seymour, whose reluctance in accepting the nomination caused him to become known as the "Great Decliner." Without a nominee who was charismatic or a national hero, the Democrats forfeited Key 13 to the Republicans. When no third party entered the contest, Key 4 fell into the incumbents' column as well.

The hero of Appomattox won 53 percent of the popular tally and 214 of 298 electoral votes. The Republicans also maintained control of Congress, although their percentage in the House slipped from 74 percent to 70 percent, jeopardizing the mandate key for 1872.

1872: The First Teflon Presidency
Incumbent-party nominee: President Ulysses S. Grant (Republican)
Challenging-party nominee: Horace M. Greeley (Liberal/Democrat)
Negative keys: 3
Result: Grant, 55.6%; Greeley, 43.9%

Key:	1	2	3	4	5	6	7	8	9	10	11	12	13
Call:	X	O	O	O	O	O	X	X	O	O	O	O	O

Although he lacked political and management skills or wisdom in the selection of his subordinates, Grant held significant advantages in his bid for reelection in 1872. Incumbency key 3 fell into place from the day of his inauguration, and unless his future performance tarnished his reputation as a war hero, he also would hold Key 12. A postwar recovery that secured both economic keys additionally boosted Grant's reelection prospects.

Despite the recovery, the restoration of southern states to the Union substantially decreased Republican representation in Congress in the midterm elections of 1870, costing the party mandate key 1. After 1870, the Republican majority in the House dropped to 55 percent.

President Grant assumed office with no program of his own; he followed the precedents set by the Republican Congresses that had guided federal policy during the Johnson years. None of his actions constituted major policy change, which meant that Key 7 would be lost to the Republicans in 1872.

As White Southerners continued to chafe under Reconstruction, social unrest continued. Grant's victory, combined with Republican control of Congress, meant the continued presence of federal troops, the sustained enforcement of the Reconstruction laws, and passage of the Fifteenth Amendment, which prohibited denial of the right to vote on the grounds of race, color, or previous servitude. But while Blacks celebrated and northern Republicans congratulated one another on passage of the amendment, southern Whites redoubled their opposition to "Africanization" and to the Republican party that seemed determined to impose it on them. Social unrest continued throughout the South, resulting in the congressional passage of three separate Force Acts authorizing the redeployment of federal troops to parts of the South to restore public order and protect voting rights. By the election year of 1872, the Ku Klux Klan and most similar White supremacist groups were in decline, but as Isaac Selley, a southern Republican leader, observed in March, "the effect, the dread—still remains."[4] Key 8 was thus turned against the administration.

When it came to the scandal key, President Grant was a lucky man. Corruption was rife in the Grant administration; cabinet members and top White House advisers made abundant use of their public authority for private gain. But the public would not learn of this widespread malfeasance until Grant's second term, thereby sparing the incumbent the loss of scandal key 9.

Another bit of luck was Grant's selection of Hamilton Fish as secretary of state, the only outstanding appointee in his cabinet. In 1871, Secretary of State Fish concluded the Treaty of Washington, which established procedures for the successful arbitration of America's wartime claims against Great Britain for the building of Confederate raiding vessels. Just in time for the election, Fish's enterprising diplomacy produced the historic "great rapprochement" between the United States and Great Britain—and gained Key 11 for Grant. With no major foreign failure during the term, the administration also secured Key 10.

Despite Grant's bright prospects for reelection, he faced opposition within his own party from a group of self-styled "Liberal Republicans" who objected to the influence wielded by the Republican machine politicians, sought a merit system of government, and favored federal disengagement from the South. The Liberals, however, lacked the standing needed to pose a credible threat to the renomination of President Grant, so they summoned their own nominating convention at Cincinnati in May and selected Horace Greeley, editor and publisher of the influential *New York Tribune*, as the Liberal Republican nominee.

The Liberals never intended to run Greeley as a third-party candidate. Even before they assembled in Cincinnati, Liberal leaders were promoting fusion with the Democrats as the only viable strategy for defeating President Grant. For many Democrats, the Greeley nomination presented an opportunity to achieve a political realignment that would free the Democrats from their identification with the Confederate cause and create a centrist coalition organized around the nonsectional issue of government reform. At their July convention in Baltimore, the Democratic party endorsed the Greeley ticket.

By removing a major third-party contender from the presidential field, the Democrats' nomination of Greeley handed the Republicans Key 4. Grant's renomination without dissent at the Republican convention turned the remaining political key, Key 2, in the Republicans' favor as well.

Although Greeley was appealing as an outspoken, crusading editor, he lacked both charisma and political experience, which meant that the final key, Key 13, was also safe for the Republicans. The party had only three negative keys on Election Day.

With 55.6 percent of the popular vote, Grant had the largest popular-vote percentage since Andrew Jackson's in 1828. Grant won all but seven states and about four-fifths of the electoral vote. In the House of Representatives, the Republicans boosted their majority from 55 percent to 65 percent, boding well for capturing mandate key 1 in the next election. Although the liberal Republican movement failed in 1872, conflict between a Republican old guard of machine politicians and reformers influenced by the liberals' ideas would continue for another twenty-five years.

1876: The "Stolen" Election
Incumbent-party nominee: Rutherford B. Hayes (Republican)
Challenging-party nominee: Samuel J. Tilden (Democrat)
Negative keys: 9
Result: Tilden, 51%; Hayes, 48%

Key:	1	2	3	4	5	6	7	8	9	10	11	12	13
Call:	X	X	X	O	X	X	X	O	X	O	X	X	O

After the results were tallied in 1872, Horace Greeley lamented, "I was the worst beaten man who ever ran for high office." Yet Republican hopes for a bright four years were dashed within months of Grant's second inauguration. In September 1873, the bankruptcy of the nation's premier banking firm, Jay Cooke & Company, triggered the failure of scores of financial institutions and paralyzed credit throughout the country. The ensuing panic precipitated an economic depression that would last throughout the term.

Grant's administration did not respond to the hard times with new policy initiatives. Congress showed greater responsiveness, passing legislation in 1874 to expand the nation's money supply through a new issue of greenback currency. But Grant, believing that too much easy money benefited debtors and irresponsible adventurers at the expense of thrifty and successful businessmen, vetoed the "inflation bill" and stiffened his commitment to tight-money policies that only exacerbated the financial crunch. This inaction would cost the incumbent Republicans both the long-term and election-year economy keys for 1876.

The deep depression, and Grant's ineffective response to it, contributed to disastrous Republican losses in the congressional elections of 1874. For the first time in nearly twenty years, the Democrats regained control of Congress, turning a 65 percent Republican House majority into a Democratic edge of 58 percent. As a result, the executive party lost mandate key 1.

The second Grant administration was as ineffectual on other domestic fronts as it was in economic policy. It took its strongest initiative in 1875, when the administration supported, and a lame-duck Republican Congress passed, a last-gasp Reconstruction measure to provide Blacks equal access to public accommodations and jury service. But the legislation omitted equal access to education—a key demand of southern Blacks—and never was vigorously enforced. (The Supreme Court would declare it unconstitutional eight years later.) Little else of consequence was accomplished, leaving policy-change key 7 turned against the party in power.

The administration narrowly avoided the loss of social-unrest key 8, as discord continued in those southern states still controlled by Reconstruction governments. Unlike violence in the South during the earlier years of Reconstruction, however, the events of the second Grant administration were confined to particular states and no longer raised questions about the restoration of the social fabric in the United States. Narrowly, the incumbent party retained the social-unrest key.

The Republicans were not so lucky on Key 9. The widespread corruption that had permeated government since the Civil War finally caught up with them. Investigations of the Grant administration found that top-level officials and close advisers had participated eagerly in what became known as the "Great Barbecue" of the 1870s. In 1875 the president's personal secretary, Orville E. Babcock, was indicted for conspiring with the notorious Whiskey Ring to defraud the federal government of revenue from the excise tax on alcohol. Babcock was acquitted only after President Grant sent the court a deposition defending his friend and adviser. The evidence of Babcock's guilt was so clear that Grant's intervention inevitably associated the president with his secretary's crime. Investigations conducted by the Democratic House of Representatives in 1876 revealed other serious misdeeds by cabinet-level officials.

The scandals deeply wounded Grant's presidency. Short of violating the law himself, the president had done his best to obstruct the investigation of wrongdoing, to defend his tainted friends and associates, and to gloss over their derelictions and crimes. The spectacle of a chief executive callously indifferent to the moral collapse of his administration not only cost his party the scandal key, but also ensured that Grant would not run for a third term.

Grant's second term was a relatively quiet period in foreign relations. The result was that the administration split the two foreign-policy keys, neither suffering major foreign-policy failure (Key 10) nor achieving notable success (Key 11).

The elimination of Grant left Senator James G. Blaine of Maine, the former Speaker of the House of Representatives, as the leading candidate for the Republican nomination. Although not a war hero like the president, the "Plumed Knight" of Congress was a brilliant orator and the most magnetic personality of his time. His nomination at least might have gained the party incumbent-charisma key 12, but his prospects were fatally damaged by accusations that he had accepted a bribe from railroad interests in return for his services as Speaker. With Blaine's star in descent, a deadlocked Republican convention turned on the seventh ballot to everyone's second choice, the moderate governor of Ohio, Rutherford B. Hayes. Although Hayes's nomination united the party, it cost the Republicans three additional keys—the candidacy of a sitting president (3), an uncontested nomination (2), and a charismatic candidate (12)—bringing their total to nine negative keys.

The Democratic party easily nominated its leading candidate, Governor Samuel J. Tilden of New York. As the state's attorney general, Tilden had gained national recognition for prosecuting Boss William Tweed, the corrupt leader of Tammany Hall, New York City's Democratic political machine. But Tilden was neither charismatic nor a national hero, which kept Key 13 from turning against the Republicans.

Several minor parties, variously dedicated to nativism, prohibition, and currency expansion, entered the field in 1876. The most significant among them—the Independent, or National Greenback, party—campaigned primarily on the need to make money available by inflating the currency, but even the Greenbackers lacked sufficient support to cost the Republicans Key 4.

Tilden achieved what appeared to be a clear popular-vote victory with 51 percent of the popular vote to 48 percent for Hayes. The tally was closer, however, in the electoral college, where Tilden apparently had secured 203 electoral votes to 184 for Hayes. The Democrats also retained their control of Congress, although their majority in the House dropped from 58 percent to 52 percent.

Before conceding defeat, however, Republican managers realized that the lame-duck Republican governors still holding Reconstruction power in Florida, Louisiana, and South Carolina might be able to invalidate enough Democratic ballots to certify their states' returns for Hayes and give the Republican a one-vote victory in the electoral college.[5]

At least two conflicting sets of returns were dispatched to Washington for each state, leaving Congress to adjudicate among the disputed results. The Democratic House and the Republican Senate arrived at a compromise plan, supported mainly by the Democrats, to refer the matter to an electoral commission consisting of seven Republicans, seven Democrats, and one independent, Supreme Court Justice David Davis. But when the state legislature of Illinois elected Davis to the Senate, another justice, Republican Joseph Bradley, took his place on the commission. Now the Democrats' own instrument was turned to their disadvantage.

On a straight partisan vote of eight to seven, the commission upheld the Republican position. If accepted by Congress, the commission's decision would give Hayes his one-vote majority in the electoral college. Although some congressional Democrats pledged to filibuster against certification of the candidate they now mocked as ''Rutherfraud'' B. Hayes, Tilden lacked the will to continue the struggle. Hayes placated southern Democrats with promises that he would withdraw the remaining federal troops assigned to enforce Reconstruction policies in southern states. Just two days before the official inauguration date of 4 March, the president of the Senate formally announced that Rutherford B. Hayes had been duly elected president of the United States.

Chapter 4

The Gilded Age

The election of 1876 marked both the end of Reconstruction and the beginning of a political stalemate between Republicans and Democrats. The stalled politics of America's late-nineteenth-century Gilded Age resulted in a seesaw series of close elections. With neither party able to gain a firm hold on government or the electorate, the White House changed hands in every contest of the era except 1880, when (following the disputed election of 1876) Republican James A. Garfield won by less than two thousand votes. This combination of major-party stasis and electoral uncertainty left the nation unable to cope with the deep depression of the mid-1890s, which shattered Cleveland's second administration. In 1896, insurgent Democratic candidate William Jennings Bryan failed to shake off the legacy of Cleveland's failures. Despite his defeat, Bryan's campaign introduced to the nation a new program of domestic reform. However, the immediate future belonged to William McKinley and his resurgent Republicans.

1880: The Toss-up Election
Incumbent-party nominee: James A. Garfield (Republican)
Challenging-party nominee: Winfield Scott Hancock (Democrat)
Negative keys: 4
Result: Garfield, 48.3%; Hancock, 48.3%; James B. Weaver (Greenback-
    Labor), 3.3%

Key:	1	2	3	4	5	6	7	8	9	10	11	12	13
Call:	O	X	X	O	O	O	O	O	O	O	X	X	O

In his inaugural year of 1877, President Rutherford B. Hayes made good his promise to southern Democrats and removed federal troops from their administrative role in southern states, although not all troops were actually removed from the South.[1] The end of Reconstruction marked a major change in federal policy, earning the incumbent Republicans Key 7 for the 1880 election. Other developments in the inaugural year were less auspicious for the party. Incumbency key 3 fell almost immediately after the election when Hayes announced that he intended to be a one-term president.

The country was still mired in a depression that threatened both economic keys. In the summer of 1877, the nation's leading railroads slashed wages and railroad workers went on strike in cities across the country. When President Hayes called out troops to restore order and get the trains moving again, dozens of strikers and a handful of soldiers were killed in the violent clashes that followed. It appeared that widespread social unrest might cost the administration Key 8.

The prolonged depression, which had begun in 1873, threatened other political consequences, too. Frustrated by the lack of administration action to stimulate the economy and provide relief to individuals, the fringe Greenback and Labor Reform parties pooled their strength in the midterm elections of 1878, forming the Greenback-Labor party. To redeem the failed promise of Reconstruction, leaders of the new party believed that labor must be freed not only from slavery, but also from an economic system that favored a privileged few at the expense of ordinary workers and farmers. A major insurgency appeared possible, jeopardizing not only Key 4 for 1880, but also mandate key 1 by clouding Republican prospects in the congressional elections of 1878.

Suddenly, however, the economic depression began to lift, brightening the Republicans' reelection prospects considerably. Although the administration initiated no new policies to stabilize the economy, it benefited from a brief but sharp upswing that would last through 1880 and secure both economic keys, 5 and 6, for the executive party. The improving economy also held down Republican losses in the congressional campaign, preserving mandate key 1. Prosperity dampened social unrest and took the sting out of a potential third-party movement, preserving Keys 4 and 8.

The upright and independent President Hayes guarded against even the hint of scandal in his administration, maintaining a steadfast hold on Key 9. Foreign affairs rarely made headlines during the Hayes administration, and once again the party in power split the two foreign-policy keys, holding Key 10 by avoiding any foreign defeat but forfeiting Key 11 by failing to achieve a major success.

As the parties prepared to select their nominees in 1880, the administration faced the near-certain loss of three keys—Key 2 for a contested nomination, Key 3 because the incumbent president would not be heading the ticket, and Key 11 for the lack of a major foreign success.

Ironically, either of the two leading contenders for the Republican nomination, the Half-Breed Senator James G. Blaine and former president Ulysses S. Grant—now seeking a political comeback—might have saved the GOP another key, charisma key 12, for their party. Grant, however, was unacceptable to most Republicans, who formed a strong anti-Grant coalition that commanded a majority of convention delegates but could not agree on a candidate. Senator Blaine was the strongest alternative to Grant, but failed to muster a first-ballot victory. The convention remained deadlocked for thirty-five ballots before turning to the darkest horse, Representative James A. Garfield of Ohio, then senator-elect from his state. He chose as his running mate Chester A. Arthur; "Boss" Arthur, considered a stalwart of the party's old guard, had held the key patronage position of Customs Collector of the Port of New York (much of the nation's tariff revenues were collected at this port) until President Hayes fired him in 1878. The contest for the nomination had cost the party Key 2, and, by spurning both Blaine and Grant, it also lost charisma key 12.

Fortunately for the Republicans, the Democrats lacked charismatic leadership, too. From a lackluster field, the Democrats came as close as they could to picking a national hero by nominating the able Civil War general, Winfield Scott Hancock. But Hancock lacked broad recognition and ran a stumbling campaign, leaving Key 13 on the side of the Republicans, who faced a deficit of four keys, not enough to predict their defeat.

For the first time in a national campaign, the Republicans, now known as the Grand Old Party, or GOP, began to supplement Reconstruction issues with an emphasis on the protective tariff, which became the party's signature issue of the Gilded Age. Garfield also ran the nation's first coordinated "front-porch" campaign, as he delivered brief, inspirational talks to carefully screened delegations visiting his home in Mentor, Ohio.

On Election Day, 4,446,158 ballots were cast for Garfield and 4,444,260 went to Hancock. With a margin of 1,898 votes, Garfield won what remains to this day the narrowest popular-vote plurality in history. As expected, Hancock carried every southern and border state but otherwise won only Delaware, California, and Nevada. In the electoral college, that translated into 155 votes to Garfield's 214. The Republican party held the White House for a sixth consecutive term since 1860, a feat that remains unmatched. By a narrow margin, the Republicans also regained control of the House, winning just over 50 percent of the seats. In the Senate, the two parties finished dead even, with thirty-seven seats each.

1884: Democratic Breakthrough
Incumbent-party nominee: James G. Blaine (Republican)
Challenging-party nominee: Grover Cleveland (Democrat)
Negative keys: 7
Result: Cleveland, 48.5%; Blaine, 48.2%; Benjamin F. Butler
  (Greenback-Labor), 1.8%

Key:	1	2	3	4	5	6	7	8	9	10	11	12	13
Call:	X	X	X	O	X	X	X	O	O	O	X	O	O

James Garfield had served less than four months as president when Charles Guiteau shot and fatally wounded him in the Baltimore & Potomac train station in Washington. When the president died on 19 September, Vice President Chester A. Arthur became the twenty-first president of the United States. In attempting to steer a middle course between his former old guard comrades and the reformers within his party, President Arthur would only alienate both factions, creating political difficulties for himself and the GOP.

The economic recovery that had begun in 1878 was in full force when Arthur assumed the presidency, but prosperity did not last. In 1883 the economy spiraled again into a cyclical downturn of the sort that plagued the country in the middle of every decade from the Civil War to World War I. The depression lasted through the election year, costing the Republicans Keys 5 and 6.

The beginning of economic troubles in late 1882, factional differences within the Republican party, and the president's own lackluster leadership contributed to congressional losses in 1882 that once again relegated the Republicans to minority status and cost the party mandate key 1.

President Arthur proved to be an unexpectedly able and conscientious administrator, but he was not a creative policymaker. The most significant change of the Arthur years was the passage in 1883 of the Pendleton Act, which established a Civil Service Commission, instituted a merit system for certain federal positions, and prohibited "kickback" political contributions by officeholders. But the civil service reform was a congressional, not a presidential, initiative and did not by itself prevent the loss of policy-change key 7.

The incumbents were luckier in other respects. Despite labor unrest and a bloody riot over law enforcement in Cincinnati that cost forty-five lives, the nation did not experience the kind of sustained unrest that would have turned Key 8 against the party in power. President Arthur's honest and competent stewardship of the government also held corruption largely in check. A scandal erupted in 1881 regarding corruption in the operation of the post office. President Arthur supported the vigorous prosecution of the conspirators—who nevertheless were acquitted by a jury in 1883—and so avoided serious damage from the scandal, holding Key 9 in the administration's favor.

In foreign relations, the Garfield-Arthur administration made several bold but abortive ventures that, if successful, might have greatly expanded the nation's involvement in world affairs. Like most other nineteenth-century presidencies, the Arthur administration split the foreign-affairs keys, holding foreign-failure key 10, but losing foreign-success key 11.

As expected, President Arthur's estrangement from both factions of the GOP undermined his chances for the 1884 nomination. The president was also suffering from Bright's disease, a debilitating and usually fatal kidney affliction that greatly diminished the vigor of his nomination campaign. (He would die of a cerebral hemorrhage two years after the 1884 election.) On the fourth ballot, the divided convention turned finally to James G. Blaine, who, though still tainted by charges of dishonesty, remained the most prominent Republican leader of the time. The nomination of the Plumed Knight gained the Republicans incumbent-charisma key 12, but it cost them contest key 2 and incumbency key 3.

The Democrats turned once again to a governor of New York, Grover Cleveland, as their nominee. Like Samuel Tilden before him, Cleveland had earned recognition through his clashes with the leadership of Tammany Hall. The Democrats' nomination of the competent but uninspiring Cleveland meant that the Republicans would retain Key 13.

With few major issues separating the Democrats and the Republicans, the Greenback-Labor party once again tried to fill the programmatic breech. But the party would gain only 2 percent of the popular vote—and the Greenbackers again did not constitute a major force in the campaign, salvaging third-party key 4 for the incumbent Republicans. The Prohibitionist party, dedicated to the banning of alcohol, also emerged as a serious and enduring third party in 1884, with a small but dedicated following.

Cleveland prevailed in a race that was nearly as close as 1880. The Democratic challenger garnered 4,874,621 votes to 4,848,936 for

Blaine, a margin of 25,685 votes. The electoral college vote was also close, with 219 for Cleveland and 182 for Blaine. For the first time since the Buchanan administration twenty-four years earlier, the southern-based Democrats occupied the White House. They also retained a majority in the House, although it slipped from 61 percent to 56 percent, jeopardizing mandate key 1 for 1888. The Senate remained in Republican hands, leaving the Democrats without firm control over the national government for at least their first two years in the White House.

1888: The Voters' Choice Reversed
Incumbent-party nominee: President Grover Cleveland (Democrat)
Challenging-party nominee: Benjamin Harrison (Republican)
Negative keys: 5
Result: Cleveland, 48.6%; Harrison, 47.8%

Key:	1	2	3	4	5	6	7	8	9	10	11	12	13
Call:	X	O	O	O	O	O	X	X	O	O	X	X	O

Soon after Cleveland's inauguration as president, the economy turned upward, spurred as in past expansions by surging railroad investment. The upturn lasted until early 1887, to be followed by a brief and relatively mild contraction that ended in the early spring of 1888. The election campaign was waged during an expanding economy, gaining for the Cleveland administration both economic keys.

As the first Democratic president in a quarter-century, Cleveland sought to change national policy, but not as vigorously as might have been expected. Cleveland saw the president's role as a limited one, devoted primarily to preserving public order and managing the executive branch. Like many Democrats of his time, Cleveland believed in states' rights, economy in government, a restrictive monetary policy, and a limited governmental role in regulating the economy or aiding individuals. Cleveland used his veto power to check the expansion of pension benefits to Civil War veterans, the largest federal welfare program prior to the New Deal. Cleveland exercised the presidential veto more than twice as many times as all his predecessors combined.

Despite his nonactivist temperament and philosophy, Cleveland also presided over an important change in the government's relationship with business and the economy. In 1887, Congress passed the Interstate Commerce Act, which established the first federal independent agency designed to regulate the conduct of corporate business in the United States. The act, however, was a product of congressional initiatives and did not bear the imprimatur of the Cleveland administration.

The president fell short of success in the only initiative that he actively pursued during the term—tariff reduction. Cleveland devoted his entire message to Congress in 1887 to the subject. Cleveland's tariff bill passed the House in 1888, but it died in the Republican Senate. In the end, Cleveland fell just short of gaining policy-change key 7 for the incumbent Democrats.

The economic upswing during the Cleveland years did not bring with it domestic tranquillity. The escalating conflict between labor and industry reached historic levels in 1886, when more than 600,000 workers were involved in over one thousand strikes and lockouts, more than double the number of the previous year. In May of 1886, the labor movement organized nationwide strikes and rallies in support of the eight-hour day, mobilizing some 300,000 demonstrators. In Chicago, police fired on protesting workers locked out of the McCormick Harvester plant, killing several of them. The following day, a bomb was thrown into the ranks of police trying to break up a protest rally at Haymarket Square, fatally wounding eight officers and injuring sixty-seven more. Stunned police charged the crowd, killing several demonstrators and wounding hundreds. The Haymarket bombing—the first time dynamite had been used as a weapon of protest in the United States—generated a climate of fear similar to the one instilled by John Brown's raid in 1859. Work stoppages, demonstrations, and general unease continued through the election year, turning Key 8 against the Democratic administration.

The midterm congressional elections of 1886 took place in a mixed political climate—the country was prosperous but troubled by labor unrest. The executive party suffered relatively modest midterm losses for the era, dropping only fourteen House seats and retaining a narrow majority of 52 percent. Democratic losses in 1884, however, meant that the incumbent party still lost mandate key 1.

Following the revelation in the 1884 campaign that he had fathered an illegitimate child, President Cleveland's private life continued to be the subject of speculation and innuendo, particularly after he married his attractive twenty-one-year-old ward, Frances Folsom, during his second year in office. But his detractors' accusations of moral turpitude failed to stick, and Cleveland's unrelenting rectitude in the conduct of his administration earned him Key 9.

The president acted with characteristic caution in foreign affairs, resisting opportunities for commercial and territorial expansion. Once again, the incumbent party gained foreign-failure key 10 but lost foreign-success key 11.

Although Cleveland's hard-money and low-tariff policies were not universally popular within the Democratic party, no rival emerged to challenge his leadership. The Democratic convention nominated the president by acclamation, securing Keys 2 and 3, but losing once again incumbent-charisma key 12. When no major third party came to the fore, the Democrats also locked up Key 4.

The Republicans chose Benjamin Harrison, grandson of President William Henry Harrison and a senator from Indiana until 1887, to oppose Cleveland. Harrison had none of the cachet that had helped propel his grandfather, old "Tippecanoe," into the White House in 1840, so the Democrats also retained challenger-charisma key 13.

In the actual balloting, Cleveland won—as the keys would have predicted—a plurality of the popular vote. Harrison, however, narrowly carried the swing states of Indiana and New York (the home states of the two candidates), with a combined 51 electoral votes. The resulting electoral college vote was 233 for Harrison to 168 for Cleveland. The Republicans also regained control of the House, winning a bare 51 percent majority. The 1888 contest would be the last presidential election to date in which the popular vote winner lost in the electoral college.

1892: An Ex-President Is Vindicated
Incumbent-party nominee: President Benjamin Harrison (Republican)
Challenging-party nominee: Grover Cleveland (Democrat)
Negative keys: 6
Result: Cleveland, 46.1%; Harrison, 43.0%; James B. Weaver (People's), 8.5%

Key:	1	2	3	4	5	6	7	8	9	10	11	12	13
Call:	X	X	O	X	O	O	O	X	O	O	X	X	O

As the first president since Grant to enjoy working majorities in both houses of Congress, Benjamin Harrison expected to preside over a successful four years and inaugurate another era of Republican control over government. At the outset of the term, circumstances seemed conducive to this goal. Economic production increased steadily, and Harrison initiated the most ambitious program of legislative change since the Civil War.

Among the Republicans' achievements was the McKinley Tariff of 1890, which fulfilled the protectionist promises made during the campaign by raising import duties to their highest levels ever. The Sherman Silver Purchase Act of 1890 obligated the federal government to purchase a substantial quantity of silver with the aim of expanding the currency. The Dependent Pension Bill of 1890, similar to legislation vetoed by President Cleveland, provided benefits to Union veterans unable to fend for themselves, as well as for widows and orphans. By 1893, pension payments accounted for almost half the federal budget. The Sherman Antitrust Act, by outlawing corporate combinations or conspiracies "in restraint of trade or commerce," made the United States the first industrial nation to attempt direct, legislative control over the size and scope of business activity. This two-year burst of federal initiative was sufficient to earn policy-change key 7 for the incumbent party.

Although the Harrison administration had taken office during a period of industrial expansion, a recession that hit the economy in mid-1890 contributed to heavy Republican losses in the congressional elections that November. The party gave up seventy-eight House seats, handing the Democrats a remarkable 71 percent majority and toppling mandate key 1.

The GOP claim that tariff protection would ensure industrial peace was dramatically refuted by the bloody labor strife that racked the nation in 1892. In a replay of the previous election year, strikers shut down America's premier steel mills at Homestead, Pennsylvania, rail yards at Buffalo, New York, coal mines at Coal Creek, Tennessee, and silver mines at Coeur d'Alene, Idaho. Militia forces and federal troops were called in to restore order and break the strikes. This labor strife, particularly the Homestead strike, which dragged on through the campaign season, cost the incumbents Key 8.

Other keys aligned more favorably for the administration. The midterm recession had played itself out by mid-1891, giving way to an expansion that continued through the presidential campaign, securing economic keys 5 and 6. The Harrison administration gained Keys 9 and 10 by avoiding major scandal and a setback abroad, but the lack of a major success in foreign affairs cost it Key 11.

Despite Harrison's relatively successful performance in office, many GOP leaders felt that the aloof and austere president had done little for his party. But they were unable to find a willing challenger. Still, Harrison garnered only 59 percent of the Republican convention's first ballot vote, thereby losing contest key 2. The president's renomination locked in incumbency key 3, but his lack of charisma cost him Key 12. Now the Republicans, with five keys down, stood at the brink of defeat.

The Democrats fielded their most popular leader, Grover Cleveland, the only former president ever renominated by his party. In retirement, Cleveland had more cachet than he had possessed as chief executive, but the plodding, stolid New Yorker still lacked the charisma needed to turn Key 13 against the incumbent GOP.

The Republicans lost a fatal sixth key with the emergence of the People's, or Populist, party as a major third-party contender. The Populists, a coalition that combined farmers' alliances in the South and upper Midwest with silver-mining interests in the Rocky Mountain states, advocated such major departures as the creation of a national currency (including monetary expansion through the unlimited coinage of silver), credit for farmers, a graduated income tax, government ownership of rail, telephone, and telegraph companies, and strict controls over corporate landholding.

James B. Weaver, the People's party candidate, fared better than any third-party candidate since 1860, polling about 8.5 percent of the popular vote. It was a disappointing performance for Populist supporters, but one that was more than sufficient to topple Key 4.

Instead of merely mobilizing the faithful through mass parades and rallies, the national committees of both parties in 1892 turned their efforts toward partisan recruitment and conversion through the centrally coordinated use of campaign literature, press relations, and speakers. These efforts were made necessary in part by the declining partisanship of the press. Even the yellow press of the day thrived on sensationalistic reporting rather than partisan or ideological appeal.[2]

Cleveland's 3.1 percent margin in 1892 constituted the largest popular-vote plurality since 1872. In a reversal of the previous election, Cleveland carried Harrison's home state of Indiana as well as his own state of New York, winning the electoral vote 277 to 145. In the congressional elections, however, the Democrats were unable to sustain the 71 percent House majority they had piled up in 1890, slipping ten points to 61 percent. Unless the party could achieve a dramatic reversal of precedent and gain seats in the off-year elections of 1894, mandate key 1 would be lost for 1896. Having recaptured the Senate, however, the Democrats returned to the White House with unified control over the national government for the first time since the 1850s.

1896: Bearing a "Cross of Gold"

Incumbent-party nominee: William Jennings Bryan (Democrat)
Challenging-party nominee: William McKinley (Republican)
Negative keys: 8
Result: McKinley, 51.0%; Bryan, 46.7%

Key:	1	2	3	4	5	6	7	8	9	10	11	12	13
Call:	X	X	X	O	X	X	X	X	O	O	X	O	O

With Cleveland's election in 1892, many observers believed that the balance of party power had shifted dramatically in the Democrats' favor. The party seemed finally to have transcended the sectionalism of Civil War politics by combining its lock on southern voters with a revived ability to compete in the North. From the perspective of the keys, however, the Democrats faced an uphill battle to retain the White House in 1896. With the lack of any clear successor to President Cleveland (who was considered unlikely to run again), the probable forfeiture of mandate key 1, and the potential for another Populist campaign, the party in power confronted the potential loss of all four political keys, portending almost certain defeat in 1896.

Within months of Cleveland's inauguration in 1893, a financial panic ignited a broader economic crisis that would become the deepest and longest depression to date. The Great Depression of the 1890s would last through the election year of 1896, costing the Cleveland administration both economic keys.

President Cleveland, the captive of his commitment to hard money and minimal government, failed to respond to the depression with new policies. Beyond a futile push for tariff reduction, his solution to the economic calamity was to maintain a currency backed by gold, chiefly through repeal in 1893 of the Sherman Silver Purchase Act. His unbending commitment to hard money only exacerbated the monetary contraction that had depressed investments, wages, and prices. It also divided the Democratic party by antagonizing the "silver Democrats" of the South and West.

As in his previous term, Cleveland continued to advocate tariff reduction, but the bill that emerged from Congress in 1894 contained so many concessions to protectionism that the president let it become law without his signature. The legislation authorized a federal income tax to compensate for any loss of tariff revenue, but Cleveland remained silent when the Supreme Court declared the tax unconstitutional, which added to his reputation as a "do-nothing" president. Cleveland's determined inaction cost his party policy-change key 7.

In the midst of economic crisis, social unrest once again swept the nation. For the first time in American history, "armies" of the unemployed gathered to march on Washington. The first of these groups, commanded by "General" Jacob Coxey, an advocate of public works for the unemployed, reached the capital on 30 April 1894, accompanied by a battalion of reporters. Spectators lined the streets as the general's five hundred "troops" marched up Pennsylvania Avenue sparking a violent response from the police.

While Coxey's army marched, labor unrest seethed. A record number of strikes and lockouts led to riots, gunplay, and the deployment of militia and troops across the country—and to America's first nation-wide labor boycott by Eugene V. Debs's American Railway Union. Key 8 would be turned against the party in power.

The Democrats, as could be expected under such conditions, suffered ruinous losses in the midterm elections of 1894. Dropping 5 seats in the Senate and 112 in the House, the party lost control of both bodies—and mandate key 1 for the next presidential election. Republican victories in 1894 foreshadowed sixteen years of Republican control of national government.

President Cleveland avoided both scandal and foreign-policy failure during the term, securing Keys 9 and 10, but he narrowly lost foreign-success key 11. Cleveland was unusually bold when, in 1895, he inter-vened in a boundary dispute between Venezuela and British Guiana. Secretary of State Richard Olney responded to Britain's involvement by declaring virtual U.S. sovereignty over hemispheric affairs—the "Olney Corollary" to the Monroe Doctrine. The British rejected Ol-ney's claim, but eventually agreed to the President's demand to arbitrate the dispute. Cleveland's victory in facing down the British was ap-plauded in the United States, but its impact was fleeting; the incident did not advance the nation's interests or prestige sufficiently to secure foreign-policy key 11 for the Democrats.

The selection of the popular but colorless William McKinley by the GOP at least left Key 13 in the Democrats' column. But their own nomination process cost the party yet another key. The Democratic fac-tion favoring inflation through the free coinage of silver had seized con-trol of the party, gaining the allegiance of nearly two-thirds of convention delegates. The "silverites" proposed economic reforms that they hoped would unite Democrats and Populists into a winning coali-tion, but they couldn't settle on a candidate. On the fifth ballot, the Democrats turned to Congressman William Jennings Bryan of Ne-braska. Bryan had stirred the passions of the silverite delegates with an extraordinary address that concluded, "you shall not crucify mankind on a cross of gold."[3] In Bryan, the Democrats had a charismatic nomi-nee—and Key 12. But the contested nomination toppled Key 2.

As the silverites had hoped, however, the threat of a third-party effort evaporated when the Populists endorsed Bryan's candidacy, keeping Key 4 in the incumbents' column. But with eight keys now turned against them, the victory was a Pyrrhic one.

The silver-Democrat/Populist alliance committed the Democratic party for the first time to a positive program of federal initiatives. Beyond free silver, Bryan embraced such reforms as a graduated income tax, arbitration of labor disputes, and stricter railroad regulation—positions at odds with the party's traditional commitment to states' rights and limited government.

The excitement of the 1896 campaign boosted voter turnout to its highest level in history (79 percent of the eligible population). In the enlarged electorate, Bryan actually polled almost a million more votes than Cleveland had in 1892, chiefly by securing 90 percent of the prior Populist vote. But McKinley polled nearly two million more votes than Harrison's 1892 total, the result both of Democratic defections and a decisive edge among new voters. McKinley garnered 271 electoral votes to 176 for Bryan. Although the Republicans maintained decisive majorities in both houses of Congress, they dropped forty congressional seats (primarily to Populist and Populist-Democratic candidates), virtually guaranteeing the forfeiture of mandate key 1 for 1900.

1900: The Republican Dynasty
Incumbent-party nominee: President William McKinley (Republican)
Challenging-party nominee: William Jennings Bryan (Democrat)
Negative keys: 3
Result: McKinley, 51.7%; Bryan 45.5%

Key:	1	2	3	4	5	6	7	8	9	10	11	12	13
Call:	X	O	O	O	O	O	O	O	O	O	O	X	X

The election of 1896 strengthened the power of the Republican party not only in Washington, but also in governors' mansions and statehouses across the country. Contrary to conventional historical thought, however, the 1890s did not occasion a political realignment comparable to those of the late 1850s and the early 1930s. The final decade of the last century did not give birth to a new party, reshuffle major party coalitions, or instigate broad policy changes. William McKinley's election and its attendant Republican gains in the states warded off the threat to politics as usual posed by the populist ideas that Bryan had championed during his campaign. Reaction to an economic collapse enabled Bryan's populist allies to take over the previously conservative Democratic party and brought to power a mainstream Republican party committed to the status quo. In domestic policy, McKinley would not depart significantly from the prevailing order of the Cleveland years. It would be in foreign policy and military ventures—nonissues in 1896—that the McKinley administration would make its mark on history and guarantee its reelection in 1900.

McKinley's inauguration was greeted by an economic rally ignited by increases in the supply of gold that ironically produced the monetary expansion that silverites had hoped to achieve by supporting Bryan in 1896. The expanded money supply, in concert with greater labor productivity, corporate investment, and foreign trade, produced four consecutive years of prosperity, securing for the party in power both the short- and long-term economy keys.

In domestic matters, McKinley's modest policy agenda focused on his party's long-standing commitment to high tariffs and sound money. He pushed successfully for higher tariffs and adoption of the gold standard. These and other domestic measures would not by themselves have secured policy-change key 7 for the GOP. Only through fundamental changes in America's relationship to the rest of the world—changes that had vast internal ramifications—did the party gain Key 7, as well as both foreign-policy keys.

Unlike Cleveland, McKinley believed that the creation of new commercial opportunities abroad required the aggressive pursuit of naval bases and coaling stations, the building of a Central American canal, and the opening of foreign markets that the imperialist nations of Europe and Asia sought to reserve for themselves. McKinley's expansionist policies included the acquisition of Hawaii (achieved in 1898) and pressure directed against Spain to end its colonial war against the nationalist rebels in Cuba. In April 1898, the Cuban dispute led to war between the United States and Spain. In the course of what Secretary of State John Hay called "a splendid little war," American naval forces destroyed Spanish fleets in Santiago Harbor, Cuba, and in the waters of Manila Bay in the Spanish colony of the Philippines. American troops quickly occupied Cuba, Guam, the Philippines, and Puerto Rico.

In the peace settlement, the United States acquired Puerto Rico, the Philippines, and Guam. For the first time, America had become a colonial power with far-flung interests to be promoted and defended. Before the Senate had even ratified the Paris accord, the United States became embroiled in a brutal colonial war to suppress nationalist rebels in the Philippines, an ironic similarity to Spain's role in the Cuban insurrection.

In 1899, the United States extended its international involvement by pursuing an "open door" policy designed to prevent the partition of China into separate spheres of influence. Almost overnight, the United States became a major player in world affairs, securing for the administration both policy-change key 7 and foreign-success key 11. By avoiding a major international setback, the administration also secured Key 10.

Even with a buoyant economy and victories in the Pacific and the Caribbean, the Republicans could not avoid the executive party's usual losses in the congressional elections of 1898, which, on top of their losses two years earlier, turned mandate key 1 against them. Still, the Republicans maintained a House majority of 52 percent, while attaining a two to one lead over the Democrats in the Senate.

Despite the return of good times, bitter labor disputes once again erupted during the term. Incidents of the McKinley years, however, were relatively isolated and did not stir the sustained fears and unrest that plagued earlier administrations, so the Republicans retained Key 8.

The only notable scandal during the term grew out of mismanagement in the deployment and supply of troops during the Spanish-American War, which resulted in thousands of noncombat deaths. A special presidential commission found ample evidence of structural weakness and incompetence in the Department of the Army, spurring many reforms, but it cleared administration officials of alleged corruption, preserving Key 9 for the GOP.

As expected after such a successful term, the Republican convention in June of 1900 unanimously renominated McKinley, thus securing Keys 2 and 3 but forfeiting charisma key 12—only the second key to be turned against the incumbent party. To replace Vice President Garret A. Hobart, who had died the year before, the convention nominated the popular favorite, New York governor Theodore Roosevelt, who had gained fame as the colorful colonel who led the Rough Riders up San Juan Hill during the war.

The Democrats' choice for president was as predictable as the Republicans'. In July, the convention turned without dissent to the party's undisputed leader, William Jennings Bryan. Bryan's charisma turned Key 13 against the GOP—it would be the third and final key to fall against the incumbent party. The dissolution of the Populist party after the disappointing "fusion" campaign of 1896 meant that no major third-party effort would be mounted in 1900, leaving Key 4 in the incumbents' column.

McKinley improved his popular- and electoral-vote majorities in 1900, becoming America's first president to win consecutive terms since Ulysses Grant. The Republicans also extended their margin in the House from 52 percent to a more comfortable 55 percent. The one-sided rematch between Bryan and McKinley, however, lacked the excitement of their first encounter. Turnout dropped from 79 percent in 1896 to 73 percent in 1900, beginning a trend toward declining voter participation that would continue through the next generation. With parties continuing to lose their ability to mobilize the faithful, presidential campaigns increasingly became top-down events, managed by professionals schooled in advertising techniques.

Chapter 5

Rise and Fall of Progressivism

For fifteen years after 1896, the Democratic party remained moribund, while the dominant Republicans underwent significant change. Bryan was the first reformist leader of a major party since Lincoln, but it took the ascendancy of Theodore Roosevelt and a new generation of Republican "progressives" to add domestic reform politics to the expansionist policies begun by McKinley. After a hiatus under William Howard Taft, the mantle of progressive leadership fell next upon a Democrat, Woodrow Wilson. Progressives in both parties for the most part rejected the Populists' anticorporatism in favor of moderate reforms designed to stabilize the new corporate economy, curb its most egregious abuses, and preserve the coexistence of small and large enterprise. Progressive-era politicians initiated an unprecedented burst of reform including government regulation of business and finance, curbs on political corruption, suffrage for women, and efforts to improve the living conditions of working-class families. There was also, however, a coercive aspect of progressivism reflected in prohibition, racial repression and segregation, and immigration restriction.

The Republican party that regained power in 1920 had become a primarily conservative party. The GOP stopped short of undoing the progressive legacy of Roosevelt and Wilson. Unlike their progressive predecessors, however, the new Republican leaders opposed activist government, believing that the free-enterprise system was a miraculous engine of progress that needed only fine-tuning and protection from misguided or malevolent reformers. Free enterprise would be both tempered and promoted by the fostering of voluntary associations and the regulation of such new industries as radio and air transport.

1904: The Perfect Election
Incumbent-party nominee: President Theodore Roosevelt (Republican)
Challenging-party nominee: Alton B. Parker (Democrat)
Negative keys: 0
Result: Roosevelt, 56.4%; Parker, 37.6%; Eugene V. Debs (Socialist),
    3.0%

Key:	1	2	3	4	5	6	7	8	9	10	11	12	13
Call:	O	O	O	O	O	O	O	O	O	O	O	O	O

McKinley's second term would last less than one year. His assassination by anarchist Leon Czolgosz in September 1901 changed the course of American political history and, ironically, improved the Republicans' political outlook for 1904 by installing the charismatic Theodore Roosevelt as the youngest and most vigorous president in history.

Early in his term, Roosevelt benefited from the same economic good fortune that marked McKinley's tenure in office. The economy surged in 1901 and 1902, driven by continued advances in domestic production and international trade. A mild recession in 1903 interrupted the six-year run of prosperity that had begun in 1897—the longest period of sustained growth since the Civil War. But a widely hailed recovery commenced in the summer of 1904, and the campaign was waged in an improving economy that turned both the short- and long-term economy keys in the administration's favor.

During McKinley's first term, the concentration of business enterprises into large corporate "trusts" had accelerated greatly. Roosevelt became the first president of either party to make federal intervention against what he called "the manifest evils of the trusts" the central theme of his administration. He endorsed the growth of corporate enterprise as a "progressive" development that would benefit America and the world. Roosevelt also embraced the responsibility of a progressive leader to protect "the public interest" from unfair and abusive corporate practices.

Although President Roosevelt's policies were milder than his rhetoric and milder than some of the legislation circulating in Congress, he did break precedent to demonstrate the supremacy of government over corporations. He prosecuted highly publicized suits against corporate giants such as the Northern Securities Company and, overall, initiated more than twice as many antitrust suits as his three predecessors combined. Roosevelt intervened to settle a major coal strike and steered an ambitious legislative program through Congress. Roosevelt's rhetoric and progressive agenda effected significant changes in the relationship between the public and private sectors, gaining policy-change key 7.

Although strikes, lockouts, and sporadic incidents of violence continued during the term, they lacked the scope or intensity of strife in previous administrations. The incumbent party secured social-unrest key 8.

With the midterm elections taking place in a time of prosperity and relative tranquillity, the Republican party suffered only a slight decline in its percentage of House seats. Its 54 percent majority exceeded the 52 percent it held at the end of the previous term, so the GOP wrapped up mandate key 1.

The only potential blemish on Roosevelt's stewardship of the executive branch involved corruption in the postal service. By vigorously prosecuting the violators, including several Republican leaders, the president turned a threatened liability into a political plus. Roosevelt also expanded the civil service and cracked down on political favoritism, leaving no chance that scandal key 9 would be turned against him.

In foreign affairs, the expansionist president crushed the nationalist rebellion in the Philippines and presided over the American withdrawal from Cuba, retaining intervention rights in the island's affairs and gaining a permanent lease on Guantanamo Bay. His major achievement was supporting a revolution in Panama, a province of the nation of Colombia, and then securing an indefinitely renewable lease on the territory needed to build a canal across the Isthmus of Panama. Roosevelt became the first president in thirty years to gain both foreign-policy keys—Key 10 for avoiding failure and Key 11 for his notable successes.

Despite the mistrust of many among the GOP's old guard, Roosevelt sailed to an easy nomination at the Republican convention, thereby gaining Keys 2 and 3. Although both the Populist and Prohibition parties nominated candidates in 1904, the most significant minor-party contender was the American Socialist party, which had first contested for the presidency in 1900 under the leadership of Eugene Debs. In 1904, Debs garnered about 3 percent of the popular vote. Although this credible showing would establish the Socialists as the leading alternative to the major parties, their campaign was not a major force in the election, leaving Key 4 in the Republicans' favor.

The Democratic party handed Roosevelt—whose charisma and nearly heroic stature easily garnered incumbent-charisma key 12—a clean sweep of the keys by failing to nominate a charismatic or heroic candidate themselves (Key 13). The conservative eastern wing had regained control by convention time. It rejected Bryan's politics of reform and nominated "safe and sane" Alton B. Parker, the taciturn and little-known chief justice of the New York State Court of Appeals.

With such a mismatch, Roosevelt won the most decisive popular-vote victory to that point in history, polling 56.4 percent of the vote to but

37.6 percent for Parker. With 336 electoral votes to Parker's 140, Roosevelt won every northern state and the border states of West Virginia and Missouri. He carried with him solid Republican majorities in Congress: The Republicans expanded their share of House seats from 54 to 65 percent, auguring well for mandate key 1 in 1908. If not for the link between White supremacy and the Democratic party in the South, Roosevelt might have swept the entire nation.

1908: Exit the Nobel President
Incumbent-party nominee: William Howard Taft (Republican)
Challenging-party nominee: William Jennings Bryan (Democrat)
Negative keys: 3
Result: Taft, 51.6%; Bryan, 43.0%; Eugene V. Debs (Socialist), 2.8%

Key:	1	2	3	4	5	6	7	8	9	10	11	12	13
Call:	O	O	X	O	O	X	O	O	O	O	O	X	O

After his triumph in 1904, Roosevelt made himself a lame-duck president by declaring, "Under no circumstances will I be a candidate for or accept another nomination."[1] Although the president soon would come to regret this commitment, he refused to reverse himself and seek another term.

Through his inimitable blend of blustery rhetoric, legislative initiative, and administrative action, Roosevelt became the symbolic leader of "progressive" movements throughout the nation. At every level of government they worked toward improving social conditions, ending corrupt political practices, conserving resources, and curbing corporate abuse. President Roosevelt committed the federal government to the pursuit of economic and social justice within the context of private property, corporate enterprise, and a market economy. Progressive reform, Roosevelt believed, was the only way to avoid a sharp turn to the Left in American political life. A firm advocate of administrative government, he won legislation authorizing the Interstate Commerce Commission to set railroad rates. He worked for the adoption in 1906 of the Meat Inspection Act and the Pure Food and Drug Act, and he helped secure passage of legislation prohibiting corporate contributions to national political campaigns. These and other initiatives proceeded from the course he set in his first term, but were broad enough to secure policy-change key 7 for his second term as well.

Two years of economic expansion helped Roosevelt's party retain mandate key 1. Although the Republicans lost twenty-eight seats in the congressional elections of 1906, they still held a 58 percent majority, well above their 54 percent level prior to the election of 1904.

The GOP's economic luck finally ran out in 1907, when sliding stock prices led to the first severe financial panic since 1893. Although the panic ended in 1907, investment and demand would continue to lag through mid-1908, costing the party in power long-term economy key 6. As in the previous election year, broad recognition of a rising economy in the late summer and fall of 1908 narrowly averted the loss of short-term economy key 5.

Social unrest intensified after the Panic of 1907, but it paled in comparison to disorders triggered by the depression of the 1890s. A major race riot that occurred in August of 1908 in Springfield, Illinois, the home of Abraham Lincoln, spurred the formation of the National Association for the Advancement of Colored People the following year. With only sporadic incidents of disorder occurring elsewhere, however, the incumbent party retained Key 8.

Executive conduct was called into question only when conservatives in Congress assailed the president's use of the Secret Service for administrative investigations and won passage of legislation limiting the service to protecting the president and investigating counterfeiting. With the White House otherwise untouched by scandal, Key 9 remained in the GOP column.

Roosevelt continued to expand the nation's role in world affairs. His greatest international success came in 1905 when he mediated an end to a war between Russia and Japan. In 1906, the president successfully interceded in the conflict among France, Germany, and Britain over the control of Morocco. These initiatives earned him the Nobel Peace Prize in 1906, making him the first American statesman to be so honored. Roosevelt's bold interventionism secured not only accolades for himself, but also foreign-policy keys 10 and 11 for his party.

As the nomination process began in 1908, Roosevelt gave the full support of his administration to his anointed successor: his loyal secretary of war, William Howard Taft. Taft swept to an easy first-ballot nomination with 702 votes to 68 for his nearest rival, gaining the party nomination key 2 while forfeiting incumbency key 3 and charisma key 12.

A coterie of minor parties entered the 1908 race, with the Socialists again the most formidable contenders. But Eugene Debs was unable to expand his appeal beyond his showing in 1904, and the Republicans retained Key 4.

After Alton Parker's embarrassing showing in 1904, the Bryan wing regained its power within the Democratic party, making the Great Commoner its near-unanimous choice for a third run at the presidency. By

1908, the once-inspiring Bryan was being lampooned in the press as the "Balding Boy Orator." The burning issues that had ignited Bryan's earlier campaigns—free silver and anti-imperialism—were now obsolete. Roosevelt had effectively expropriated much of Bryan's reform program, whose faded appeal meant that Key 13 would not be turned against the GOP.

With voting machines in extensive use for the first time, rapid returns showed Bryan suffering his most emphatic defeat. He won only 43 percent of the popular vote and 162 electoral votes to 52 percent and 321 for Taft. The GOP continued to dominate Congress, although small losses in the House portended the loss of mandate key 1 for 1912.

1912: A Party Divided
Incumbent-party nominee: President William Howard Taft (Republican)
Challenging-party nominee: Woodrow Wilson (Democrat)
Negative keys: 6
Result: Wilson, 41.8%; Theodore Roosevelt (Progressive), 27.4%; Taft, 23.2%; Eugene V. Debs (Socialist), 6.0%

Key:	1	2	3	4	5	6	7	8	9	10	11	12	13
Call:	X	X	O	X	O	O	X	O	O	O	X	X	O

Shortly after Taft's inauguration in March of 1909, ex-president Roosevelt embarked on an African safari in the belief that his handpicked successor would follow the policies of his own seven years in office. By the time the Rough Rider returned to a hero's welcome the following year, he would be disappointed. Taft, he believed, was neither advancing the progressive agenda nor exercising leadership. The conflict between Taft and Roosevelt would divide the GOP and create an opening for a Democratic party that had last held the presidency during the depression of the 1890s.

The economic recovery that had begun in 1908 continued through the early months of the new term. Although recovery faltered during the middle of the term, the economy would spurt ahead in 1912, gaining both economic keys for the administration.

More than Roosevelt would admit, Taft basically followed the policy agenda of the previous seven years. Favoring judicial over administrative review of economic activity, he would initiate more antitrust suits in his four years than Roosevelt had in seven, including the successful prosecution of the largest of the trusts, the Standard Oil Corporation. Unlike Roosevelt, however, Taft lacked the imagination, rhetorical skills, and political ability to rally the public or the Congress behind a distinctive policy of his own. His accomplishments, while significant, were seen largely as a continuation of the policies put forward by his predecessor, toppling Key 7 for 1912.

Taft's patronage policies, his support for high tariffs, his opposition to the recall of judges, and his lukewarm support for the direct election of U.S. senators also alienated the progressive wing of the party. Any semblance of comity between Taft and the Progressives disappeared when the president launched a campaign against Progressive legislators in the 1910 Republican primaries. With a lackluster economy and a divided party, the GOP gave up fifty-eight House seats in the midterm elections of 1910, sealing the loss of mandate key 1.

The Taft years were marred by several outbreaks of labor unrest, but militant activities had subsided by 1912. The nation was much less agitated during the election year than it had been, for example, during the depression of the 1890s or would be during the Red Scare and racial riots following World War I. The GOP narrowly retained Key 8.

Allegations of corruption under Interior Secretary Richard Ballinger were the only serious challenge to Taft's probity in the conduct of his administration. After a congressional investigation cleared Ballinger of wrongdoing, scandal key 9 stayed safely in line for the incumbent party.

In foreign affairs, Taft replaced Roosevelt's "Big Stick" approach with "Dollar Diplomacy," the use of American influence to increase American investment overseas. His policies produced no major successes, turning Key 11 against the GOP for 1912. The lack of a major foreign defeat, however, preserved Key 10.

Progressive Republican leader Senator Robert M. La Follette of Wisconsin planned to challenge Taft for the Republican nomination in 1912. But the frustrated and still-vigorous Roosevelt undercut La Follette by deciding that he himself would run for the Republican nomination. In 1912, Taft, Roosevelt, and La Follette fought the first primary-election campaign in American history, battling one another in the dozen states that had recently established party primaries. The results decidedly favored Roosevelt, who garnered more primary votes than Taft and La Follette combined. State conventions and caucuses, however, still selected the majority of convention delegates. Taft's control over the party machinery resulted in a first-ballot victory in the convention, but he fell short of a two-thirds vote, thereby losing contest key 2.

Even before the convention balloting, Roosevelt—incensed that his ambitions and the will of Republican primary voters were being thwarted—had decided to abandon the GOP and run for president as the candidate of a new Progressive party, turning a lethal sixth key, third-party key 4, against the incumbent nominee.

On the forty-sixth ballot, the Democratic convention nominated New Jersey governor Woodrow Wilson. Although erudite, articulate, and sometimes inspirational, Wilson lacked the broad popular appeal needed to turn Key 13 against the party in power. The GOP's deficit would stand at six negative keys.

In addition to Roosevelt's Progressive party (dubbed the "Bull Moose"), yet another contender entered the fray. "This is our year," Eugene Debs told his Socialist followers in 1912. The Socialists still called for the revolutionary overthrow of capitalism and denounced the Progressives as a party dedicated to the survival of capitalism through reforms that would keep the working class enslaved. Debs would nearly double his 1908 totals, gaining about 6 percent of the popular vote. It was a measure of the progressive tenor of the times that even Taft, the most conservative of the four major candidates, affirmed the duty of government to serve the general welfare.

Roosevelt outpolled Taft 27 percent to 23 percent in popular ballots and eighty-eight to eight in electoral votes. Whereas Roosevelt and Taft split the 1908 Republican majority, Wilson held the Democrats together, retaining more than 80 percent of Bryan's 1908 tally. Wilson captured a popular vote plurality of 41.8 percent and about 80 percent of the electoral vote. The Republican split also helped the Democrats capture the Senate for the first time in nearly thirty years and expand their House majority from 58 percent to 67 percent, putting the party in a strong position to win mandate key 1 for the 1916 election.

1916: The Democratic Progressive
Incumbent-party nominee: President Woodrow Wilson (Democrat)
Challenging-party nominee: Charles Evans Hughes (Republican)
Negative keys: 3
Result: Wilson, 49.2%; Hughes, 46.1%; Allan L. Benson (Socialist), 3.2%

Key:	1	2	3	4	5	6	7	8	9	10	11	12	13
Call:	X	O	O	O	O	X	O	O	O	O	O	X	O

In his inaugural address, Woodrow Wilson signaled his commitment to an activist government empowered to regulate the financial system, improve social conditions, promote international trade, and spur business competition at home. In pursuit of these goals, Wilson became the most active and sophisticated legislative leader yet to serve in the White House.

But the bright promise of Wilson's presidency appeared to darken early, as the economic revival of 1912 petered out during the first months of his inaugural year. By mid-1913, unemployment was rising, production was slumping, and stock prices were falling. Real per-capita GNP declined about 1 percent in 1913, a prelude to the depression that would set in the following year.

However, the faltering economy did not stall Wilson's agenda. He succeeded in effecting initiatives that had eluded a generation of reformers: tariff reduction, regulation of the banking and currency system, and enactment of a graduated income tax. The president sponsored the Clayton Antitrust Act that prohibited specific business practices and also banned unspecified activities that had the general effect of lessening competition. The act also prohibited the use of federal court injunctions against strikes by labor unions.

By the end of his second year, Wilson's tariff, banking, and antitrust initiatives had already won Key 7 for the Democrats. But his legislative gains did not translate into victory for his party in the midterm elections of 1914, the first elections in which the number of House seats was fixed at 435. During a steep midterm recession, the executive party dropped 61 House seats, falling from a 66 percent to a 53 percent majority and losing mandate key 1.

Fortunately for the Democrats, the economy began to revive in late 1915, led by the munitions industry and booming exports to the Allied Powers in Europe, who had gone to war against Germany in 1914. Wartime demand continued to stimulate both industry and agriculture in 1916. The incumbent Democrats retained short-term economy key 5, but the war-driven growth was insufficient to salvage long-term economy key 6.

The social-unrest key also was put in jeopardy in 1914 by the Ludlow massacre, an incident in which state militiamen and mine guards killed more than a dozen wives and children of striking miners in the coalfields of Colorado. No similarly violent incidents followed the Ludlow massacre, but, with a labor market tightened by wartime production, strike activity markedly increased in 1916. Still, in contrast to earlier periods, the largely nonviolent strikes produced little anxiety about the preservation of public order. Even the Ludlow massacre had raised questions about the leadership of industry rather than sparking fear of insurrection. The incumbent Democrats retained social-unrest key 8.

The moralistic and meritocratic President Wilson avoided even the hint of scandal in his administration, securing Key 9 as well. In foreign affairs, Wilson sought to replace Taft's Dollar Diplomacy with a policy more responsive to moral concerns. For Latin American countries, this was a distinction without a difference, as Wilson intervened in the internal affairs of several nations, most notably Mexico. Although the results of his Latin American diplomacy were mixed, Wilson suffered no major setback and so retained Key 10.

The president was more successful in dealing with the primary challenge of his administration: developing an American response to the outbreak of World War I in the summer of 1914. In the election year of 1916, Germany capitulated to Wilson's demand that it cease attacking merchant ships without warning. The clouds of war lifted, and the president could credibly campaign on the slogan "He Kept Us Out of War." Foreign-success key 11 lined up in the incumbent's column.

In the election year, Wilson also worked to unite progressives behind his leadership, sponsoring yet another burst of reform. So distinctively had Wilson placed his stamp on national policy by the nominating season that even his potential rivals acknowledged that the party would fare best by uniting behind the president. At the June convention, delegates renominated him by acclamation and adopted a platform, drafted by Wilson himself, that for the first time committed the Democrats to a combination of internationalism abroad and social and economic reform at home. Keys 2 and 3 were locked in for the incumbent party. Wilson had proven his oratorical skills in rallying public support for his programs in Congress, but he still lacked the common touch necessary for mass appeal; incumbent-charisma key 12 was the third and final key to be counted against his reelection.

With neither Taft nor Roosevelt becoming contenders for the GOP nomination, the party turned to Charles Evans Hughes, an associate justice of the U.S. Supreme Court who had established a mildly progressive record in two distinguished terms as governor of New York. But the austere Hughes—dubbed the "bearded iceberg" by Roosevelt—was hardly the dynamic personality that the party would need to turn Key 13 against the Democrats.

Roosevelt's Progressive party, despite having outpolled the Republicans in 1912, had not developed an enduring organization capable of challenging the major parties. When Roosevelt, uninterested in pursuing lost causes, declined nomination, the Progressive convention dissolved without putting forth a candidate. Like the Progressives, the Socialists had seen some of their thunder stolen by Wilsonian reforms, and the party was suffering from factional disputes. Membership had tailed off after 1912, and Socialist success in local elections had diminished. The party's presidential tally would decline from 6 percent of the popular vote in 1912 to 3 percent in 1916. With no significant third party in the field, the Democrats retained Key 4.

On election night, early returns from the East Coast appeared to favor Hughes; by 10:00 P.M. that evening he had garnered 247 electoral votes, just 19 short of a majority. The *New York Times* awarded the election to Hughes, the *New York World* followed suit, and several late-edition newspapers headlined the Republicans' victory the next morning. But returns from the West that began filtering in after 2:00 A.M. favored Wilson heavily. Not until two days after the polls had closed were the returns complete enough to call the election definitively for Wilson. Wilson gained 49 percent of the popular vote to 46 percent for Hughes. The electoral college tally was closer: 277 to 254. Although the Democrats retained control of the House and the Senate, they lost fourteen seats in the House, reducing their majority from 53 percent to 50 percent and virtually guaranteeing the loss of Key 1 for 1920.

1920: Return of the Conservative GOP
Incumbent-party nominee: James M. Cox (Democrat)
Challenging-party nominee: Warren G. Harding (Republican)
Negative keys: 8
Result: Harding, 60.3%; Cox, 34.2%; Eugene V. Debs (Socialist), 3.4%

Key:	1	2	3	4	5	6	7	8	9	10	11	12	13
Call:	X	X	X	O	X	X	O	X	O	X	O	X	O

Despite Wilson's pledge to keep us out of war, German U-boats checked his diplomatic initiatives by sinking three U.S. merchant ships early in 1917. Within a month of his second inauguration, the president appeared before a special joint session of Congress to ask for a declaration of war against Germany.

America's entry into the European conflict required the mobilization of the entire economy. The federal government nationalized the rail, telegraph, and telephone systems, built merchant ships, took over the distribution of coal, and directly purchased and sold agricultural staples. The government established new wartime agencies, drafted soldiers for the first time since the Civil War, raised individual and corporate income taxes, ran up huge budget deficits, and marshaled public opinion in support of the war. Federal officials censored the mails and prosecuted dissenters under new espionage and sedition laws. The spirit of sacrifice and common purpose hastened passage of Constitutional amendments to prohibit the manufacture and sale of alcohol and grant voting rights for women. These many dramatic changes easily secured policy-change key 7 for the Democrats, but the war triggered the loss of several other keys.

America's wartime economic boom gained even greater force after the United States entered the conflict. However, the end of the war in 1919 produced an economic tailspin that would continue throughout the remainder of the term. As a result, the Democrats lost both economic keys.

World War I was not universally popular among Americans, many of whom believed that the nation had foolishly become involved in an imperialistic quarrel among European powers. More than 300,000 men evaded the draft, and antiwar protests provoked arrests, beatings, and prosecutions. The government also used wartime legislation to crack down on socialists and radical unionists. Discrimination against Blacks in the military and the tensions resulting from the migration of 450,000 rural Blacks to northern and western cities sparked racial violence. The end of the war in November 1918 intensified the unrest. Race riots erupted in more than twenty-five northern cities during the summer of 1919, leaving more than one hundred people dead. The dismantling of wartime arbitration in 1919 also led to major labor upheavals. In addition, hostility formerly directed against Germans during the war now was turned against foreign radicals. Thirty-six mail bombs addressed to government officials were discovered in 1919 and a bomb was exploded outside the home of Attorney General A. Mitchell Palmer, a man with presidential ambitions of his own. Palmer exploited fears of subversion to raid the headquarters of radical organizations, deport aliens, and arrest suspected revolutionaries. This Red Scare, combined with racial and labor unrest, turned Key 8 against the incumbent party.

Despite ample opportunity for corruption in the intermingling of public and private activity during the war, no significant scandal tarnished the Wilson administration. The war produced tens of thousands of new millionaires as business benefited from high demand, government assistance, and lucrative contracts. After the armistice, private interests also profited by purchasing government land, plants, and equipment at cut-rate prices. But most of those who grew rich during the war operated within the law, and the incumbent party retained scandal key 9.

Wilson would pay a political price for the tensions and sacrifices of war. Even as American troops pressed toward victory in the Argonne, Wilson—hoping to increase support for his peacemaking policies when the fighting was over—abandoned the bipartisanship that had marked the wartime period and campaigned aggressively for a Democratic Congress in the elections of 1918. The electorate reacted negatively, returning Republican majorities in both houses and toppling mandate key 1 for the executive party.

A week after the elections, the war was over, with the entry of American ground troops playing a decisive role in the Allied victory. Foreign-success key 11 was thus turned in favor of the administration.

Wilson sought to achieve a just peace on the basis of his "Fourteen Points." But European leaders shattered most of Wilson's high-minded plans. Although the peace process preserved his dream of an international body to prevent war (the League of Nations), Wilson failed to gain Senate ratification of the treaty incorporating the League. His botched peacemaking cost the Democrats foreign-failure key 10.

After forty-four ballots, a dispirited Democratic convention nominated Ohio Governor James M. Cox as the candidate to succeed Woodrow Wilson. For vice president the convention picked a relative unknown with a magic name, Franklin D. Roosevelt of New York, assistant secretary of the Navy. Nomination of the uncharismatic Cox in a divided convention cost the Democrats contest key 2, incumbency key 3, and incumbent-charisma key 12.

The Republicans also suffered from a crisis of leadership in 1920. Theodore Roosevelt was dead, Taft was unelectable, and Charles Evans Hughes had no zest for another race. After ten ballots, the convention turned to another Ohioan as a compromise candidate: Senator Warren G. Harding. For vice president, the convention chose Massachusetts Governor Calvin Coolidge, whose firm stand against the striking Boston police force in 1919 had earned him national prominence. The GOP's failure to select a charismatic candidate left Key 13 in the incumbent Democrats' hands.

The nomination of Harding and the adoption of a conservative platform also marked an important transition for the Republican party. Although a progressive faction remained within the GOP, no longer would the party be a vehicle for progressive policies.

The failure of a significant third-party movement to emerge in 1920 decided Key 4 in favor of the incumbents. The Socialist party, weakened by wartime repression and divided over its response to the Soviet revolution, would not again in this century be a major force in presidential politics.

In 1920, voters handed Harding the most decisive popular-vote victory in American history. He garnered 60 percent of the popular vote and 404 electoral votes to 34 percent and 127 for Cox. He would enter the presidency with a 22-vote majority in the Senate and a 169-vote majority in the House, where the GOP's gain of sixty-one seats pointed to the likely retention of mandate key 1 for 1924.

Women, newly enfranchised in every state by the Nineteenth Amendment, turned out in a much lower proportion than men, accelerating a trend toward lower voter participation that had begun in 1900. For the first time since 1824, turnout of eligible voters dipped below 50 percent. It would climb again in 1928 but would never again reach the levels of the late nineteenth century. Contrary to preelection predictions of a progressive women's vote, women actually supported the conservative Harding in greater proportion than men. A progressive-oriented women's vote would not emerge until the 1960s.

1924: "A Fat and Happy World"
Incumbent-party nominee: President Calvin Coolidge (Republican)
Challenging-party nominee: John W. Davis (Democrat)
Negative keys: 4
Result: Coolidge, 54.1%; Davis, 28.8%; Robert M. La Follette
   (Progressive), 16.6%

Key:	1	2	3	4	5	6	7	8	9	10	11	12	13
Call:	X	O	O	X	O	O	O	O	X	O	O	X	O

Despite his triumph in 1920, Warren Harding was poorly equipped for the presidency. He was an indecisive leader, a lax administrator, and often a poor judge of character. But Harding also appointed to crucial cabinet positions several of the ablest persons to serve an American president: Herbert Hoover at Commerce, Charles Evans Hughes at State, and Andrew Mellon at Treasury. The tenure of Harding and Calvin Coolidge, who would become president upon Harding's death in August of 1923, would prove to be an era of prosperity, achievement abroad, and relative tranquillity within America.

By 1922, the postwar recession had decisively ended. The resulting economic growth secured both economic keys for the Republican administration.

Under Harding and Coolidge—and their leading domestic advisers, Hoover and Mellon—the Republicans adopted some limited progressive initiatives. Overall, however, the GOP rejected the Roosevelt-Wilson philosophy of government as an instrument of reform. Rather than trying to dismantle the administrative state, they reined it in with probusiness appointments to regulatory agencies and a virtual cessation of action against abusive business practices. The administration also restored protective tariffs, restricted immigration, and slashed the income tax. These policies, representing an about-face from the progressivism of previous administrations, locked in policy-change key 7 for the GOP.

Despite the booming economy of 1922, the Republicans lost heavily in the midterm congressional elections. Faced with weak presidential leadership and divisions between progressives and conservatives, the Republicans lost seventy-six House seats in 1922, barely retaining a majority of 52 percent and losing mandate key 1.

The conflicts of the immediate postwar years cooled during the early part of the decade. Despite scattered incidents of racial and ethnic conflict, spurred by America's second Ku Klux Klan, relative calm prevailed during the term, especially in comparison to the postwar disorders of 1919 and 1920. As a result, social-unrest key 8 stayed in line for the incumbent Republicans.

In early 1923, the nation learned that top officials of the Harding administration had abused their public trust in ways reminiscent of the Grant years. Most shocking was the discovery that Interior Secretary Albert B. Fall had secretly leased government oil reserves at Teapot Dome in Wyoming and at Elk Hills in California in exchange for "loans" and "presents" totaling about $400,000. The price was a cheap one for the two lessors, oilmen Harry Sinclair and Edward Doheny: Each lease was worth an estimated $100 million in profits. In 1928, Fall became the first cabinet officer in history to serve time in a penitentiary.

After his death in August of 1923, Harding became a convenient scapegoat for what was known as the "Teapot Dome" scandals. Although Harding and the leaders of his cabinet—Mellon, Hoover, and Hughes—were probably free of personal corruption, the president clearly had failed to supervise the executive branch adequately or to take decisive action when he learned of wrongdoing within his administration. The GOP lost scandal key 9 for 1924.

The Republican administration spurned the League of Nations, but it could not return America to its relative isolation from great-power affairs, especially in the economic realm. Americans advanced new loans abroad and expanded foreign investment. In 1924, a plan developed by banker Charles Dawes for payment of Germany's postwar reparations earned its author the Republican nomination for vice president and later the Nobel Peace Prize. Still, what turned the foreign-success key 11 in favor of the GOP was the Washington Disarmament Conference of 1921–22. Under the leadership of Secretary Hughes, the world's major powers agreed to major limitations on naval armaments and other initiatives designed to forestall conflict among them. Historians would later criticize the Washington Conference for a lack of enforcement mechanisms and for neglecting to control aircraft and submarines. But the treaties represented America's most successful venture yet in promoting the security of nations, and the administration received almost universal acclaim. Nowhere in its conduct of foreign affairs did the administration confront a major crisis, so foreign-failure key 10 was also secure.

Upon assuming the presidency in 1923, Calvin Coolidge continued on the course established by his conservative predecessor. Untainted by the Harding scandals, Coolidge quickly became a popular, if uninspiring, president. A united Republican convention gave him a near-unanimous nomination, locking in Keys 2 and 3, but forfeiting Key 12.

The challenging Democrats could reach no consensus on a nominee. With the party divided between its northeastern and southern bases, the Democratic convention droned on for a record 103 ballots before nominating a compromise candidate, John W. Davis. Davis was a leading constitutional lawyer, with a long record of service to the Democratic party. But he was a little-known and unexciting candidate whose selection gave challenger-charisma key 13 to the incumbent Republicans. A highlight of the convention—the first ever broadcast to a nationwide radio audience—was Franklin Roosevelt's return to the national political scene following a bout with polio.

A third and final key fell when Senator La Follette organized a Progressive party campaign in hopes of rallying former Roosevelt and Wilson supporters. La Follette's followers did not believe he could win the presidency, but they hoped that he might precipitate a realignment of the parties by denying either the Republicans or the Democrats a majority in the electoral college. Although La Follette would be a significant force in the campaign—turning Key 4 against Coolidge—his campaign failed to reshuffle the American party system. Eight years later, however, La Follette voters would be part of the coalition that installed Democrat Franklin Roosevelt in the White House.

Neither La Follette nor Davis came close to mounting a challenge to the incumbent president. Coolidge polled an outright majority of the popular vote (54 percent) and 382 electoral votes to 136 for Davis and 13 for La Follette (all from his home state of Wisconsin). The GOP also captured solid majorities in the House and Senate; with a gain of twenty-two seats in the House, the party would be able to withstand modest losses in the midterm elections of 1926 and still retain mandate key 1.

1928: Sitting Pretty
Incumbent-party nominee: Herbert Hoover (Republican)
Challenging-party nominee: Alfred E. Smith (Democrat)

Negative keys: 3
Result: Hoover, 58.2%; Smith, 40.8%

Key:	1	2	3	4	5	6	7	8	9	10	11	12	13
Call:	O	O	X	O	O	O	X	O	O	O	O	X	O

Like Theodore Roosevelt twenty years earlier, Coolidge would re-move himself from consideration for a second term shortly after his 1924 triumph. Fortunately for the Republicans, Secretary of Commerce Herbert Hoover, the leading light of domestic policy since 1921, emerged as the dominant contender in 1928, sparing the GOP a con-tested nomination.

The economy grew briskly during the first two years of the Coolidge administration. Lagging consumer demand in an economy in which wealth increasingly was concentrated at the top slowed growth during the third year of the term. The economy would narrowly avoid an elec-tion-year recession, gaining Key 5 for the Republican party. Real per-capita GNP grew just enough during the term also to secure long-term economy key 6.

By 1925, the Republican party had largely completed the policy agenda of the Harding-Coolidge era. During the next four years of "keeping cool with Coolidge," the administration would reduce taxes further and expand regulation only to such new industries as aviation and radio broadcasting. This minimal innovation pleased Republicans but cost the party policy-change key 7.

The late 1920s were tranquil times for the nation. The domestic peace that accompanied prosperity kept social-unrest key 8 in the incumbents' column. Likewise, domestic calm and prosperity helped the GOP in the 1926 midterm elections. The party dropped a modest ten House seats for a net gain of twelve over the previous term; mandate key 1 was in hand for 1928.

Although the nation was still sorting out the Teapot Dome scandals of the Harding years, no new evidence of misconduct came to light during Coolidge's term. There were incidents of corruption among minor officials responsible for the enforcement of prohibition, but this was an ongoing problem that had begun with the start of prohibition in 1920. Scandal key 9 stayed in line for the GOP.

In foreign policy, President Coolidge emphasized Latin American affairs, disarmament, and international treaty agreements. The adminis-tration suffered no major setback, which meant that the GOP retained Key 10. An unexpected foreign-policy triumph would come in 1928 with the successful negotiation of a treaty, the Pact of Paris, renouncing war as "an instrument of national policy." In retrospect, the purely voluntary character of the agreement seems naive, but the treaty, an extraordinary popular success, earned Key 11 for the incumbent party.

The Republicans selected the leading light of the Coolidge administration, Secretary of Commerce Herbert Hoover, as their consensus nominee, securing Key 2. But the nominee's popularity still did not translate into charisma, so the incumbent party forfeited Key 12.

The Democrats turned to their most successful vote-getter of the Republican-dominated 1920s, multiple-term governor Al Smith of New York. But Smith also lacked charisma, leaving Key 13 in line for the GOP.

The Progressive party had rapidly declined after La Follette's defeat in 1924. As organized labor continued to lose power and the socialist movement faded away, third-party candidates would receive less than 1 percent of the vote in 1928, the smallest proportion since 1872. Key 4 remained in the incumbents' column. Only three keys—3, 7, and 12— would be counted against the Republicans' bid for a third consecutive term. Al Smith's nomination marked the first time a major party had selected a Catholic candidate. The issue of his religion would dominate the presidential campaign, but not determine its outcome.

In the November balloting, Herbert Hoover cruised to a near-landslide victory, with 58 percent of the popular vote and forty-four electoral college votes to 41 percent and eighty-seven for Smith. With victories in both houses of Congress, the Republicans controlled the national government for a third consecutive term. The party picked up thirty House seats, raising its majority from 54 to 61 percent and putting it in a strong position to retain mandate key 1 for 1932.

The emotions churned up by the religious issue boosted voter turnout in 1928. After thirty years of steady decline, turnout increased from 49 percent in 1924 to 57 percent in 1928, with the GOP gaining 5.7 million votes and the Democrats 6.6 million. Turnout increased particularly among women; for the first time since their enfranchisement in 1920, the participation of women approached that of men.[2]

Chapter 6

Depression, War, and Cold War

Herbert Hoover's 1928 triumph turned into bitter defeat just seven months after his inauguration. For more than three years, he would preside over a devastating economic depression. The collapse of the American economy returned the Democrats to power and kept Republicans out of the White House until the nomination of war hero Dwight Eisenhower in 1952. For all but six years after 1932, Democrats also controlled the House of Representatives. Once in office, Eisenhower was no innovator. He promoted a "modern Republicanism" that took a middle course between Democratic liberals and the right wing of the Republican party. However, modern Republicanism neither stole the thunder of the Democrats nor attracted independents to the Republican camp. With the failure of modern Republicanism, Eisenhower found himself governing against the grain of a Democratic Congress for most of his eight years in office.

1932: The End of an Era
Incumbent-party nominee: President Herbert Hoover (Republican)
Challenging-party nominee: Franklin D. Roosevelt (Democrat)
Negative keys: 8
Result: Roosevelt, 57.4%; Hoover, 39.6%; Norman Thomas (Socialist), 2.2%

Key:	1	2	3	4	5	6	7	8	9	10	11	12	13
Call:	X	O	O	O	X	X	X	X	O	O	X	X	X

Hoover entered the White House fully expecting the economy to continue its advances of the past seven years. From 1921 to 1929, real growth, stock prices, wages, and corporate profits had made strong gains, and only about 3 percent of the workforce was unemployed. Beginning in the late summer of 1929, industrial production began to slide. Suddenly, in October, a wave of panic selling hit the stock market. Although the crash did not itself precipitate the depression, both the market and the economy would decline steadily over the next three years, plunging the nation into the deepest and most prolonged depression in its history. Both the short- and long-term economy would be lost to the incumbent Republicans.

Given Hoover's philosophical commitment to limited government, the president showed some boldness in responding to the crisis. His program included federal loans to businesses and banks, purchases of farm commodities, selected increases in federal spending, and banking reform. Even these relatively ambitious measures did little to allay the unprecedented economic crisis. Other Hoover initiatives (as well as some actions of the Federal Reserve Board) exacerbated the problem. In 1930, the Republicans had enacted the Hawley-Smoot Tariff, which raised import duties to the highest levels ever, constricting an already reduced flow of international commerce. Two years later, fearful that budget deficits would choke off private credit, Hoover pushed through a major tax increase that further diminished the funds available to consumers and investors.

Historians have rightly noted that Hoover did much more to combat economic depression than any previous president.[1] Yet his program did not measure up to the magnitude of the crisis and fell short of what many Democratic leaders—including newly elected Governor Franklin D. Roosevelt of New York—were proposing. Hoover's promises of recovery had become a standing joke by the election year; policy-change key 7 was turned against the party in power.

The deepening depression precipitated a dramatic partisan reversal in the congressional elections of 1930. The Democrats gained fifty-three House seats, earning a majority (51 percent) for the first time in more than a decade and toppling mandate key 1. They also came within a single seat of a Senate majority.

Although the revolutionary activity anticipated by some observers never materialized, social unrest was unavoidable. The trouble of the 1930s began among farmers rather than among mine, factory, or railroad workers. In 1931, farmers organized picket lines, blocked roadways, and battled law officers in efforts to halt bank foreclosures and boost farm prices by preventing the marketing of agricultural goods. In December, hundreds of "hunger marchers" descended on Washington, D.C., where police barred them from delivering their petition for employment to the White House. Strikers, unemployed workers, and radical demonstrators disrupted public order in cities across the country in 1931 and 1932, when a "wandering population" of some two million displaced Americans were on the nation's roads and highways. In the spring of the election year, protest came to Hoover's doorstep as ten thousand members of a "Bonus Expeditionary Force" set up camp in the capital and demanded that they be allowed to cash in World War I veterans' bonuses. The harsh treatment by the police and army of men who had served their country in war raised a storm of protest against the already beleaguered president. Social-unrest key 8 turned against the administration, at least partly as a result of its own blunders.

Although it was difficult to see in the midst of economic calamity, Hoover was an able executive—far more effective as an administrator than as a national leader. He ran a scandal-free administration and even improved the previously corruption-ridden enforcement of prohibition. Scandal key 9 stayed solidly in the GOP's favor.

In foreign relations, as in economic life, the Hoover years marked a transition from one era to another. The international arbitration and disarmament agreements won in the aftermath of the world war began to crumble, and China's invasion of Manchuria in 1931 foreshadowed a new period of international conflict. Although Hoover arguably was more aggressive in foreign than in domestic affairs, the collapse of the economy overshadowed both his successes and failures abroad. The president split the foreign-policy keys, neither suffering a major defeat (gaining Key 10) nor achieving a major victory (losing Key 11).

In June of the election year, a dispirited Republican convention renominated President Hoover with but four dissenting votes. The nomination did not reflect party unity and strength. For the first time in history, the uncontested selection of an incumbent candidate meant that no party leader believed the nomination was worth fighting for. Nonetheless, Hoover's renomination secured for the GOP both contest key 2 and incumbency key 3. Charisma key 12, however, would be turned against the party once again.

The Democrats, confident of victory, turned to Franklin D. Roosevelt, the party's leading light since his election as governor of New York in 1928. After winning reelection by the largest margin in state history in 1930, Roosevelt established a solidly progressive record during the economic crisis of 1931–32. Despite a commanding lead in the primaries, however, Roosevelt did not coast to the nomination. In a deft bit of deal making that gave the vice-presidential slot to favorite-son John Nance Garner of Texas, Roosevelt won the nomination on the fourth ballot.

Fears of social revolution notwithstanding, no third party representing either the Right or the Left tapped effectively into popular discontent. The American Socialist party—strengthened by the leadership of Norman Thomas, the most dynamic radical politician since Eugene Debs—advocated reforms that would become staples of the New Deal, including unemployment and old-age insurance and a minimum wage. Thomas, however, went beyond reform to propose the nationalization of private industry. The 1932 electorate preferred to give mainstream politics another chance; Thomas was a minor figure in the campaign, leaving Key 4 in line for the incumbent party.

In the popular balloting, Roosevelt swamped Hoover by roughly the same margin Hoover had achieved against Al Smith in 1928. Democrats won ninety House seats, boosting their majority from 51 to 71 percent and practically assuring the party mandate key 1 for 1936. Roosevelt's seemingly contradictory pronouncements of his campaign kept people guessing about the course he would follow as president. Roosevelt and his Brain Trust, however, already had mapped out changes in national policy that not only would revitalize the moribund Democratic party, but also would transform the role of the federal government in American life.

1936: A New Deal—and a New Majority

Incumbent-party nominee: President Franklin D. Roosevelt (Democrat)
Challenging-party nominee: Alfred M. Landon (Republican)
Negative keys: 1
Result: Roosevelt, 60.8%; Landon, 36.5%; William Lemke (Union), 2.0%

Key:	1	2	3	4	5	6	7	8	9	10	11	12	13
Call:	O	O	O	O	O	O	O	O	O	O	X	O	O

Roosevelt's victory in 1932 was the first of two stages in the realignment of the American electorate. The "depression effect," manifest from 1930 to 1932, was primarily a negative reaction to the failure of the Hoover administration to deal with the economic crisis. It gave the Democrats a mandate for change and an opportunity to expand their partisan base with recruits drawn from new voters and the ranks of disaffected Republicans. The "Roosevelt effect," a popular response to the new president's policies and leadership, manifested itself between 1934 and 1936 in the emergence of a distinctive Roosevelt coalition comprised of Blacks, immigrants, city-dwellers, union members, and traditional southern Democrats.

During his first one hundred days in office, Franklin Roosevelt became the most active legislative initiator in presidential history. Roosevelt proposed and Congress enacted new programs of cash assistance and work relief. He extended precedents of the progressive years by strengthening federal controls over the banking and credit system, insuring savings-bank deposits, mediating labor disputes, regulating the securities and communications industries, and instituting home-mortgage refinancing. He also established the Tennessee Valley Authority (TVA) to provide federally generated power and economic planning for the underdeveloped region in parts of seven southern states. Roosevelt promoted industrial and agricultural recovery primarily through three programs—the National Industrial Recovery Act (NIRA), the Agricultural Adjustment Act (AAA), and the Reconstruction Finance Corporation (RFC) established during the Hoover years. These programs, in effect, put the government into partnership with the dominant elements in the struggling industrial and agricultural sectors of the private economy.

Reflecting the broad but diffuse mandate he had won in 1932 and his determination to bring together a "concert of all interests," FDR did not set the nation on a radically new course. He tried to keep spending under control, deferred to local traditions (including racial segregation), and steered clear of programs to redistribute wealth and income.

Despite these limitations and contradictions of early New Deal programs, FDR had effected a policy revolution by 1934, vastly expanding the commitments of the federal government to aiding individuals, expanding the economy, and regulating enterprise. Policy-change key 7 was already in hand for the administration, and even more initiatives were to come.

Efforts to expand the money supply, and the increased federal spending that resulted from New Deal programs, spurred some economic recovery. The economy improved steadily during the term. Unemployment dropped by a third, manufacturing production and farm parity prices increased by 50 percent, and wholesale and retail trade nearly doubled. Real per-capita economic growth soared an average of about 7 percent for each year of Roosevelt's tenure. This record pace of expansion would secure both economic keys (5 and 6) for the party in power, but it did not put an end to the depression. The economic collapse of 1929 to 1933 had been so complete that, even after nearly four years of recovery, unemployment remained above 15 percent in 1936.

With the economy improving and the president establishing a close rapport with the public through his innovative "fireside chats" on radio, the New Deal was a political success. The Democratic party reaped the benefits in the congressional elections of 1934, which occasioned an extraordinary turnout and resulted in unprecedented midterm gains in the House of Representatives for the party in power, easily securing mandate key 1. The 1934 elections remain the only midterm elections in history in which the executive party increased its percentage of House seats.

This new Democratic coalition helped stimulate a second wave of policy innovation in 1935 and 1936.[2] The Social Security Act of 1935 established the new principle of government entitlements for American citizens. The Works Progress Administration (WPA) established a federal jobs program designed to provide useful, remunerative work to large numbers of the unemployed. The Wagner National Labor Relations Act gave collective bargaining by employees the sanction and protection of a federal agency, critically assisting the growth of the Congress of Industrial Organizations (CIO), the first union to recruit millions of factory workers without regard to their craft affiliations.

As the economy recovered, protest abated among farmers and unemployed workers. Roosevelt's policies helped revive an American union movement that had been waning since the early 1920s. From 1933 to 1936, union membership rose 45 percent to 4.2 million, a prelude to the even larger increases of the next decade. The revival of unionism did not lead to the violent confrontations that had marked earlier periods of union expansion. Social-unrest key 8 stayed in the incumbent's column.

Despite the explosion of alphabet agencies outside the jurisdiction of cabinet departments, the New Deal was virtually untouched by corruption during FDR's first term. An occasional official was dismissed for bribery or kickbacks, but no scandal tarnished the reputation of any high government official. Key 9 also would stay in the Democrats' favor.

Although Roosevelt's first priority was domestic policy, he took a lively interest in events abroad. Roosevelt was most successful in extending the Good Neighbor policy in Latin America. Beyond the hemisphere, FDR was unable to respond effectively to international economic problems or to check the rise of fascist aggression in Europe, Africa, and Asia. By the end of Roosevelt's first term, however, the impact of international conflict had not yet struck home in the United States. Once again the incumbent administration neither suffered a major failure nor achieved a major success in foreign policy, thereby retaining Key 10 but forfeiting Key 11.

The Democrats enthusiastically renominated President Roosevelt at their 1936 convention, securing contest key 2, incumbency key 3, and incumbent-charisma key 12. The Republicans, routed in the elections of 1930, 1932, and 1934, had to draw from a limited leadership base for their 1936 nominee. With neither controversy nor enthusiasm, the party presented a first-ballot nomination to Governor Alfred M. Landon of Kansas, who lacked the charisma to turn Key 13 against the incumbent party.

The assassination of a potentially formidable third-party contender—Senator Huey Long of Louisiana—in September of 1935 and the reinvigoration of FDR's New Deal policies blunted the potential impact of any insurgent campaign. Critics who felt that the New Deal did not go far enough organized a Union party to challenge Roosevelt, but the party lacked a coherent alternative to the New Deal, and its candidate, North Dakota congressman William "Liberty Bell" Lemke, generated little popular support. Key 4 stayed in line for the Democrats.

The only cloud on the otherwise sunny Democratic horizon was a straw poll conducted by the *Literary Digest* (which had correctly forecast the previous three presidential elections) that predicted a smashing Landon victory with about 57 percent of the popular vote. Coincidentally, three pioneers of scientific polling—George Gallup, Elmo Roper, and Archibald Crossley—in their first forecasting efforts, showed what Roosevelt's own polls were showing: a comfortable victory for the president.

As more than three-fifths of the nation's eligible voters cast ballots, the largest participation rate since 1916, Roosevelt polled 61 percent of the popular vote to but 37 percent for Landon. The Democrats padded their already lopsided majority in the House from 73 percent to 76 percent—although the gain of only twelve seats left them vulnerable to the loss of mandate key 1 in the midterm elections. The Democrats also captured 79 percent of the Senate, reducing the GOP to but sixteen members.

1940: War on the Horizon, Salvation at Hand
Incumbent-party nominee: President Franklin D. Roosevelt
   (Democrat)
Challenging-party nominee: Wendell Willkie (Republican)
Negative keys: 2
Result: Roosevelt, 54.7%; Willkie, 44.8%

Key:	1	2	3	4	5	6	7	8	9	10	11	12	13
Call:	X	O	O	O	O	O	O	O	O	O	X	O	O

In taking the oath of office for the second time in 1937, Franklin Roosevelt became the first president to be inaugurated after the Twentieth Amendment had changed the traditional 4 March inauguration date to 20 January. After four years of recovery from the trough of the depression in March of 1933, Roosevelt believed that the control of inflation and the restoration of business confidence now required balanced budgets and monetary restraint. The administration ceased pushing the Federal Reserve Board to expand the money supply and cut back sharply on WPA relief and public-works projects. Late in the inaugural year, the economy began to slide. The decline, which continued until mid-1938, was one of the most brutal in the nation's history. By early spring of 1938, the unabated crisis finally had convinced FDR that federal initiatives were needed to stimulate the economy. The president steered major relief and public-works appropriations through Congress, expanding consumer demand and helping to reignite the economy. (The experience ultimately led Roosevelt to modify his orthodox views and to accept, at least tacitly, both deficit spending and monetary expansion as proper means of promoting economic growth.) By mid-year the contraction had halted, but it resulted in a 6 percent decline in real per-capita GNP for 1938.

Beset with economic problems and divided over the future of the New Deal, the Democrats lost seventy House seats in the congressional elections of 1938, reducing their majority from 76 percent to 60 percent and forfeiting mandate key 1. Roosevelt found it difficult to control the new Congress. His attempt to purge conservatives from party ranks in the 1938 primaries had weakened the fragile alliance between the Democrats' northern and southern wings, contributing to the emergence of a "conservative coalition" of Republicans and southern Democrats.

Halfway through Roosevelt's second term, the Democrats' prospects for reelection in 1940 looked doubtful. Mandate key 1 was down, and sentiment against a third Roosevelt term augured the possible loss not only of incumbency key 3 but also of contest key 2 and charisma key 12. The recent "Roosevelt depression" had put long-term economy key 6 in jeopardy, the administration had effected no major new policy innovations, and it had yet to make a mark in foreign or military policy.

Although the conservative coalition in Congress blocked major Roosevelt initiatives, including far-reaching proposals for reorganizing the federal government and expanding its capacity to engage in comprehensive national planning, the president did win passage of several important new programs. These included minimum-wage and maximum-hour legislation, the creation of a federal housing authority, a revised Agricultural Adjustment Act, and a reorganization bill creating the Executive Office of the President. The Democrats secured policy-change key 7, however, only through unprecedented military-preparedness measures undertaken late in the term, as Europe appeared poised to fall to Nazi aggression.

Civil disorder had bubbled to the surface in 1937 as the newly formed CIO challenged some of the nation's largest and most powerful corporations. Although some deadly violence resulted, these were isolated incidents in what was otherwise a remarkably bloodless transfer of economic power as industrial unionism became established in the United States. The Democrats retained social-unrest key 8 for the election of 1940. As unions gained legitimacy, the activities of labor would not again become the source of major social unrest.

Although controversy emerged during FDR's second term when congressional investigators uncovered instances of political activity by workers on the payroll of the WPA, the administration remained largely free of scandal. Passage of the Hatch Act in 1939, which generally prohibited political activity by federal employees, quieted the WPA controversy. Scandal key 9 was secure for the incumbent party.

In foreign policy, a largely isolationist Congress and public muted the president's responses to the German takeover of Austria and Czechoslovakia, and even the outbreak of the European war in 1939. Only after the fall of France in June of 1940 did the president take major steps to aid Great Britain and to build up America's own defenses. Roosevelt pushed measures through Congress that elevated military spending to the highest peacetime levels in history. He initiated America's first peacetime draft and agreed to send fifty aging American destroyers to Britain in exchange for basing rights on British possessions. In a move that would lead indirectly to America's entry into the war the following year, Roosevelt embargoed the export of vital raw materials to Japan, which, mired in its lengthy war of conquest in China, was now a formal ally of Nazi Germany. Roosevelt's military aid and preparedness measures began a dramatic reversal of the nation's isolationist stance and—in combination with his domestic policy successes—finally secured policy-change key 7 for the incumbent Democrats.

The economic keys, too, were solidly back in the Democrats' camp. Spurred by Roosevelt's renewed pump-priming in the second half of 1938, growth resumed strongly in 1939. The whopping increases in defense spending in 1940 helped boost real per-capita GNP an average of more than 7 percent for the last two years of the term. Although unemployment remained in double digits during the election year, the administration gained short-term economy key 5 and achieved growth for the four-year period that secured long-term economy key 6 as well.

By the time of the 1940 campaign, public opinion had caught up with the president's policies of strengthening U.S. defense capabilities and aiding Britain while avoiding involvement in the war. The president would appeal to the "mothers and fathers" of America by pledging that "your boys are not going to be sent into any foreign wars," but, given the lack of direct provocation, he could not credibly claim a foreign-policy triumph, as Woodrow Wilson had in 1916. By avoiding a major foreign or military failure the administration had retained Key 10, but the lack of a notable success toppled Key 11.

The Republicans lacked a strong candidate for 1940. Spurning career politicians, the GOP turned to the darkest horse in their stable, Wendell L. Willkie, a utility executive and former Democrat with no previous experience in politics. Willkie was an articulate speaker with an engaging and folksy style; against a lesser opponent than FDR, and in circumstances other than the war crisis, the amateur nominee might have emerged as a charismatic candidate. In 1940, however, he had difficulty developing a campaign theme and was outclassed by the campaigner Willkie himself called "the Champ." The Democratic party would retain challenger-charisma key 13.

Once Roosevelt signaled his willingness to accept a third nomination, other contenders melted away, and the president won an easy first-ballot victory. The nomination of the charismatic president and the failure of a third party to emerge locked up nomination key 2, incumbency key 3, third-party key 4, and incumbent-charisma key 12 for the Democrats. In a dramatic reversal of the outlook at midterm, only two keys— mandate key 1 and foreign-success key 11—were counted against the incumbent president.

Roosevelt prevailed by a smaller margin than in either of his previous campaigns. But he still achieved a fairly comfortable 55 percent victory. The president won thirty-eight states with 449 electoral votes; Willkie took ten states and 82 electoral votes. The Democrats retained strong majorities in Congress, although their gain of only seven seats in the House portended the loss of mandate key 1 for 1944.

1944: Sticking with a Winner

Incumbent-party nominee: President Franklin D. Roosevelt (Democrat)
Challenging-party nominee: Thomas E. Dewey (Republican)

Negative keys: 2
Result: Roosevelt, 53.4%; Dewey, 45.9%

Key:	1	2	3	4	5	6	7	8	9	10	11	12	13
Call:	X	O	O	O	O	O	O	O	O	X	O	O	O

After his defeat in 1940, Republican candidate Wendell Willkie pleaded for national unity in the face of the international emergency. Willkie's support for Roosevelt's policies during World War II would contribute to his defeat in the campaign for the Republican nomination in 1944. Like Willkie, however, a majority of the electorate would unite behind the wartime leader.

Even before the Pearl Harbor invasion thrust the United States into war, Roosevelt and Congress had transformed the nation into an "arsenal of democracy," providing arms and materiel for the European Allies. Following Pearl Harbor, Japanese forces quickly overwhelmed American possessions in the Pacific, including Wake Island, Guam, and the Philippines. Shortly thereafter the Japanese navy inflicted heavy casualties on American forces in the Java Sea. The disastrous losses in the Pacific turned military-failure key 10 against the administration.

The early military setbacks—combined with an initial mobilization effort that seemed hopelessly enmeshed in confusion and inefficiency—also contributed to the loss of a second key. Roosevelt's party suffered heavy losses in the midterm congressional elections of 1942, with Democrats barely maintaining majorities in both chambers. Their fifty-seat decline in the House constituted a net loss of forty-three seats since the previous term and cost the party mandate key 1. Even so, America's military fortunes, and the administration's, already were on the upswing.

The prosecution of total war transformed the policies of government, easily securing policy-change key 7 for the Democrats. Meeting the material demands of World War II required the greatest mobilization of manpower and production capacity in history. In 1940, federal spending had totaled less than $10 billion. During the next five years, the federal government spent nearly $300 billion on the war effort. With taxes financing about 40 percent of this amount, personal and corporate levies reached their highest levels in history, and the government began withholding taxes from paychecks. Federal agencies curtailed the output of civilian goods and directed the conversion of plants to military production, rationed raw materials, controlled prices, financed investment in new plants and equipment, set wage scales, and arbitrated labor-management disputes. To aid returning veterans, Congress passed the GI

Bill of Rights in the election year of 1944, eventually providing unprecedented federal benefits to ex-servicemen.

The many billions of dollars pumped into the economy during FDR's third term sparked a boom that quickly eliminated unemployment and in just four years raised real per-capita GNP more than 50 percent. Not until the 1960s would real per-capita GNP rise significantly above the level attained at the height of wartime prosperity in 1944. The economic boom secured both economic keys, 5 and 6, for the party in power.

Domestic support for the war and government supervision of relations between labor and capital minimized domestic turmoil. Racial tensions arising from the migration of large numbers of Blacks to northern cities was a mainspring of social unrest during the early 1940s. The U.S. government also placed some 120,000 Japanese-Americans in internment camps during the war. The events of the term, however, did not lead to widespread disorder, and the Democrats retained social-unrest key 8 in 1944.

The military mobilization was conducted in the spotlight of an ongoing Senate investigation headed by Senator Harry Truman of Missouri. The committee's exposure of deficiencies in the planning and execution of the mobilization brought Truman to national prominence. Although the Truman committee uncovered instances of corruption in some of the wartime agencies, no high administration official was involved, and the party in power retained scandal key 9.

By mid-1942, the military initiative in the Pacific passed to the American forces; major victories were achieved in 1943 when, island by island, the United States began recapturing territory held by the Japanese. Not until late 1942 did America become heavily involved in the war against Germany. The Allies eventually stymied Axis attempts to capture the Suez Canal and assert control over the region. By the end of 1943, the Allies had rolled back German armies in North Africa and forced the surrender of Italy. On D-Day, 6 June 1944, Allied forces launched the massive Operation Overlord, crossing the English Channel to invade the European continent. By the time of the election, the American-led Allies had swept through France and penetrated the German border, and Allied troops from the second front in Italy had driven Hitler's army to the German-Italian border. The end of the war in Europe was in sight. In the Pacific, American forces were beginning the liberation of the Philippines. Although some of the most ferocious fighting of the war still lay ahead, American triumphs had been plentiful enough to secure military-success key 11 for the incumbent Democrats.

Just prior to the Democratic convention, President Roosevelt announced his intention to seek an unprecedented fourth term. When the Democrats renominated the president by a nearly unanimous vote, they gained nomination key 2, incumbency key 3, and incumbent-charisma key 12.

With rumors that Roosevelt's health was failing circulating through the party, the selection of a new vice president took on particular importance. The most influential party professionals rejected incumbent vice president Henry Wallace as too radical and outspoken. Despite considerable popular and delegate support for Wallace, the convention nominated Senator Harry Truman as FDR's running mate on the second ballot.

The only possible way to beat Roosevelt after twelve extraordinary years in office, some Republican leaders believed, was to nominate a war hero. But a boom for General Douglas MacArthur had collapsed when he removed himself from consideration in May of 1944. The Republican nominee, Thomas E. Dewey, now governor of New York, was a good speaker and an efficient administrator, but he lacked both charisma and heroic stature; Key 13 remained in line for the incumbent Democrats. No third party came forward in wartime to mount a serious challenge to the president, so the Democrats also secured Key 4. On 7 November 1944, FDR amassed 53 percent of the popular vote to 46 percent for Dewey. The president garnered 432 electoral votes to but 99 for Dewey. In the House of Representatives, the Democrats gained twenty-four seats, giving them a fair chance to hold on to mandate key 1 for 1948.

1948: The Surprise Election

Incumbent-party nominee: President Harry S Truman (Democrat)
Challenging-party nominee: Thomas E. Dewey (Republican)
Negative keys: 5
Result: Truman, 49.5%; Dewey, 45.1%; J. Strom Thurmond (States' Rights), 2.4%; Henry A. Wallace (Progressive), 2.4%

Key:	1	2	3	4	5	6	7	8	9	10	11	12	13
Call:	X	O	O	X	O	X	O	O	O	X	O	X	O

After the death of FDR, President Harry Truman attempted to revive and expand the legacy of the New Deal. But the defection of southern Democrats, the declining influence of labor, and the exigencies of foreign affairs weakened the president's ability to enact new domestic programs. As a result, Truman accomplished only modest changes in domestic policy during his nearly eight years in office. However, Truman presided over the most significant transformation of American foreign policy since the 1890s. America emerged from the war as the world's dominant power, both determined and obliged to defend its security and economic interests around the globe.

On 12 April 1945, less than three months after taking the presidential oath of office for the fourth time, Franklin Roosevelt died of a cerebral hemorrhage. Many Washington insiders viewed the new president, Harry S Truman, as a provincial Midwestern politico ill-equipped to be chief executive. The perception of a doomed presidency would persist through the 1948 campaign, masking the critical achievements that narrowly, but assuredly, secured Truman's election to a second term despite the almost universal prediction of a Republican victory.

Twenty-five days after Roosevelt's death, Germany had surrendered unconditionally. Victory in the Pacific came three months later, but only after the United States had devastated the Japanese cities of Hiroshima and Nagasaki with the newly developed atomic bomb. Foreign-success key 11 was locked in the administration's favor.

In the aftermath of war, President Truman faced two new realities: the devastation of much of Europe and the Far East, and the sudden status of the United States and an expansionist Soviet Union as the world's two superpowers. America quickly began assuming new responsibilities. In 1945, the United States took the lead in founding and nurturing the United Nations. Within the UN framework, America supplied the lion's share of funding for a World Bank dedicated to development projects in less-developed nations and an International Monetary Fund designed to maintain currency stability in the world economy. The United States also strengthened the Export-Import Bank to provide foreign loans for the purchase of American goods.

The exultation of victory over the Axis powers was short-lived. With the end of the conflict in Europe, the Soviet Union—abrogating pledges made at a February conference in Yalta—brutally imposed pro-Soviet regimes in Poland and Hungary and began solidifying communist influence in Czechoslovakia and the Balkan states of Bulgaria, Romania, Yugoslavia, and Albania. Even as Americans were still savoring their triumph in war, foreign-failure key 10 was turned against the incumbent administration.

At home, the wartime economic boom collapsed in the summer of 1945, as the government canceled seventy thousand contracts and companies laid off 2.5 million workers. The economy continued to slide during the next two years, largely as a result of steep price increases following the end of wartime controls, but it never sank into the deep depression that many authorities anticipated. Growth picked up again in 1948, securing short-term economy key 5 for the Truman administration, but real per-capita growth for the term was negative, turning long-term economy key 6 against the Democrats.

The postwar economic letdown contributed to massive losses for the executive party in the midterm congressional elections of 1946. Voters responded to the Republican query as to whether they had "Had Enough?" of high prices and high taxes by returning control of the Congress to the GOP for the first time since 1930. In addition to dropping eleven Senate seats, the Democrats lost fifty-four seats in the House of Representatives, more than twice the number it had gained in 1944. Mandate key 1 was turned against the incumbent administration.

Without Democratic control over Congress, President Truman's chances for a successful presidency seemed almost hopeless. Ironically, the Soviets aided his cause through their aggression in Europe and the Middle East. Public opinion lined up behind the president when, on 12 March 1947, he proposed a policy of "containment" to halt the spread of communism to nations not already under Soviet control. The Truman Doctrine committed the United States to providing military and economic assistance to targets of communist aggression. The National Security Act of 1947 reorganized the American military under the supervision of a civilian Secretary of Defense and created the Joint Chiefs of Staff, the Central Intelligence Agency (CIA), and the National Security Council. Finally, the United States implemented the Marshall Plan, a massive and unprecedented aid program proposed by Secretary of State George C. Marshall to rehabilitate the war-torn economies of Western European nations and blunt the appeal of communism. Overall, the new, outward-looking foreign policy forged in the aftermath of the war clearly constituted a major redirection of national purpose, securing policy-change key 7 for the administration.

Racial unrest after World War II did not lead to a reprise of the urban rioting that followed the First World War. Given the profound changes that took place in the nation's economic and social fabric after the war, domestic turmoil was surprisingly moderate. A rash of strikes in 1946 eroded public support for labor, however, and contributed to the passage (over Truman's veto) in 1947 of the Taft-Hartley Act, which instituted new controls over unions and work stoppages. Still, the domestic scene was predominantly tranquil, keeping Key 8 in the Democrats' column.

The Truman administration avoided high-level scandals during its first term. No misdeeds of consequence surfaced prior to the election, leaving Key 9 standing for the party in power.

Pessimism about Truman's chances in the election led some Democrats to push for the nomination of the D-Day hero, General Dwight David Eisenhower. Eisenhower rebuffed their advances, leaving Truman without a serious challenger to the nomination. Truman's selection gained the Democrats nomination key 2 and incumbency key 3 but cost them incumbent-charisma key 12.

The Republicans also courted General Eisenhower, but he declined their appeals, too, so the GOP turned again to the dapper New York governor, Thomas Dewey, as its presidential nominee. Dewey was neither a national hero nor a charismatic candidate capable of turning Key 13 against the incumbent party.

The Democrats lost Key 4 when independent movements split off from both left and right wings of the party. In 1946, President Truman had fired Secretary of Commerce Henry Wallace—his predecessor as vice president—after Wallace accused the United States of bearing responsibility for the Cold War. Wallace had formed the new Progressive party and now sought to unite liberals, socialists, and communists. Polls taken late in 1948 showed that Wallace was likely to garner about 6 percent of the popular vote, much of it in cities crucial to a Democratic victory. From the other end of the spectrum, a states' rights Democratic party, the Dixiecrats—harkening back to nineteenth-century traditions—nominated South Carolina Governor Strom Thurmond. The Dixiecrats objected to Truman's support for civil rights and activist government. Although Thurmond had little potential as a contender for popular votes, he had a chance to win several southern states that were normally solid for the Democratic nominee.

The emergence of these splinter candidacies brought the incumbent Democrats' final tally to five negative keys—mandate, third party, long-term economy, foreign failure, and incumbent charisma. No matter what the polls or the pundits said, it was one short of the number necessary to count the president out.

On 9 September 1948, esteemed pollster Elmo Roper announced that the margin in favor of Dewey was so large that he would "stop reporting" his polling results "unless something really interesting happens."[3] The two other national pollsters, George Gallup and Archibald Crossley, continued polling through late October; their identical findings showed Dewey ahead by five percentage points. Both Crossley and Gallup concluded a week before the election that opinion had solidified, and they joined Roper in proclaiming Dewey president-elect.

The pollsters apparently convinced the nation's newspaper editors and journalists. On election eve, *Life* magazine observed, "If the '48 campaign has seemed to have less fireworks than usual, it is because Dewey has known all along that he would win.'' [4] The next night, editors were quick to see their belief confirmed when early returns favored the Republican. As in 1916, the headlines of several major newspapers echoed the page-one banner of the *Chicago Tribune*: ''Dewey Defeats Truman.''

When the final tally was posted, however, Truman had garnered 49.5 percent of the popular vote to 45.1 percent for Dewey. The Progressive and Dixiecrat nominees together garnered nearly 5 percent of the popular ballots. Thurmond won four Deep South states with 39 electoral votes. In the electoral college, the president gained 303 votes to 189 for Dewey. The election also restored Democratic majorities in both chambers of Congress. In the House of Representatives, the Democrats gained seventy-five seats, showing that Truman's victory was no fluke and making it likely that the Democrats would gain mandate key 1 for 1952.

1952: The Buck Passes
Incumbent-party nominee: Adlai E. Stevenson (Democrat)
Challenging-party nominee: Dwight D. Eisenhower (Republican)
Negative keys: 8
Result: Eisenhower, 55.1%; Stevenson, 44.4%

Key:	1	2	3	4	5	6	7	8	9	10	11	12	13
Call:	O	X	X	O	O	X	X	O	X	X	O	X	X

Fresh from his ''upset'' victory in 1948—and with a new Democratic Congress on Capitol Hill—President Truman began his second term by outlining a new domestic program he called the ''Fair Deal.'' Truman's plans included sweeping proposals for national health insurance, development of public power, increased farm supports, low-income housing, fair-employment practices, federal aid to education, and government control of prices, commodities, exports, wages, and rents.

Truman achieved some domestic policy results, but not the major changes he envisioned. He was hampered by the conservative coalition of Republicans and southern Democrats in Congress, recurring diplomatic crises, the opposition of powerful interest groups such as the American Medical Association, and ultimately the distraction of the Korean War. The Fair Deal would succeed primarily in expanding New Deal programs, such as Social Security and the minimum wage, rather than in advancing new policies. For the first time in the twentieth century, policy-change key 7 would be turned against a Democratic administration.

For all his efforts on the domestic front, Truman saw foreign affairs dominate his second term. Major accomplishments of the term included the establishment of the North Atlantic Treaty Organization (NATO), the breaking of the Russian blockade of West Berlin, and a successful campaign against internal communist movements in Western Europe.

Success in Europe was accompanied by failure in Asia. The announcement in September 1949 that the Soviet Union had exploded an atomic bomb of its own set the stage for a succession of foreign surprises. More disturbing news arrived before the end of that year: Chinese Communist forces under the command of Mao Zedong defeated the Nationalist armies of Chiang Kai-shek, and Mao quickly proclaimed his alignment with the Soviet bloc. The "loss" of China—which the American government hardly could have prevented—nevertheless gave critics an opportunity to lambaste Truman for his inability to halt the communist menace.

This pattern of success mixed with failure also characterized America's response to the invasion of South Korea. After the intervention of Chinese forces, the war stalled at the 38th parallel, the original boundary between North and South Korea. Truce talks began in the summer of 1951 after Truman, wary of igniting a third world war, had fired General Douglas MacArthur for insubordination in pressing for an all-out campaign against China. Inconclusive fighting and deadlocked negotiations would continue through the election of 1952. Once again, international developments earned the administration foreign-success key 11 and cost it foreign-failure key 10.

The midterm elections of 1950 took place under mixed circumstances for the party in power. The Truman administration had been tagged with the loss of China but, after a slight recession in 1949, was enjoying prosperous times and riding the crest of MacArthur's early success in Korea. The twenty-nine House seats that the Democrats lost in 1950 fell far short of the gains they had made in 1948; they retained both their majority in Congress and mandate key 1 for the 1952 election.

A frantic hunt for communists within America's own borders disrupted national harmony during Truman's second term. Republican senator Joseph McCarthy of Wisconsin and others charged that communists had infiltrated the federal government and other national institutions. What became known as "McCarthyism" created a national hysteria over internal subversion and affected the lives of thousands of persons, but it did not generate violent protests or mass arrests, and so did not turn Key 8 against the incumbent party. Nor did a nationwide steel strike in the summer of 1952, which seriously hampered war production but did not spur civil disorder.

However, a series of scandals, worse than any since the Harding years, rocked the Truman administration. Investigations led by Democratic senators uncovered influence peddling by General Harry H. Vaughn, the president's military adviser and friend. Far more serious were revelations that officials of the multibillion-dollar Reconstruction Finance Corporation had dealt out loans for questionable activities and accepted gifts and favors from the recipients. The trail of graft also led to high officials of the Democratic party and to political appointees in the Bureau of Internal Revenue and the Tax Division of the Justice Department. The president's inept handling of the scandals magnified the widespread perception of a "mess in Washington." He did not act quickly against wrongdoers, although he did reform the RFC and reorganize the Bureau of Internal Revenue as the Internal Revenue Service, whose personnel came under the civil service. To defuse criticism, he called for a Justice Department commission to investigate corruption, a forerunner of the special prosecutor appointed to investigate the Watergate scandal. But the commission was sidetracked by a squabble between Truman and Attorney General Howard McGrath, whom the president eventually fired. Key 9 would be lost to the incumbent party.

The economy picked up after a brief slump in 1949; per-capita GNP increased in real terms during the next three years, stimulated by the military spending brought on by the Korean War. The election-year economy would hand the Democrats Key 5, but the pace of post-recession growth was sluggish, costing the party Key 6.

Although Truman was exempt from coverage of the newly passed Twenty-second Amendment barring third presidential terms, he had confided to friends that he would not be a candidate for reelection in 1952. The president did not formally withdraw from the race, however, until Senator Estes Kefauver of Tennessee defeated him in the New Hampshire primary. Despite Kefauver's strong showing in the primaries, the party professionals who controlled the Democratic convention rejected his candidacy. On the fourth ballot, the Democrats chose insider favorite Adlai Stevenson, the governor of Illinois. Stevenson had sat out the primaries and proclaimed disinterest in the nomination. The witty and urbane Stevenson articulated liberal principles more eloquently than any other Democrat of his generation. But he lacked the common touch and seemed plagued by indecision. The governor's nomination in a contested convention cost the incumbent Democrats nomination key 2 and incumbent-charisma key 12.

No significant third party emerged in 1952. The Progressive party, revived in 1948 by Henry Wallace, stayed in business but never recovered from the disappointments of the 1948 campaign. The Dixiecrats, mollified by a weaker civil-rights plank than in 1948 and by the selection of Senator John Sparkman of Alabama as the vice-presidential nominee, stayed within the party. The Democrats retained Key 4.

In a bitterly divided Republican convention—the first to be televised live to a nationwide audience—General Dwight D. Eisenhower, the war hero both parties had courted in 1948, wrested the nomination from Robert A. Taft, the champion of the party's conservative wing. Eisenhower's nomination cost the Democrats Key 13, the eighth key to fall against the incumbent party.

As election day approached, pollster George Gallup took special care not to repeat the "errors" of 1948. Gallup's final poll, taken just a few days before the election, showed 47 percent for Eisenhower, 40 percent for Stevenson, and 13 percent undecided. This time there would be no mistake. Having missed the powerful Democratic drift of the undecided vote in 1948, Gallup now concluded that the large undecided vote meant that the 1952 race was too close to call.[5]

"Wrong again," hooted *Time* magazine after Eisenhower swept to an easy victory at the polls. "The scientific pollsters who were so famously wrong in 1948, were even more wrong (in a different way) in 1952. This year, they were right and did not have the courage to believe themselves."[6]

Eisenhower received 55 percent of the popular vote and 442 electoral votes compared to Stevenson's 44 percent and 89 electoral college votes. For only the second time since 1930, the Republicans also gained control of both chambers of Congress, winning twenty-two seats in the House, enough to give the party a chance at holding mandate key 1 for 1956.

1956: We Still Like Ike
Incumbent-party nominee: President Dwight D. Eisenhower (Republican)
Challenging-party nominee: Adlai E. Stevenson (Democrat)
Negative keys: 1
Result: Eisenhower, 57.4%; Stevenson, 42.0%

Key:	1	2	3	4	5	6	7	8	9	10	11	12	13
Call:	O	O	O	O	O	O	X	O	O	O	O	O	O

The presidential contest of 1956 was a reprise of the election of 1900, in which the defeated nominee of the incumbent Democratic party would return to challenge his conqueror, now a popular sitting president. Dwight Eisenhower, like William McKinley before him, would have nearly all the keys lined up in his favor. The outcome on Election Day would surprise no one; this time, not even the pollsters would be fooled.

In December of 1952, the president-elect fulfilled his campaign pledge and went to Korea, where he toured the front lines of American troops. Six months after his inauguration, he negotiated an armistice ending the war at the same place it had begun, the 38th parallel. The end of the three-year conflict, which had cost more than fifty thousand American lives, was a great relief to the nation and a notable success for the new administration, but it was not the kind of clear-cut victory that America had enjoyed in the two world wars.

Although current mythology casts the 1950s as an era of comfort and prosperity, economic performance was one of the weaker aspects of the Eisenhower presidency. Several recessions retarded economic growth during his two terms; at the end of Eisenhower's tenure in 1961, real per-capita GNP was only 5 percent higher than it had been at the beginning of his first term. A brief recession occurred early in the Eisenhower years. The economy briskly recovered in 1955, but the expansion was not broad based and the economy quickly began to falter again. The economy grew just enough in the election year to salvage the short-term and long-term economic keys.

As a modern Republican, Eisenhower supported the containment policies, alliances, and foreign economic commitments established by his Democratic predecessors. Eisenhower did depart from previous policy in some areas. He curbed the regulatory zeal of federal agencies by appointing probusiness advocates to head them, and tax policy became an instrument for stimulating business investment as well as for raising revenue and redistributing income. The major positive initiative of the term was the Federal Highway Act, which authorized the construction of an interstate highway system. Eisenhower's middle-of-the-road initiatives fell well short of the major redirection needed to secure Key 7.

President Eisenhower hoped that his modern Republicanism would become the basis for a new party coalition of moderate Republicans, independents, and centrist Democrats. Such hopes were dampened, however, by Republican losses in the off-year elections of 1954. After almost a year of recession, the Democrats recaptured both houses of Congress and made gains in state and local elections as well. The Republicans lost only eighteen seats in the House, however—four fewer than they had gained in 1952—and so, while forfeiting their majority, they retained mandate key 1 for 1956.

The anticommunist crusade promoted by Senator McCarthy continued during the Eisenhower regime. Party loyalty did not restrain McCarthy from "exposing" alleged subversives in the new Republican administration, although McCarthy's ill-advised attack on the U.S. Army led to his censure by the Senate and the discrediting of his crusade. With the formation of the combined AFL-CIO in 1955 and a membership of nearly eighteen million workers, organized labor reached the zenith of its economic power. Negotiating from a position of relative strength, unions won major gains from corporations without sparking the industrial strife of earlier times. A fledgling civil-rights movement began organized protest activities, but major civil-rights demonstrations—and the violent reactions that often met them—were still in the future. The lack of domestic turmoil during the term locked in Key 8 for the incumbent Republicans.

Despite revelations of apparent conflicts of interests arising from the close relationship between the administration and the business community, the GOP also retained scandal key 9. Imbroglios of the Eisenhower years had little impact compared to the "mess" in Washington of the Truman years.

By negotiating an end to the Korean War, President Eisenhower had captured foreign-success key 11 in his first year in office. But he had to steer a steady course through three difficult Cold War years to avoid a major foreign-policy failure and the loss of Key 10. To maintain the struggle against communism worldwide, Eisenhower found that he had to sustain defense spending at levels close to those of the Korean War—three times the amount devoted to defense in 1949. The administration used the CIA to wage the Cold War in the Third World, overturning leftist governments in Iran and Guatemala. In Indochina, however, American aid failed to prevent the defeat of French colonial forces by the nationalistic Marxist leader, Ho Chi Minh. After deciding not to intervene militarily against Ho, the United States managed to salvage Western influence in Vietnam by supporting a noncommunist government in the southern half of the country, which was partitioned under UN auspices.

Two major crises emerged in the election year. Just a few days before the election, Soviet tanks and troops crushed a revolution in Hungary, killing thousands. The Eisenhower administration, realizing its logistical disadvantage in Eastern Europe and unwilling to risk all-out war with Russia, could only condemn the Soviet actions that outraged the world. A week before the election, Eisenhower also denounced an invasion of Egypt by Israel, Britain, and France. These nations sought to topple Egyptian leader Gamal Abdel Nasser, who had seized control of the Suez Canal. On the evening of the U.S. election, the invading forces agreed to a cease-fire, having stopped short of the canal. Two election-eve crises with the potential to inflict serious foreign-policy setbacks on the administration may instead have strengthened a president widely regarded as America's most reliable helmsman in a time of crisis. Foreign-failure key 10 was solidly in the administration's favor.

Other keys lined up for the Republicans. Only possible health problems stood between Eisenhower and renomination in 1956. Although Ike had suffered a serious heart attack in 1955, his doctors gave him a clean bill of health the following year. A unanimous convention vote for the president secured contest key 2, incumbency key 3, and incumbent-charisma key 12. The continued absence of any significant third-party movement left Key 4 standing for the incumbent party. The Democrats' renomination of Adlai Stevenson secured challenger-charisma key 13 for the incumbent party as well.

Eisenhower's 57 percent majority in the popular vote exceeded even the expectations of his own campaign. In electoral votes, Ike outpaced his rival 457 to 73, but the election results also disclosed his failure to achieve a realignment of political loyalties in the United States. The Democrats retained control of Congress with approximately the same margins they had secured in 1954, leaving the Republican party vulnerable to the loss of mandate key 1 for 1960.

Chapter 7

New Directions, War, and Scandal

Despite his promise of a new direction for America, President John F. Kennedy proceeded cautiously on the domestic front. It was in defense and foreign policy that JFK became an activist chief executive, expanding military budgets, facing down the Russians in Berlin and Cuba, and negotiating the first arms-control agreement of the Cold War. Political logic pushed the Democrats in new directions during the 1960s, as Black voters expanded their role in the party and White Southerners began defecting to the GOP. Even before Kennedy's successor, Vice President Lyndon Johnson, won reelection on his own in 1964, he had sponsored watershed civil-rights legislation and an unprecedented "war on poverty."

Johnson's early achievements appeared to presage the rise of another Democratic dynasty, but his expansion of the Vietnam War divided and weakened the party, leading to another Republican victory in 1968. As president, Richard Nixon would contradict his own conservative rhetoric and for the most part extend the domestic policy initiatives of his Democratic predecessor. Despite Nixon's landslide reelection in 1972, the Watergate scandal ended his presidency and thwarted the efforts of his appointed successor, Vice President Gerald Ford, to steer the economy, manage what had become a vast patchwork of domestic programs, and defend the nation's far-flung interests abroad.

1960: The Unmaking of a Presidency
Incumbent-party candidate: Richard M. Nixon (Republican)
Challenging-party candidate: John F. Kennedy (Democrat)
Negative keys: 9
Result: Kennedy, 49.7%; Nixon, 49.6%

Key:	1	2	3	4	5	6	7	8	9	10	11	12	13
Call:	X	O	X	O	X	X	X	O	O	X	X	X	X

In 1960, for the first time since the Democrats nominated Martin Van Buren in 1836, the incumbent party selected its vice president, Richard Nixon, to head the campaign ticket. The Democratic nominee, Massachusetts senator John Fitzgerald Kennedy, was also a "second": the second Catholic, after Al Smith in 1928, to win the nomination of a major party. More than thirty years after Smith, Catholicism remained a divisive issue, reducing Kennedy's popular vote margin over Nixon.

GOP troubles began with a double whammy in the fall of 1957, when a Soviet-launched satellite soared into space and the U.S. economy crashed to earth. At home, a tight monetary policy by the Federal Reserve Board and a drop in private investment led to a brief but sharp recession. The Soviets' launching of Sputnik—the first orbiting vehicle in space—in October 1957 was a painful blow to the administration and a global propaganda triumph for the Soviets. The feat called into question what Americans had smugly taken for granted: their nation's technical and scientific superiority over the Soviet Union. The launching also added to the credibility of an alleged "missile gap" between the United States and Russia.

The sour economy and the humiliation of Sputnik set the tone for the congressional elections of 1958. Despite six years of Eisenhower moderation, surveys found that a majority of Americans still viewed the GOP as favoring "big business" at the expense of the "common man." The Republicans dropped forty-seven House seats—and mandate key 1—in the midterm elections, becoming but a 35 percent minority for Eisenhower's last two years. The party fared no better in the Senate, where it retained only thirty-four seats.

Despite his guaranteed lame-duck status and a heavily Democratic Congress, Ike enjoyed some legislative successes, including a modest voting-rights bill, the establishment of the National Aeronautics and Space Administration (NASA), initiatives in science education, and new labor laws. But the president's modern Republicanism called for no bold departures in domestic policy. The limited policy change achieved during Ike's second term turned Key 7 against the party in power.

Despite recurrent labor unrest and resistance to Black demands for civil rights in the South, social order largely prevailed during the second half of the decade. In 1957, President Eisenhower dispatched federal troops to Little Rock, Arkansas, to protect nine Black children entering the city's previously all-White Central High School. From 1958 through 1960, sit-ins by protesters seeking to integrate all-White lunch counters and other facilities sparked attacks on Blacks and the arrest of demonstrators by local police. But the sit-in movement did not produce the sustained unrest or dramatic episodes of violence that would have turned Key 8 against the GOP.

The appearance, at least, of conflicts of interests did mar Eisenhower's second term. In 1958, a House investigating committee uncovered evidence suggesting that the president's most trusted aide, White House chief of staff Sherman Adams, had accepted gifts from businessman Bernard Goldfine in return for intervening on Goldfine's behalf with federal regulatory agencies. Eisenhower yielded to the entreaties of fellow Republicans and reluctantly accepted Adams's resignation. The incident was an isolated one, and the president's integrity remained unquestioned, so the administration narrowly retained scandal key 9.

In the wake of the Sputnik humiliation, a "crash" U.S. rocketry program let America join the Russians in space just four months later. Eisenhower and his unblinking secretary of state, John Foster Dulles, scored several other small foreign-policy victories in 1958. The president successfully applied the Eisenhower Doctrine, committing U.S. support to Middle Eastern nations threatened by communist aggression, when he sent troops to protect the pro-Western government of Lebanon from the alleged threat of a Soviet-inspired revolution. The administration defused threats by mainland China to move against the nationalist government on Taiwan and coolly stared down Nikita Khrushchev's demand that the United States, Britain, and France abandon West Berlin to East German rule.

These successes, however, were overshadowed by other crises played out under the mounting threat of nuclear annihilation. Promising diplomatic developments—including a 1959 visit by Khrushchev to the United States—in Eisenhower's efforts to negotiate the first arms-control agreement with the Soviets ended precipitously in 1960. Just prior to a summit meeting in Paris, the Soviets shot down an American U-2 reconnaissance plane and captured its pilot, Francis Gary Powers. The administration first denied conducting surveillance flights, then did an embarrassing about-face when Khrushchev exhibited photos of the downed spy plane and its pilot. Progress on arms control, Berlin, and other issues would have to await another administration. The White House suffered another blow late in the term when Fidel Castro, the newly triumphant leader of the Cuban revolution, expropriated American property and moved Cuba into the Soviet orbit. With no major foreign-policy triumphs to its credit and several international setbacks, the administration forfeited both foreign-policy keys, 10 and 11.

The GOP's troubles were not over. To counter the 1957–58 recession, the Federal Reserve Board finally had acted to lower interest rates, and a reluctant Eisenhower had grudgingly boosted federal spending. As a result, the economy turned upward again in mid-1958 and 1959. As the economy began to slow again in 1960, Vice President Nixon tried to persuade the administration to adopt an expansionist fiscal policy. Eisenhower, however, was determined to achieve a budget surplus in his final year, and Nixon's plea fell on deaf ears. The resulting fiscal drag, combined with the Fed's tight-money policy, contributed to a mild election-year recession, toppling short-term economy key 5. Overall, real per-capita growth increased an average of less than 1 percent a year during the term, costing the GOP Key 6 as well.

The Democrats' nomination of the young, handsome, and charismatic junior senator from Massachusetts, John F. Kennedy, cost the incumbent party charisma key 13. As his vice-presidential choice, Kennedy took the unusual step of choosing one of his rivals for the nomination, Senator Lyndon Baines Johnson of Texas, the Senate majority leader.

Vice President Nixon, although not Eisenhower's first choice, cruised to an almost unanimous nomination. His selection secured nomination key 2 but cost the party Key 12; popular though Nixon was, he clearly lacked charismatic appeal. The absence of a notable third-party contender gave the GOP Key 4.

The Democratic nominee confronted the matter of his Catholic religion head-on, boldly choosing for the occasion of his major speech what many considered enemy turf: a gathering of the Greater Houston Ministerial Association. Kennedy said succinctly that he favored the strict separation of church and state and would not be influenced in any presidential decision by Roman Catholic dicta.

In two ways, television—which was expanding its news programming and its audience—assumed a new role in presidential campaigns. More than ever before, the candidates competed for coverage on the nightly news and, for the first time, confronted one another in televised debates.

In one of the closest elections in history, Kennedy garnered 34,221,344 popular votes (49.7 percent) to 34,106,671 (49.6 percent) for Nixon. The Democrats also retained majorities in both houses of Congress, but the loss of twenty House seats after the huge gains of 1958 virtually ensured that mandate key 1 would be lost for 1964. Although the religious issue undoubtedly cost Kennedy several percentage points in the popular vote, it may actually have bolstered his electoral-college majority. Catholic voters were concentrated in the urban areas of states with large numbers of electoral votes. Kennedy garnered 303 votes to 219 for Nixon. Kennedy's margins of victory in the key states of Texas and Illinois were so close, however, that some Nixon associates, believing that Democratic machine politicians had stolen the election, urged Nixon to challenge the results in court. The vice president demurred on the grounds that a legal battle would only disrupt the transition to the new administration.

Kennedy's winning campaign of 1960 would become the model for subsequent political campaigns—and for the conventional wisdom that the sophisticated application of modern technology and marketing techniques could be decisive in a presidential contest. Pundits attributed Kennedy's narrow victory to his innovative use of television, polling, personal organization, and image making—an impression that Theodore White's influential best-seller, *The Making of the President, 1960,* strongly reinforced.[1] From then on, presidential campaigns typically became frenzied, almost contradictory, affairs—conducted in every corner of the nation yet geared toward maximum television coverage—dominated by the candidates' personal retinues of pollsters, organizers, press handlers, advertising specialists, and other consultants.

1964: A New Frontier, a Greater Society
Incumbent-party nominee: President Lyndon B. Johnson (Democrat)
Challenging-party nominee: Barry M. Goldwater (Republican)
Negative keys: 3
Results: Johnson, 61.1%; Goldwater, 38.5%

Key:	1	2	3	4	5	6	7	8	9	10	11	12	13
Call:	X	O	O	O	O	O	O	O	O	X	O	X	O

John Fitzgerald Kennedy brought a new look, a new style, a new vitality to the presidency. Despite the supposed ''good times'' of the 1950s, the United States was not fulfilling its promise. America was falling behind in competition with the Soviets. Poverty, illiteracy, and injustice were to be found not just in foreign lands but within our own borders as well.

The extent of what Kennedy might have done for his country will never be known. An assassin's bullet cut down the youngest president ever elected less than three years after he took office. The task of fulfilling his bright promise fell to a man despised by many in the slain president's inner circle. Yet the task could not have fallen more fortuitously. While JFK's liberal followers mourned their martyred leader, they feared that Lyndon Johnson—America's first chief executive from the Deep South—would steer the nation in a conservative direction. Few remembered that Johnson was a disciple of FDR or that, despite cultivating a moderate image during the 1950s, as Senate majority leader he had helped sustain vital elements of the liberal agenda. Johnson guided through Congress the stalled initiatives of the Kennedy administration, assuring JFK's place in history and Johnson's own reelection in 1964.

Kennedy had campaigned on the need to get the economy moving again, but he resisted pressure from his Council of Economic Advisers for expansive spending and tax policies. To restart the stalled economy of 1961, he won an investment tax credit and modest spending hikes for domestic and foreign programs. Although the economy was growing rapidly by 1962, a midyear tumble in the stock market sparked concern about the economy's future and prompted Kennedy to become the first American president to propose an avowedly Keynesian approach to economic expansion. He called for a major cut in personal and corporate income taxes to stimulate the economy. Although Congress passed the tax cut late in the term (after Kennedy's death), the economy grew fairly briskly in the early 1960s, securing keys 5 and 6 for the incumbent Democrats.

President Kennedy himself was responsible both for the administration's most devastating foreign-policy blunder and for its greatest international success. In April of 1961 the United States launched an exile invasion of Cuba planned by the CIA during Eisenhower's final year in office. Despite misgivings about its potential for success—and on the condition that there be no "direct" U.S. involvement—Kennedy authorized the invasion; intelligence reports indicated that this would be the last opportunity to overthrow the increasingly powerful Castro regime. The invasion was too little, too late. Castro's seasoned troops easily defeated the invaders, who lacked American air support, taking most of them prisoner. The Bay of Pigs fiasco was a major blow to the credibility of the new administration; within three months of his inauguration, Kennedy had lost Key 10.

Encouraged by the Bay of Pigs to test the mettle of the young president, Soviet Premier Nikita Khrushchev threatened to sign a treaty with East Germany abrogating Western rights in Berlin and bringing the entire city under Communist party control. Kennedy responded to the Berlin crisis by mobilizing reserve U.S. forces, and Khrushchev backed down—a reversal tacitly acknowledged in mid-August when the communists began building a massive concrete and barbed-wire wall to stem the flood of refugees from the Soviet-dominated eastern sector to the West.

However, Khrushchev was not finished. In the fall of 1962, intelligence flights revealed that the Soviet Union was installing offensive missiles in Cuba, expanding its capacity to strike at the United States.

Rejecting suggestions of a bombing raid against the missile sites, President Kennedy imposed a naval blockade against Russian vessels headed for the island. With the Strategic Air Command on a full war alert, America—perhaps on the brink of nuclear war—waited to see if the Soviets would attempt to run the blockade. But the Soviet ships stopped short of the blockade, enabling the superpowers to reach an agreement that called for the removal of the missiles in return for an American pledge not to invade Cuba. In the most dangerous confrontation of the Cold War, the callow president had stood eyeball-to-eyeball with the seasoned Khrushchev, and the Russian had blinked first. Foreign-policy success key 11 was now secure for the Democrats.

The Cuban missile crisis persuaded President Kennedy to try to ease superpower tensions. In 1963, the United States and Russia signed the first arms-control accord of the Cold War, a treaty prohibiting nuclear tests in the atmosphere and under the seas. Meanwhile, communist elements backed by the Chinese were threatening governments in Southeast Asia. With the lesson of Korea in mind, Kennedy declined to commit American military support to Laos, which shared a border with China. But he continued support, begun under Truman, for South Vietnam, whose government was now under pressure from a guerrilla war led by communist infiltrators from North Vietnam. By autumn of 1963, the number of U.S. advisers was about fifteen thousand.

The congressional elections of 1962 closely followed the successful resolution of the Cuban missile crisis. With the economy booming as well, the Democrats fared better than any executive party had in a mid-term election since 1934, losing only five House seats. But combined with the loss of twenty seats in 1960, these results still toppled mandate key 1 for 1964.

Notwithstanding his bold campaign vision of a "new frontier" for America, Kennedy proved to be a cautious leader at home, mindful both of polls showing the moderate tenor of public opinion and of his dependence on the conservative southern Democrats who, by virtue of seniority, controlled the crucial committees of Congress. He also feared that liberal policies would undermine the business confidence he deemed essential to economic expansion. The president did not resurrect Fair Deal proposals for national health insurance, revamped farm programs, or major civil-rights legislation. Despite his chiding of the Eisenhower administration during the campaign, he hesitated for nearly two years before signing an executive order ending racial discrimination in federally supported housing.

When the president was shot and killed while riding in a motorcade in Dallas, Texas, on 22 November 1963, his most ambitious programs were in the works, including an omnibus civil-rights law, new antipoverty initiatives, and tax-cut proposals. But in a year of extraordinary accomplishment—aided no doubt by Kennedy's martyrdom—President Johnson, the consummate legislative leader of his time, cashed in on all of these major programs.

In February of 1964, Congress approved the tax cut, just in time to boost the election-year economy. But the burning issue of the Kennedy-Johnson term was racial justice. In 1963, the one hundredth anniversary of the Emancipation Proclamation, civil-rights organizations began the most widespread campaign of demonstrations in the nation's history. The violent response of local police to demonstrations led by Martin Luther King in Birmingham, Alabama, generated national outrage and moved Kennedy to draft the new civil-rights legislation. As Congress debated the civil-rights bill in August of 1963, more than 200,000 Black and White citizens joined in the "March on Washington for Jobs and Freedom," one of the largest demonstrations in the capital's history. Finally, under Johnson's firm guidance, Congress in June of 1964 passed the most significant civil-rights bill since Reconstruction. The Civil Rights Act of 1964 prohibited racial segregation in government facilities and "public accommodations" such as restaurants and hotels. It strengthened voting-rights enforcement, established programs to hasten school integration, banned discrimination in federally assisted programs, and outlawed employment discrimination.

Johnson was not content, however, with fulfilling JFK's legacy. To move the nation toward a "great society" characterized by economic security for all Americans, Johnson also pushed through Congress the Economic Opportunity Act of 1964, a multipronged attack on poverty. Having achieved the most significant domestic-policy innovations since the New Deal, the Democrats gained policy-change key 7.

Gains in civil rights had been spurred by racial confrontations that sometimes turned violent, especially after the 1963 March on Washington. In September of that year, a church bombing in Birmingham had killed four Black girls. In the summer of 1964, as civil-rights groups mounted voter-registration drives in the South, members of the Ku Klux Klan murdered three volunteers in Mississippi. In all, fifteen civil-rights workers were murdered in the South during the "Freedom Summer" of 1964. Mob violence also erupted in several northern cities—notably New York, Rochester, and Jersey City—during the long hot summer of 1964. The demonstrations and riots contributed to general unease about race relations in America, but they did not lead to widespread social disorder. In a close call, the Democrats retained social-unrest key 8 for the 1964 election.

The moral tone for the Kennedy administration had been set by an executive order in April of 1961 promulgating the most exacting regulations on conflict of interest in the history of the federal bureaucracy. Kennedy and Johnson generally presided over a scandal-free administration, keeping Key 9 in line for the Democrats.

The Democrats nominated by acclamation the author of the Great Society, thereby securing nomination key 2 and incumbency key 3. But Johnson, though a master politician, lacked his predecessor's charisma, so the Democrats forfeited Key 12.

For a contest that virtually no one believed the GOP could win, the Republicans nominated Senator Barry Goldwater of Arizona, their first genuinely conservative candidate since Herbert Hoover. Goldwater inspired ardent support from his conservative followers, but his views were not in step with majority opinion, and he lacked the charisma needed to turn Key 13 against the incumbent Democrats. No third party challenged the dominant two in 1964, leaving Key 4 in the Democrats' column as well, for a final deficit of three keys.

As anticipated, Johnson won overwhelmingly in November, with 61 percent of the popular vote and 90 percent of the electoral college vote. The Democrats also earned better than two-to-one majorities in Congress, giving Johnson control of the legislative agenda for at least two more years. The Democrats' gain of thirty-seven House seats augured well for their holding mandate key 1 for 1968.

Ironically, in one of the party's worst defeats, the GOP had finally broken the opposition's hold on the once solidly Democratic South. During the next quarter century, the Democrats would win the South only in the presidential election of 1976, when the party nominated Jimmy Carter of Georgia. By the 1970s, the Republicans would also make inroads into the South's once solidly Democratic contingent in Congress.

1968: Losses in the Quagmire
Incumbent-party nominee: Hubert H. Humphrey (Democrat)
Challenging-party nominee: Richard M. Nixon (Republican)
Negative keys: 8
Result: Nixon, 43.4%; Humphrey, 42.7%; George C. Wallace (American Independent), 13.5%

Key:	1	2	3	4	5	6	7	8	9	10	11	12	13
Call:	X	X	X	X	O	O	O	X	O	X	X	X	O

Events at the outset of LBJ's first full term seemed to confirm a rosy outlook for the Democrats in 1968. The Kennedy tax cut pushed through by Johnson the previous year had the economy humming, and the president had used his robust mandate to expand the Great Society. Civil-rights and antipoverty legislation headed Johnson's domestic agenda, most of which he implemented in the first two years of the term. The president's crowning achievement in civil rights was the Voting Rights Act of 1965, which prohibited literacy tests for determining voter eligibility and sent federal registrars and election observers to many parts of the South, truly opening the ballot box to Blacks in the region for the first time in this century. Johnson's civil-rights initiatives reflected political as well as moral considerations. Blacks, who were voting in ever-increasing numbers, were a major component of the Democratic party, and effective voting-rights legislation promised to boost Black turnout in the southern states. Johnson also took new directions in his war on poverty, shifting his emphasis from self-help to direct-benefit programs that would contribute to a vast increase in federal spending in the late 1960s and 1970s.

In a significant departure from the New Deal approach of targeting groups such as the elderly or the unemployed, the administration began targeting categories of need as well, notably housing, medical care, education, and nutrition. Johnson and the Democratic Congress authorized federally sponsored medical insurance for the elderly (Medicare) and the poor (Medicaid). They expanded the coverage of the food-stamp program and initiated the most ambitious aid programs for housing and education in history. Overall, Lyndon Johnson brought the authority and resources of the federal government to bear on a wider range of domestic problems than any president since Franklin Roosevelt. His second-term initiatives easily won policy-change key 7 for 1968.

The president was not so successful abroad. Johnson sought to gain the upper hand in Vietnam, first through intensive bombing of the North, then through a major commitment of American combat forces. By the end of 1965, Johnson had dispatched 185,000 troops to Vietnam, a number that more than doubled to 385,000 in 1966. The war in Vietnam became Johnson's preoccupation during his last three years in office. Despite public optimism, Johnson and his key advisers recognized that military escalation was not achieving their objectives. Fighting a limited, defensive war against a well-organized and often "invisible" guerrilla force, as well as a powerful conventional army from the North with heavy Soviet and Chinese backing, U.S. forces were unable either to secure strategic objectives or to wear down the ideologically motivated enemy.

nationally

The war at first contributed to economic growth at home. Increased military outlays, combined with the effects of the 1964 tax cut and spending on new domestic programs, boosted growth substantially during the first two years of the term. For a while it seemed as though America really could afford both guns and butter. Despite such prosperity and Johnson's legislative accomplishments, frustration over the Vietnam War contributed to the Democrats' loss of forty-nine House seats in 1966. Although the party still retained a majority in the House, it lost mandate key 1.

During the next year and a half, the administration drew no closer to a resolution of the war. In the winter of 1968, the Viet Cong and North Vietnamese launched a surprise offensive during Vietnam's Tet (New Year) holiday. American and South Vietnamese troops technically won the Tet engagement, but the intensity of the attack made continued predictions of victory sound hollow. By March, most of the president's key advisers had concluded that the administration had neither the time nor the political support necessary to achieve its military objectives in Vietnam. The stalemate in Vietnam cost the Democrats foreign-failure key 10.

The war also diverted attention from other foreign-policy endeavors. Vietnam drove a wedge into the Atlantic Alliance, as America's European friends expressed growing distaste for U.S. conduct in Southeast Asia, and it diminished American prestige in the Third World. The president achieved some success in arms-limitation talks, reaching agreement with the Soviets on a nonproliferation treaty banning the distribution of nuclear weapons to nonnuclear nations. Further progress in superpower negotiations was stalled after the Tet offensive and the Soviet invasion that crushed Czechoslovakia's move toward democratic reform. In the end, the administration could boast no major success in foreign relations, and the Democrats lost Key 11.

Nor were Johnson's prodigious efforts in fighting discrimination and poverty rewarded at home. For Blacks burdened with low-wage jobs, high unemployment and crime rates, dilapidated housing, and inferior schools in the ghettos of America's big cities, the civil-rights revolution raised unreachable expectations. Dashed hopes for a better quality of life led to an unprecedented outbreak of urban disorders during the term. The riots—along with the formation in 1966 of the heavily publicized Black Panther party, portrayed by the government and the media as the violent vanguard of Black revolution—created fears of racial insurrection. Ironically, the Democratic party, which had championed racial progress, had now fallen victim to racial unrest.

Demonstrations against the Vietnam War and an American establishment accused of responsibility for racism, violence, and repression also began during Johnson's second term. Throughout the nation, college students who believed that America had reneged on its promise of a just society began organizing protests. Student takeovers of campus buildings at Columbia and Boston Universities in the spring of 1968 foreshadowed a more militant phase of demonstrations that would begin after the election. Before then, however, the cumulative impact of social disorder had turned Key 8 against the incumbents.

For all the problems that beset him, President Johnson managed to avoid major scandal in his administration. Although in 1968 Johnson withdrew his nomination of Abe Fortas as chief justice of the Supreme Court after revelations of personal financial improprieties on Fortas's part, the party in power still retained scandal key 9.

On the economic front, the price of financing both the war and the Great Society was increased inflation. Not until 1967 did Johnson propose a tax surcharge to begin covering the costs of the war, and not until mid-1968 did Congress accede to his request—too late to halt the inflationary spiral that was already built into the economy. Through 1968, however, the pace of economic growth exceeded the rise in inflation, earning the Democrats both economic keys, 5 and 6. Democratic difficulties in 1968 were unrelated to economic performance. The problems generated by rising inflation would not fully manifest themselves until the next administration.

In the election year, the war in Vietnam splintered the majority Democratic party. Johnson, his party's unanimous champion four years earlier, faced heated opposition from Senator Eugene McCarthy of Minnesota and from JFK's brother Robert, who was now a U.S. senator from New York. On 31 March, a visibly dispirited and exhausted president announced on nationwide television that he would not seek reelection; he would concentrate instead on bringing peace to Vietnam. Peace talks began in May of 1968, but peace itself would elude Johnson for the remainder of his administration.

The Democrats, already down mandate key 1, campaigned without the sitting president as their candidate, and hence with Key 3 turned against them as well. The contest to replace him at the head of the ticket also toppled Key 2. Robert Kennedy's assassination, just after his victory in the California primary, locked up the nomination for Vice President Hubert Humphrey. Although Humphrey was an enthusiastic campaigner with an ebullient personality, he was not a commanding presence and had the burden of campaigning in the shadow of Lyndon Johnson. Key 12 was also lost to the incumbent party.

The Democratic convention became the bitter symbol of an era of social unrest, as police and demonstrators battled on the streets of Mayor Richard Daley's Chicago. In a concession to the antiadministration forces, the convention established a commission to reform the nominating process. With South Dakota senator George McGovern at its head, the commission instituted wide-ranging changes that affected every subsequent nominating contest, Republican as well as Democratic. No longer would an insider candidate like Humphrey be able to win a nomination without competing state-by-state in open delegate contests. The reformers had largely taken the nomination process out of the hands of party pros and placed it in the hands of primary-election voters, usually the most activist members of each party.

To challenge the Democrats in 1968, the GOP looked to the center of the party, rejecting California governor Ronald Reagan on the Right and New York governor Nelson Rockefeller on the Left. Once again the party nominated Richard Nixon. The nomination of the uncharismatic Nixon handed the Democrats Key 13, but it was too little, too late.

The third-party campaign of the former governor of Alabama George C. Wallace toppled an eighth and final key—Key 4. This populist conservative campaigned against the establishment of both parties, calling for lower taxes, states' rights, and escalation of the war against communism abroad and crime at home. Tapping into the reservoir of disaffection among White Southerners and blue-collar workers in the Northeast and Midwest, Wallace received about 20 percent support in early polls; ultimately he would garner nearly 14 percent of the popular vote, by far the most for any third-party contender since Robert La Follette in 1924.

In the popular balloting, Nixon barely edged Humphrey, 31,785,148 (43.4 percent) to 31,274,503 (42.7 percent). His electoral-college margin was more substantial, 301 to 191. The Democrats, however, held on to both houses of Congress. Having gained only five House seats, the Republicans were almost certain to lose mandate key 1 for 1972.

Was a new Republican realignment in the offing with the Nixon victory? GOP analyst Kevin Phillips made that case in an influential 1969 book, *The Emerging Republican Majority*.[2] The new Republican hegemony, Phillips argued, would be anchored in the conservative and increasingly populous states of America's Sun Belt. Phillips was correct in identifying the Sun Belt as a source of future Republican strength. Yet the GOP had made little inroad on Democratic majorities in Congress; a plurality of Americans still identified themselves as Democrats; and southern congress members, governors, state legislators, and local officials remained primarily Democratic despite GOP presidential success in the South.

1972: The Turnaround President
Incumbent-party nominee: Richard Nixon (Republican)
Challenging-party nominee: George McGovern (Democrat)
Negative keys: 4
Result: Nixon 60.7%; McGovern 37.5%

Key:	1	2	3	4	5	6	7	8	9	10	11	12	13
Call:	X	O	O	O	O	X	X	O	O	O	O	X	O

Although stalemate in Vietnam had propelled Richard Nixon to victory, the president-elect had no innovative plan for ending the war, and
he soon found himself searching for a way out of the quagmire.

In domestic policy, the administration's most daunting challenge was
to control inflation while sustaining economic growth. For two years,
Nixon resisted pressures for price-control measures, relying instead on
monetary restraint to keep inflation in check. The unwelcome result was
both a sluggish economy and rising prices.

To offset economic woes and the lack of progress in Vietnam, Nixon
sought to turn still simmering fears of social disorder (sparked by violent campus demonstrations) to the GOP's advantage by pushing a law
and order theme in the midterm congressional elections. Democrats
counterattacked by accusing the GOP of demagoguery and reaffirming
their party's dedication to upholding the law. The result was something
of a standoff. Although the executive party's loss of twelve House seats
was modest by historical standards, it padded an already substantial
Democratic majority and turned mandate key 1 against the GOP.

Despite Nixon's conservative rhetoric, like Eisenhower in the 1950s,
he did not try to dismantle the programs adopted by his Democratic
predecessors. More than any Republican president of the last half-century, he actually strengthened and extended Democratic programs.
Among the measures enacted with Nixon's support were tax-reform
legislation that reduced individual rates and removed several million
low-income persons from the tax rolls, the Equal Rights Amendment
(which failed to gain ratification by the states), and a new Environmental Protection Agency to oversee pollution controls. The administration
established "affirmative-action" programs setting numerical goals and
timetables for minority hiring by federal contractors. The president supported a plan to tie Social Security benefits to increases in the cost of
living and initiated a program of general-revenue sharing with the

states. Despite the scope and expense of this expansion of government under Nixon, it represented not a redirection but an extension of previous domestic policies. Key 7 was lost to the GOP.

The reality of 1971 was that Nixon's prospects for reelection looked bleak. Besides the loss of mandate key 1 and policy-change key 7, he lacked a success in foreign affairs (Key 11) and still faced failure in Vietnam (Key 10), the threat of renewed social unrest (Key 8), and a troubled economy (Keys 5 and 6). With his lack of charisma (Key 12), Nixon confronted a potentially fatal deficit of eight keys.

Nixon salvaged reelection through new initiatives in foreign and economic policy. In 1971, the administration reversed course economically and moved to stem inflation through federal price controls, while stimulating the economy through an expansive fiscal policy. The New Economic Policy was a short-term success. After another lackluster year in 1971, the economy spurted ahead in 1972, saving short-term economy key 5 for the Republicans. This improvement, however, was insufficient to earn the administration long-term economy key 6.

By the spring of 1972, Nixon's policy of turning the war over to the Vietnamese had reduced American ground forces from a peak of 543,000 in 1969 to around 66,000; U.S. involvement was limited primarily to air strikes. With the stepped-up bombing, Nixon hoped to pressure the North Vietnamese into making a deal. Just a few days before the election, National Security Council Director Henry Kissinger announced dramatically, "peace is at hand." Although progress in Vietnam did not constitute a major foreign-policy success, the disengagement of American troops, combined with improved prospects for a negotiated settlement, kept it from counting as a major administration failure, preserving Key 10 for the party in power.

The winding down of the war, along with Nixon's shrewd support for an all-volunteer army, helped avert the reemergence of social unrest. Campus disorders disappeared from the polls as a public concern after 1970, and on Election Day, social-unrest key 8 would be lined up for the incumbent Republicans.

Nixon's foreign-policy triumph would come in his dealings with the major communist powers. His twenty-year record of militant anticommunism gave him more flexibility in foreign affairs than previous presidents had enjoyed. Nixon and Kissinger mapped out a pragmatic strategy designed to achieve a new era of relaxed tensions, or "détente," with the Soviet Union and a surprise opening of relations with Red China. Nixon's overture to China was both a public-relations and a foreign-policy coup, warmly received in the United States and abroad.

It led quickly to the seating of Communist China in the United Nations and ultimately to American recognition of the People's Republic. With this dramatic rapprochement, the Nixon administration had secured Key 11 for the upcoming election. The China opening led to yet another administration success by increasing pressure on the Soviets for arms control. Nixon returned from an unprecedented presidential trip to Moscow with two major agreements, one placing strict limits on antiballistic missile (ABM) systems, the other restricting certain types of strategic weapons (SALT).

The Nixon administration remained relatively free of scandal until June of 1972, when White House aides became implicated in a break-in at Democratic National Headquarters in the Watergate Building in Washington, D.C. Through the presidential election, Nixon was able to deny any involvement by himself or his personal staff. Although the Democratic nominee, George McGovern, would try to make Watergate a campaign issue, his charges of corruption simply would not stick in the midst of a partisan presidential campaign. The Republicans retained scandal key 9.

The Republicans nominated Richard Nixon in late August at Miami Beach with but a single dissenting vote, gaining nomination key 2 and incumbency key 3 but forfeiting incumbent-charisma key 12. With the threat of a major third-party campaign eliminated by an assassination attempt in May of 1992 that left George Wallace partially crippled, the GOP also retained Key 4, leaving the incumbent with a final deficit of four keys.

Under previous circumstances, Senator Edmund Muskie of Maine, Hubert Humphrey's running mate in 1968 and the overwhelming choice of party professionals, would have easily wrapped up the Democratic nomination. But the 1972 primary campaign was different from any that had come before. Under the new party rules drafted by the McGovern Commission, candidates now had to compete for delegates selected in primaries or open caucuses. As the author of these reforms, McGovern understood the new rules better than any other contender and used them to advantage in his own bid for the nomination. Using his staunch opposition to the Vietnam War to build a grassroots organization and gain recognition, McGovern garnered just enough delegates to control the Democratic convention and stave off a late challenge from former vice president Hubert Humphrey. The Democrats' nomination of the passionate but hardly magnetic McGovern gave challenger-charisma key 13 to the incumbent GOP.

The magnitude of Nixon's victory lived up to Republican expecta-

ᐳ*C* ?

tions, as he won all states except Massachusetts. Still, the GOP failed to win a majority in either house of Congress. The Democrats actually gained two Senate seats in the midst of the Nixon landslide, while the GOP picked up only a dozen House seats, placing mandate key 1 in jeopardy for 1976.

The anticipated realignment of the American electorate did not occur in 1972. The Democrats' continued strength in Congress would have profound consequences when Watergate burglar James McCord began implicating top administration officials just weeks after Nixon's second inauguration.

1976: The Watergate Defeat
Incumbent-party nominee: Gerald Ford (Republican)
Challenging-party nominee: Jimmy Carter (Democrat)
Negative keys: 8
Result: Carter 50.1%; Ford 48.0%

Key:	1	2	3	4	5	6	7	8	9	10	11	12	13
Call:	X	X	O	O	O	X	X	O	X	X	X	X	O

Tape-recordings of conversations in the Nixon White House reveal that, during his first term, the president and his closest advisers had placed first priority on winning reelection in 1972. They planned in the second term, however, to wield ''the power'' of an incumbent administration to advance more conservative domestic policies, as well as to punish their political enemies and reward their friends. The opportunity to use that power never arrived. From a third-rate burglary, the break-in at Democratic Headquarters in the Watergate escalated into a scandal that crippled the Nixon administration and triggered the only resignation of a U.S. president in history.

The dam of silence that had shielded the administration from Watergate through the 1972 campaign gave way early in the second term as revelations surfaced that high officials of the Nixon administration had directed the break-in and were being protected by a subsequent cover-up. A special prosecutor began investigating Watergate-related crime and a Senate committee began dramatic televised hearings. The committee's investigation, aided by taped White House conversations, revealed that the burglary had been part of an illicit program of political intelligence-gathering and sabotage directed by top White House and cabinet officials, including former attorney general John Mitchell. It also found that Nixon's campaign committee had raked in illegal donations from major corporations and cash contributions from wealthy individuals.

In 1973, Spiro Agnew became the first vice president since John C. Calhoun to resign the office. To avoid likely imprisonment for extortion and bribery unrelated to Watergate, he resigned and pleaded nolo contendere (no contest) to a single count of federal income-tax evasion. To replace Agnew, the president appointed House Republican leader Gerald R. Ford of Michigan.

Ultimately, the Watergate matter landed in the House Judiciary Committee. After two months of hearings and a series of televised debates, the committee voted to recommend three articles of impeachment against the president. In early August, the release of new tape transcripts included the "smoking gun" necessary to tie Nixon to criminal conduct: In a conversation of 23 June 1972, the president had ordered the CIA to quash an investigation of the Watergate affair. Faced with likely impeachment by the full House and conviction by the Senate, the president resigned on 9 August 1974.

The new president, Gerald Ford, quickly appointed former New York governor and presidential aspirant Nelson Rockefeller as his vice president. For the first time in history, appointees filled the nation's two highest offices. A month later, Ford issued a full pardon for Richard Nixon. The press immediately questioned whether the pardon had been part of a "deal" between Nixon and Ford, who, previously untainted, became slightly sullied by the scandal, too. In all, some twenty-five administration officials received prison terms for violating federal law, including Nixon's closest advisers. Key 9 was turned decisively against the Republican party.

The prolonged Watergate affair took a heavy toll on the nation, as the government's preoccupation with the scandal all but halted effective responses to other pressing matters. Nixon's New Economic Policy had succeeded just long enough to aid his reelection in 1972. By the end of 1973, with unemployment and inflation both on the rise, the economy was succumbing to the worst bout of "stagflation" in American history. An oil embargo imposed by the Organization of Petroleum Exporting Countries (OPEC) in 1973 added a tremendous inflationary shock. Real per-capita growth fell 2 percent in 1974, and inflation hit 11 percent, its highest level since 1947.

In the midterm congressional elections of 1974, which took place only three months after Richard Nixon's resignation, the Republican party paid the price both for Watergate and stagflation. The GOP lost forty-eight House seats, turning mandate key 1 against the incumbent party.

Upon taking office in 1974, President Ford had found himself confronting the most daunting economic problems since the Great Depression without a coherent strategy for coping with them. Calling at first for tax increases to moderate soaring prices, Ford reversed course in 1975 and agreed to a package of tax reforms and reductions drafted by the Democratic Congress. Fiscal and monetary stimuli finally sparked real growth in 1976, when per-capita GNP increased 5 percent, securing short-term economy key 5 for the GOP. But the recovery was not sufficient to prevent the loss of long-term economy key 6.

The embattled Nixon-Ford administration effected minimal changes in national policy. Watergate had prevented Nixon from pursuing his programmatic agenda and Ford, besides lacking innovative ideas, faced overwhelming Democratic majorities in Congress. Among Ford's disappointments were his failures to curb federal spending and to enact a national energy policy for dealing with the oil embargo. Unable to effect changes of its own or block Democratic initiatives, the Republican administration lost policy-change key 7 for the upcoming election.

The beleaguered regime fared as poorly in foreign affairs as it did domestically. Ironically, an event that the administration first heralded as a triumph—the end of American participation in the Vietnam War—ultimately became one of the most humiliating foreign-policy failures in U.S. history. Just three weeks after Nixon's second inauguration, Henry Kissinger had signed a pact providing for a cease-fire in Vietnam, the final withdrawal of American forces, and the freeing of all American prisoners of war. With no mechanism to enforce the cease-fire, fighting continued to rage in Vietnam. By 30 April 1975, South Vietnam had surrendered and the remaining American personnel had completed a desperate and humiliating evacuation. At virtually the same time, Cambodia fell to a brutal communist guerrilla force, the Khmer Rouge. With the exceptions of Hong Kong, Thailand, and South Korea, the Americans and Europeans had been driven out of mainland Asia, the very goal that the Japanese had sought to achieve in World War II. Foreign-failure key 10 was turned against the incumbent party.

Other foreign-policy ventures by the administration yielded mixed results at best. Ongoing talks with the Soviets produced no major new breakthroughs, and two years of inconclusive "shuttle diplomacy" by Secretary of State Kissinger following the Arab-Israeli war of 1973 failed to relieve Mideast tensions. In May of 1975, Ford had a minor success with the military rescue of a U.S. cargo ship, the *Mayaguez*, which had been seized by Cambodia's Khmer Rouge government, but the lack of a significant international advance cost the Republicans Key 11.

Social unrest, already on the wane in the last two years of the first

Nixon administration, did not reemerge after 1973. The end of the war stalled political protests and student unrest, and the sour economy seemed to quell other forms of dissent. Although the plight of minorities in the inner cities improved little during the 1970s, residents no longer expressed their discontent through rioting and looting. Instead of exploding in flames, ghetto communities continued to deteriorate through neglect, rising crime, and increased drug trafficking. Nevertheless, social-unrest key 8 stayed in the incumbents' column.

With the Republicans widely perceived as vulnerable in 1976, a host of Democrats competed for the party's nomination. The successful contender was a little-known former governor of Georgia, Jimmy Carter. The Georgian had a refreshing, dynamic demeanor, but it fell short of charisma; his nomination handed the GOP Key 13.

Although Gerald Ford had succeeded in restoring order to the White House and faith in the American system during its greatest crisis of the century, as an appointed president with few accomplishments to his credit and limited popular and party support, he was unable to stave off a challenge from former California governor Ronald Reagan. Reagan appealed forcefully and emotionally to the party's conservatives, falling just a few delegate votes short of wresting the nomination from Ford. With Vice President Nelson Rockefeller unacceptable to conservatives, Ford picked Kansas senator Robert Dole as his running mate. Ford's contested nomination cost the GOP Key 2 and incumbent-charisma key 12, while securing incumbency key 3. With no substantial third party on the horizon, the party in power retained Key 4 as well.

In the final tally, Carter edged out Ford, 50 percent to 48 percent in the popular vote and 297 to 240 in the electoral college. The election conferred no new mandate: Although Carter still enjoyed substantial majorities in Congress, the Democrats merely held even in the Senate and gained only one seat in the House—a showing that boded ill for the Democrats' chances of holding mandate key 1 in the next election.

Largely overlooked in the 1976 campaign was internal change within the Republican party. The repudiation of Vice President Rockefeller and the near miss of Ronald Reagan's candidacy marked the continuing decline of the party's once formidable moderate wing, based largely in the Northeast and the Midwest, and the rise of a new, southern- and western-based conservatism.

Chapter 8

Reagan and Beyond

President Jimmy Carter proved unable to respond effectively to profound changes that had taken place in America's economic and international standing—sagging productivity, increased foreign competition, and an unprecedented convergence of high unemployment, high interest rates, and high inflation. Superpower relations had deteriorated since the Nixon era, and the United States found it increasingly difficult to exert its will over less-developed nations.

In 1980, it was the Republicans—led by a sixty-nine-year-old Ronald Reagan—who emerged as the activist party. In a second philosophical reversal of party positions in the twentieth century, Reagan Republicans effectively combined their anti-government message with selected elements of the Kennedy-Johnson legacy: free trade, aggressive anticommunism, and deficit spending. The Republican revolution would run out of steam during President Reagan's second term. Although Republicans gained another four years in office, President George Bush failed to govern effectively on the domestic front, leading to the election of the first Democratic president in twelve years.

1980: The Politics of Malaise
Incumbent-party nominee: President Jimmy Carter (Democrat)
Challenging-party nominee: Ronald Reagan (Republican)
Negative keys: 8
Result: Reagan, 50.7%; Carter, 41.0%; John Anderson (National Unity), 6.6%

Key:	1	2	3	4	5	6	7	8	9	10	11	12	13
Call:	X	X	O	X	X	O	X	O	O	X	O	X	X

Lacking a clear direction for the country and skill in the give and take of legislative politics, Carter won few domestic achievements in his first two years. He managed to gain the creation of the Department of Energy in 1977 and pushed legislation through Congress to put the Social Security system on a sounder financial footing. The signal achievement of Carter's first two years was ending a long-simmering dispute with Panama by negotiating treaties that would turn over the canal to Panama in the year 2000. Conservatives charged that Carter had "given away" the canal, but the administration pushed the treaties through the Senate by a single vote in early 1978. The economy remained strong through 1978, as real per-capita GNP increased an average of nearly 4 percent per year—the best two-year record of economic growth since the mid-1960s. But growth was accompanied by persistent inflation, a trade deficit, and high unemployment and interest rates. The Democrats lost sixteen House seats in the 1978 midterm elections, not a lot by historical standards but, having gained only one in 1976, fifteen more than were necessary to topple mandate key 1.

The economy deteriorated rapidly in 1979. A steep hike in OPEC oil prices pushed fuel costs up and propelled inflation to its highest levels since the end of World War II. To combat inflation, Paul Volcker, Carter's new appointee as chairman of the Federal Reserve Board, adopted a tight-money policy. The result was the worst of all economic worlds: In Carter's last two years, real growth slowed, inflation soared to double-digit levels, and budget deficits climbed to peacetime records.

As economic conditions deteriorated, the president achieved several of his initial goals. Congress granted his requests for standby gasoline-rationing powers, a windfall-profits tax on oil companies, and an enhanced synthetic fuels program. He won approval of new environmental legislation, the Department of Education, limited reorganization of the civil service, and deregulation in such key industries as trucking and banking. Carter failed, however, in his efforts to rewrite the tax code, reform the welfare system, revise the labor laws, or reshape the federal bureaucracy. Almost like Hoover, Carter achieved several notable legislative successes, but they had little impact on the nation's most pressing problems and did not constitute a significant departure from past policies; Key 7 was lost to the incumbent Democrats.

In the tradition of Woodrow Wilson, Jimmy Carter approached foreign affairs with missionary zeal, emphasizing the protection of human rights. The president found it difficult to reconcile morality with the pragmatic realities of international affairs. He settled the Panama Canal dispute and negotiated a new superpower agreement on strategic-arms limitations (SALT II) in 1979. But the treaty languished in the Senate and was withdrawn by Carter after Soviet troops invaded Afghanistan in late 1979. The invasion, mounted to preserve a Marxist, pro-Soviet regime, led to the promulgation of a new "Carter Doctrine" declaring that any attempt by a foreign power to gain control of the oil-rich Persian Gulf region would be considered a threat to America's vital interests. But U.S. allies, by refusing to join in boycotting the 1980 Moscow Olympics or in imposing economic sanctions against the Soviet Union, undercut Carter's effort to pressure the Soviets to withdraw from Afghanistan.

The administration's greatest triumphs and failures occurred in the Middle East. President Carter intervened decisively in negotiations between Egypt and Israel in 1978 and 1979 to achieve a treaty ending the state of war that had existed between these two nations since Israel's creation in 1948. The resulting Camp David Accords were hailed in the United States and around the world as a major breakthrough, garnering foreign-success key 11 for the administration.

However, failure ensnared Carter elsewhere in the Islamic world. A revolution toppled the Shah of Iran in 1979 and established in his place a fundamentalist Islamic republic under the leadership of Ayatollah Ruhollah Khomeini. In November of 1979, after President Carter allowed the deposed shah into the United States for medical treatment, Iranian radicals seized the American embassy in Tehran, taking sixty-six Americans hostage. Neither diplomacy nor the launching of an abortive military rescue effort helped to resolve the crisis, which dragged on through the election, costing the administration foreign-failure key 10.

Back home, despite mounting economic troubles, there was little social disorder during the Carter years. In May of 1980, a bloody race riot erupted in Miami after a jury acquitted four White police officers charged with murdering a Black insurance executive. But Miami was an isolated incident that failed to generate the widespread unrest necessary to topple Key 8.

The Carter administration also held on to the scandal key. A succession of incidents during the term embarrassed the president. These included the resignation of his longtime friend, budget director Bert Lance, over the disclosure of irregularities in the conduct of his banking business; allegations of cocaine use and other unseemly behavior by his chief of staff, Hamilton Jordan; and revelations during the campaign that the president's brother Billy had capitalized on his sibling relationship to become a paid agent of the government of Libya. But the incidents revealed no pattern of corruption within the administration, and Carter's moral rectitude never was called into question, so the Democrats retained Key 9.

By the summer of 1979, Carter's approval rating had plummeted to below 30 percent. The president seemed vulnerable not only to defeat in the next year's general election, but to rejection by his own party. A troubled Carter retreated to Camp David, seeking to reevaluate his leadership in the solitude of the mountain retreat. In a subsequent televised address that became known as the "malaise speech," Carter suggested that America's problems stemmed from a national "crisis of confidence," not from a lack of leadership.[1] In November, just days after the hostage-taking in Iran, Senator Edward Kennedy of Massachusetts decided to challenge the president's renomination, and pundits instantly gave him the edge over the faltering Carter. However, the hostage crisis briefly rallied Americans around the embattled chief executive, and, combined with an upturn in the economy in the first quarter of 1980, stymied Kennedy's efforts. Still, the Kennedy challenge cost the Democrats contest key 2. Carter's nomination kept incumbency key 3 in line, but forfeited incumbent-charisma key 12.

Carter's troubles continued with a steep economic slide in the second quarter of the election year that led the National Bureau of Economic Research to declare that the economy had entered a new recession. Growth would remain flat in the third quarter before turning upward again in the fourth quarter of 1980, but the upswing would come too late to convince the economists or the public that recovery was under way prior to the November election. Short-term economy key 5 would be lost to the party in power for the first time since 1960. Still, the strong economic performance of Carter's first two years was sufficient to salvage long-term economy key 6.

The Republicans confirmed their party's move to the right with a nearly unanimous nomination of Ronald Reagan. The nominee worked to conciliate the party's shrinking moderate wing, first by negotiating to bring former president Ford onto the ticket as his running mate and, when that failed, by choosing George Bush.

The Democrats lost an eighth and final key when John Anderson, complaining that the leaders of both parties were shirking the hard choices needed in an era of economic austerity and energy scarcity, announced his candidacy as an independent. Polls showed initial support for Anderson at about 15 percent, a figure that dropped to less than 10 percent after a one-on-one debate with Ronald Reagan. Ultimately, Anderson would poll just under 7 percent of the popular vote.

Despite ambiguous polls on election eve, the electorate handed Reagan a decisive victory with 51 percent of the popular votes, 44 states, and 489 of 538 electoral college votes. The election provided mixed signals, however, as to whether a political realignment was in the offing. Surveys taken after the balloting did not show a sharp shift to the right, and the ideological composition of the vote for the conservative Reagan was no different from that for the moderate Ford in 1976. Still, fewer Americans than in the past were identifying themselves as liberals. The GOP also gained thirty-five House seats—auguring well for its chances of gaining the mandate key in 1984—and seized control of the Senate for the first time since 1954. The Democrats, however, remained the nation's majority party, controlling the House of Representatives and holding most of the elective offices in state and local governments.

1984: Morning in America
Incumbent-party nominee: President Ronald Reagan (Republican)
Challenging-party nominee: Walter Mondale (Democrat)
Negative keys: 2
Result: Reagan, 58.8%; Mondale, 40.5%

Key:	1	2	3	4	5	6	7	8	9	10	11	12	13
Call:	O	O	O	O	O	X	O	O	O	O	X	O	O

In the first year of his presidency, Ronald Reagan departed sharply from the precedent of earlier Republican presidents—Harding, Eisenhower, and Nixon—who had declined to challenge the policy systems erected during the Progressive, New Deal, and Great Society eras. True to his bold campaign promises, the new president launched an assault on the taxation, spending, regulatory, and defense policies of his predecessors. He pledged to rebuild America's defenses and face down the Soviets abroad while trimming a bloated government at home. Rather than continuing the twentieth-century tradition of solving domestic problems through an expanded government, Reagan sought to limit the role of government and promote opportunity in the private sector.

The president's exceptional personal qualities were dramatically underscored in March of 1981, when he showed remarkable courage and humor after a gunman gravely wounded him in an assassination attempt. Reagan developed a public aura of warmth and invincibility that both enhanced his clout with Congress and helped deflect criticism of his shortcomings—making him, in the words of Democratic representative Patricia Schroeder, a "Teflon" president.

In a series of startling legislative triumphs during his first year in office, President Reagan put his stamp on national life, easily capturing policy-change key 7. His most consequential victory came when Congress passed the president's proposal for deep cuts in federal income taxes. A conservative coalition of Republicans and southern Democrats, dubbed "boll weevils"—the kind of coalition traditionally dedicated to blocking rather than passing legislation—came together to enact the tax program in the Democratic House. Reductions in many domestic programs followed the tax cut. Although legislators resisted the deep cuts proposed by the Reagan administration, they still sliced into real spending for such programs as grants to the states, aid to education, mass transit, and housing assistance. In contrast, military budgets rose dramatically as Congress agreed to Reagan's plans for shoring up America's allegedly sagging defenses. Jimmy Carter actually had initiated the defense buildup in response to the Soviet invasion of Afghanistan. Reagan's promise that the stimulative effects of the tax cuts, combined with reductions in domestic outlays, would result in a balanced budget by 1984 was quickly abandoned as the new policies produced record budget deficits instead.

For all of Reagan's early personal and legislative triumphs, he still had to confront a severe economic crisis. The uptick at the end of 1980 lasted only through the first quarter of 1981, after which the Federal Reserve Board's restrictive, anti-inflation policies plunged the economy into a deep recession that would not abate until 1983. The pain of recession contributed to the Republicans' loss of twenty-seven House seats in the 1982 midterm elections, a sizeable decline, but one that still left them with a net eight-seat gain over the previous term and secured mandate key 1.

Early the next year the economy rebounded, fueled largely by borrowed money. The recovery lasted through the election year, securing campaign-economy key 5 for the GOP. But the recession had taken its toll and the administration lost long-term economy key 6.

The recession did not provoke civil disorder, and, despite the embarrassing resignations of several high-level officials and the indictment of Labor secretary Raymond Donovan for activities prior to his appointment (he subsequently was acquitted), what came to be known as the "sleaze factor" during Reagan's first term neither touched the president himself nor pointed to a pattern of corruption in his administration. The party held on to both social-unrest key 8 and scandal key 9.

The first Reagan term was a time of relative quiet in international relations, as the president assumed a harder foreign-policy line but, at the same time, tread more carefully than his bellicose rhetoric led many to expect. In late 1981, the administration proposed a "zero option" plan for the elimination of Intermediate Range Nuclear Forces (INF) in Europe and subsequently began the Strategic Arms Reduction Talks

(START) with the Soviets. But Reagan's continued military buildup, ideological opposition within the administration, and the announcement of efforts to build a new space-based strategic defense system (SDI, popularly known as "Star Wars") limited progress on arms control. American endeavors elsewhere also fell short of major triumph. In October of 1983 the United States invaded the tiny Caribbean nation of Grenada, ostensibly to rescue American medical students on the island, and dismantled a leftist regime that the administration believed was turning the island into a base for Soviet and Cuban forces. Although popular, the invasion hardly qualified as a noteworthy achievement for the world's greatest power, and Key 11 remained beyond the executive party's grasp.

The administration suffered its greatest setbacks in the Middle East. In April of 1983, terrorists blew up much of the American embassy in Beirut, Lebanon, killing more than sixty people. In October, just days before the launching of the Grenada operation, a terrorist truck bomb exploded at U.S. Marine headquarters in Beirut, killing 241 Americans. Although Reagan pulled American troops out of Lebanon, the Teflon president escaped responsibility for the tragedy, and foreign-failure key 10 remained in line for the party in power.

With the economy humming along, the nation relatively tranquil, and Reagan highly rated in the polls, no Republican would contest his bid for a second term. The GOP's protectionist and internationalist factions had been reconciled since the 1980 campaign, and there was little anti-Reagan dissent within the party. The president's age—campaigning at seventy-three, he would be eight years older than Eisenhower had been in 1956—was a potential problem. But Reagan had achieved a remarkable recovery from the 1981 assassination attempt and appeared to be in excellent health. His near-unanimous renomination secured contest key 2, incumbency key 3, and charisma key 12 for the GOP. John Anderson's inability to generate enthusiasm for another third-party campaign also gave the Republicans Key 4, making Reagan the first candidate since FDR to hold all four political keys. When the Democrats selected their uninspiring former vice president, Walter Mondale, the GOP also gained challenger-charisma key 13, leaving a final deficit of only two keys—long-term economy key 6 and foreign-success key 11.

The most notable aspect of an otherwise lackluster Mondale campaign was his decision to shatter political precedent by selecting a woman—Representative Geraldine A. Ferraro of New York—as his running mate. Women constituted the majority of presidential voters and were favoring Democrats in greater proportion than men. However, the potential pluses of Ferraro's candidacy were lost amidst allegations of illicit business activities on the part of her husband, John Zaccaro.

It was "morning in America," Reagan told the public and the voters seemed to agree, giving him 59 percent of the vote, forty-nine states and all but thirteen electoral college votes. Despite this decisive win, the election of 1984 confirmed that the GOP was still the minority party. The Republicans picked up only seventeen seats in Congress, putting the party in a fair position to win the mandate key for 1988, but leaving it with only 42 percent of the House, lower than its representation in 1981. The GOP actually lost a Senate seat in the midst of Reagan's landslide, leaving it clinging to a 53 percent majority.

1988: Passing on the Legacy
Incumbent-party nominee: George Bush (Republican)
Challenging-party nominee: Michael Dukakis (Democrat)
Negative keys: 3
Result: Bush, 53.4%; Dukakis, 45.6%

Key:	1	2	3	4	5	6	7	8	9	10	11	12	13
Call:	O	O	X	O	O	O	X	O	O	O	O	X	O

In 1988, the GOP had to find a successor to a charismatic two-term president. To retain the White House that year, the Republicans could not withstand any of the usual mishaps of a president's second term. Since World War II, second-term presidents on average had lost five of the seven performance keys. Most second-term presidents to date had lost at least one of the two economic keys, and it appeared that Reagan would be no exception. In 1985 the economy was entering a third year of expansion after recovering from the deep recession of 1981–82. Given the usual turning of the business cycle, many economists anticipated another recession, perhaps lasting until the election. At least through the first two years of Reagan's second term, the economy grew at a steady pace. Economic expansion helped the GOP retain mandate key 1 by dampening GOP losses in the House during the midterm elections of 1986; the Republicans lost only five seats after gaining seventeen in 1984. Still, the GOP suffered heavy losses in the higher-visibility Senate elections, changing their 53 percent majority to a 45 percent minority.

A paucity of new ideas doomed administration hopes for retaining policy-change key 7. When it came to the emerging issues of the late 1980s—budget and trade deficits, deterioration of the global environment, failing financial institutions, loss of industrial jobs, rising racial tensions, drug abuse and its attendant crime, AIDS, persistent poverty—Reagan seemed to lack either interest or ideas. President Reagan did realize a top domestic priority of his second term—overhauling the federal tax system. The Tax Reform Act of 1986 reduced income-tax rates for many individuals, lowered the number of tax brackets, and eliminated dozens of loopholes. The new law, however, was not a Reagan innovation, but a bipartisan measure that originated from ideas proposed by two Democrats, Senator Bill Bradley of New Jersey and Missouri representative Richard Gephardt. Even so, the measure did not represent a sweeping policy innovation or a significant new direction for the nation, so the Republicans lost Key 7.

The continued absence of civil disorder in the 1980s meant that, for the fifth consecutive election, the incumbent administration retained social-unrest key 8. Scandal key 9 was a much closer call. The "sleaze factor" continued to plague the Reagan administration; by the end of 1987 more than a hundred current or former officials had either resigned or been forced from office under charges of misconduct. But the excesses of past and present officials still did not seem to tarnish the presidency in the public's mind or reveal a pattern of official corruption.

Most serious was the Iran-Contra fiasco involving the secret sale of arms to Iran—ostensibly to gain influence with moderate elements within the Iranian government, but also to elicit the release of American hostages held by Islamic fundamentalists in Lebanon—and the illicit diversion of the profits to the Contra resistance movement in Nicaragua. The Iran-Contra operation was to be the springboard for a larger scheme, known as "Project Democracy," to create an independent covert-operations organization accountable to no one but its creators, not even the president.[2] Although the Iran-Contra affair entailed illegality on the part of administration officials, it differed from past scandals in being motivated by ideological goals, not by the pursuit of personal or narrow political gain.[3] The illegal actions of subordinates were never linked directly to President Reagan, whose popularity rebounded strongly in the election year. Remarkably, the scandal fizzled and the GOP retained Key 9.

As a foreign-policy venture, the failed Iran-Contra initiative did not constitute a major blow to America's interests and prestige. The arms sale did not get the hostages released, increase American influence in Iran, or provide more than token aid to the Contras. When the dust settled, however, the United States was not appreciably worse off than before. In fact, tensions eased in trouble spots around the world during the election year, earning the administration foreign-failure key 10.

In relations with the Soviet Union, the administration achieved the foreign-policy triumph that had eluded it for nearly seven years. In 1985 the new Soviet leader, Mikhail Gorbachev, undertook a dramatic reversal of past policy, promoting a modicum of democracy, civil liberties, economic reform at home, and a more conciliatory approach to relations abroad. The superpowers nearly agreed to deep cuts in their nuclear arsenals and did sign an accord, similar to Reagan's first-term ''zero-option'' proposal, eliminating intermediate-range ballistic missiles in Europe. The Senate ratified this INF treaty in the summer of 1988, concluding the first actual arms-reduction agreement of the nuclear age and heralding what Americans hoped would be a permanent easing of tensions between the United States and the Soviet Union. Foreign-success key 11 was now in hand for the GOP.

In October of 1987, the five-year stretch of prosperity had suddenly seemed threatened when the Dow Jones Industrial Average plunged a record five hundred points in a single day, losing about 20 percent of its value and wiping out tens of billions of dollars in shareholder equity. Unlike 1929, however, the crash of 1987 did not spread to the overall economy. The economy grew robustly in the fourth quarter of 1987 and continued to grow at least moderately throughout the election year of 1988. For the first time since 1968 an incumbent administration secured both economic keys.

The anticipated battle to succeed Ronald Reagan appeared to be shaping up in 1988 as six candidates took to the hustings for the Republican primary campaign. Vice President George Bush and Senate Republican leader Bob Dole quickly emerged as the front-runners. The heated nomination contest ended abruptly on 8 March 1988, when George Bush swept all sixteen of the primaries held on ''Super Tuesday.'' These victories guaranteed Bush a consensus nomination at the August convention in New Orleans. The vice president's surprising strength earned the GOP contest key 2 but, as expected, his nomination cost the party, already forced to run without incumbency key 3, incumbent-charisma key 12 as well.

The battle for the Democratic nomination was much tighter. Massachusetts governor Michael Dukakis was the clear front-runner, but Jesse Jackson—the first African American to contest seriously for a major-party presidential nomination—was conducting a professional, reassuring campaign that had largely shaken off earlier allegations of extremism and anti-Semitism. Only when the Massachusetts governor won a crucial showdown in the New York primary on 19 April did he gain a clear path to the nomination. The nomination of the articulate but bland Dukakis meant that challenger-charisma key 13 would favor the GOP.

With no significant third-party candidate in the race, Bush campaigned with only incumbency key 3, policy-change key 7, and incumbent-charisma key 12 turned against him. Of all incumbent-party nominees who were not also sitting presidents, only war hero Ulysses S. Grant in 1868 had sought the presidency with fewer negative keys than George Bush in 1988.

The polls, however, were conveying a message much different from that of the keys through the spring and midsummer of 1988. Dukakis's consistent lead ballooned to seventeen percentage points in the Gallup Poll of late July. The auspicious polls and the apparent weakness of the often inarticulate Bush enticed Dukakis to run a safety-first campaign that would avoid errors and give Bush room to self-destruct. Yet his cautious strategy—this would be a campaign of competence rather than ideology, he declared—hardly befitted a challenger seeking election under circumstances so conducive to incumbent-party success. Sure enough, by the end of the Republican convention, Bush had overtaken Dukakis in the polls and suddenly led by substantial margins. The polls had finally caught up with the keys.

Bush's biggest mistake, according to conventional analyses, was choosing the inexperienced and lightly regarded junior senator from Indiana, Dan Quayle, as his running mate. In the only vice-presidential debate of the campaign, Lloyd Bentsen trounced the often faltering Quayle. The most memorable sound bite of the campaign came when Quayle compared his own experience in Congress with that of John F. Kennedy and Bentsen snapped, ''Senator, you are no Jack Kennedy.''

As always, voters responded to the top of the ticket, not to the second spot. Bush carried forty states and 53.4 percent of the popular vote. But the Republican victory was a narrow one. The GOP lost one seat in the Senate and three in the House, virtually assuring the loss of mandate key 1 for 1992. About half of the potential electorate actually rejected both Bush and Dukakis in 1988. Voter turnout in 1988 was just 50 percent, the lowest since 1924.

1992: Governing without Vision
Incumbent-party nominee: George Bush (Republican)
Challenging-party nominee: Bill Clinton (Democrat)
Negative keys: 6
Result: Bush, 38%; Clinton, 43%; Perot (Independent), 19%

Key:	1	2	3	4	5	6	7	8	9	10	11	12	13
Call:	X	O	O	X	X	X	X	O	O	O	O	X	O

If Dan Quayle was no Jack Kennedy, George Bush was no Ronald Reagan. The new president not only lacked his predecessor's persuasive skills but, in Bush's own words, he didn't have "the vision thing." Without bold new ideas for America, Bush viewed himself as an honest and competent guardian of a status quo already transformed by the Reagan presidency.

For three years, this seemed more than good enough. In 1990, following the final collapse of the Soviet Union, Bush's popularity passed 70 percent and conventional analysts began to consider whether he had a lock on reelection. Although his popularity declined to just over 50 percent as the economy faltered in late 1990, it soared to a record 89 percent in the aftermath of the 1991 Gulf War. By then, conventional analysts had assured Bush of victory the following year. The most prominent Democrats—Ted Kennedy, Tennessee senator Al Gore, New York governor Mario Cuomo, and Jesse Jackson—would all decline to fight for what seemed to be a worthless Democratic nomination for president.

Attention to the fundamentals of governing, as revealed by the keys, told a very different story of the Bush presidency, revealing a far more vulnerable opponent than the conventional wisdom would suggest. Bush began his incumbency with the near certain loss of three keys. His party's House losses in 1988 virtually assured the toppling of mandate key 1. His limited programmatic vision would likely cost him policy-change key 7 and his lack of personal charisma meant the loss of Key 12. Only three more keys would have to fall to predict the president's defeat.

When George Bush took the oath of office in 1989, the economy had been growing for five years, without the interruption of a recession. Few economists believed that sustained growth could continue for another four years. The economy plunged into recession in July of 1990, jeopardizing long-term economic key 6 and even short-term economic key 5 if the recession lasted long enough.

In contrast to his diffidence in domestic policy, Bush acted boldly in foreign affairs. In his first year, he authorized an invasion of Panama that captured the dictator General Manuel Noriega, who was being charged with drug trafficking; but the real action of the early Bush presidency took place in Eastern Europe, where the Soviet empire was coming apart. Once the Soviets withdrew their troops, satellite regimes crumbled overnight. Then the Soviet Union itself disintegrated in 1990. 1991 Although Bush was obviously not personally responsible for these momentous events, in effect, America had completed its victory in the Cold War on his watch.

The midterm elections of 1990 took place under the mixed conditions of a faltering economy and victory abroad. Republican losses in the House were limited to a modest seven seats. But combined with the three seats lost in 1988, the result was sufficient to turn mandate key 1 against the party in power.

Despite a still ailing economy, 1991 would be the high point of the Bush presidency. An international crisis precipitated by an Iraqi invasion of oil-rich Kuwait, an American ally, showed President Bush at his best. He organized an extraordinary international coalition in support of American opposition to the invasion. Even the Soviet Union and moderate Arab states were brought on board. He gained United Nations approval to expel Iraqi armies from Kuwait and, with difficulty, support of the U.S. Congress as well.

When the time for military action against Iraq had come, Bush amassed overwhelming military force. He would decisively avoid the Vietnam-era mistake of engaging in limited, protracted war. The United States rapidly defeated the Iraqi armies and liberated Kuwait with little loss of American life. Bush was later criticized for not taking the road to Baghdad and toppling Iraqi dictator Saddam Hussein. However, Bush had no mandate to do so from the UN, the Congress, or the American people. On its own terms, the war was a stunning success, the first decisive triumph of American arms since World War II. Not only George Bush, but field commander General Norman Schwarzkopf and Joint Chiefs of Staff chairman General Colin Powell emerged as war heroes. The war easily earned Bush foreign-success key 11. The lack of any major foreign failure also preserved Key 10, giving the administration a sweep of both foreign-policy keys.

Far less propitious was the president's performance at home. The most notable domestic initiative of the term actually came at the behest of Democrats in Congress. In June of 1990, George Bush reached a "budget deal" with Democratic leaders that sought to curb the deficit through a mix of tax increases and spending restraint. Not only was the impact of deficit control lost as the economy plunged into recession, but conservatives lambasted Bush for abandoning his famous election pledge: "Read my lips. No new taxes."

Beyond the budget deal, Bush professed concern for education but offered no major proposals to Congress. He vetoed a civil-rights bill that he said went too far in attempting to expand protection against employment discrimination. Yet he subsequently signed a bill with most of the same provisions. He took no decisive action to reverse the sliding economy in 1990–91. Bush and his advisers believed that the normal turning of the business cycle would rescue the economy by the beginning of the election year. In the worst case of a weak election-year economy, Bush believed that he could still ride his foreign-policy accomplishments to reelection against a little-known Democratic challenger. The most immediate result of presidential inaction was the loss of policy-change key 7.

Late in the term there also emerged the possibility that the social-unrest key would fall for the first time since 1968. In reaction to the acquittal in state court of police officers accused in the videotaped beating of Rodney King, rioting erupted in south-central Los Angeles during the spring of 1992, taking some fifty-eight lives. However, Los Angeles remained an isolated incident, much like the Miami disorder of 1980, and the party in power held on to Key 8.

Throughout the term and into the presidential election, critics charged that President Bush had lied about his degree of involvement in and knowledge of the Iran-Contra scandal. During the election, media reports also alleged that officials of the Bush administration had illicitly sought to examine challenger Bill Clinton's passport records. Overall, however, the upright and fastidious George Bush ran a scandal-free administration, securing Key 9.

Just as George Bush's popularity was peaking in mid-1991, his reelection prospects were becoming precarious. The still sluggish economy made it nearly certain that the long-term economy key would be lost and raised the possibility of losing the election-year economy key as well. Already, Bush had dropped the mandate, policy-change, and incumbent-charisma keys. If both economy keys fell, it would take just one more negative key to bring the total to six and a predicted defeat in the November election.

This is precisely what came to pass, making 1992 the first six-key election since 1912. In a close call reminiscent of 1960 and 1980, the short-term economy key did turn against the party in power. With 2.9 percent growth in the first quarter of 1992, the economy seemed on the rebound from recession. But second-quarter growth slowed to 1.4 percent, barely enough to keep pace with population growth. Unemployment rose and consumer and business confidence plummeted. A preliminary report on the third-quarter economy, released just days before the election, showed the economy had rebounded to a rate of 2.7 percent. Employment reports released before the election, however, failed to show that the economy had made the upturn needed to create jobs. According to the National Bureau of Economic Research, the recession had technically ended in 1991, but the bureau did not reach this conclusion until seven weeks after the election.[4] Most decisive in making the short-term economic call for 1992 was the overwhelming public perception that the economy remained mired in recession through the election campaign. According to a Gallup Poll in September of 1992, 79 percent of respondents said that the economy was in recession. A nationwide *Los Angeles Times* Poll taken ten days before the election showed that a nearly identical 76 percent agreed that the economy remained in recession.[5]

With no charismatic Democrat on the horizon in 1992, Bush could still survive the loss of the short-term economy key, provided he dropped neither of the two keys still very much in play at the beginning of the election year: contest key 2 and third-party key 4. Former Nixon speechwriter and well-known political commentator Patrick Buchanan took the conservative case against George Bush to the Republican primary electorate. Buchanan attracted a loyal following and generated vast media coverage, but he won no primaries and amassed few delegate votes. Ultimately, George Bush swept to a nearly unanimous nomination. Key 4 remained in place for the incumbent party.

But third-party key 4 would tumble in 1992 as a result of the insurgent campaign launched by Ross Perot, a self-made billionaire with no prior political experience. Perot became the first major third-party candidate in history without either a track record in public office or a grassroots movement with a specific platform and philosophy. Insurgent campaigns count against incumbent parties because they are barometers of discontent with the state of the nation. This was graphically demonstrated in the spring of 1992 when Perot became the first third-party candidate in history to win a presidential preference poll. Perot embodied people's discontent with politicians and their ways, even though he was lacking in specific solutions to national problems. The Perot insurgency also meant that the incumbent president would be attacked on two fronts by two candidates with very different styles.

Within a few months after bursting dramatically onto the presidential scene, Perot enigmatically withdrew his candidacy. Yet he continued to spend millions of dollars to keep his state-level operations going and to get his name on individual state ballots. The noncandidate still scored up to 15 percent in national opinion polls, far more than necessary to topple Key 4. Showing his continued flair for the dramatic and the bizarre, Perot hurdled back into the presidential campaign just in time to participate in the three televised debates. Never again would he threaten to overtake the major contenders, but he still won an amazing 19 percent of the popular vote. Only one prior insurgent candidate, former president Teddy Roosevelt, had captured a larger share of the popular balloting.

From a field of little-known candidates, the Democrats chose Bill Clinton, the governor of Arkansas. Clinton had shaken off charges of marital infidelity to amass a solid majority of Democratic convention votes. It did not matter that Clinton lacked the heroic stature or charismatic appeal needed to topple challenger-charisma key 13. With six keys against him, Bush was already a one-term president.

Clinton won the presidency with a decisive margin of 370 electoral votes to 168 for Bush, but his popular vote plurality of 43 percent (compared to 38 percent for Bush and 19 percent for Perot) was the least for any winning candidate since Woodrow Wilson in 1912. With the Democrats losing nine House seats in the presidential year, mandate key 1 would be almost certain to fall in 1996. Still, the Democrats regained unified control of government for the first time since the Carter administration of the late 1970s.

Chapter 9

A False Dawn for Democrats: 1996–2004

Bill Clinton's victory in 1992 restored unified Democratic control over national government for the first time since the Carter administration. However, Democratic dominance would not last. Unlike Carter, President Clinton won re-election to a second term, but failed to revitalize the Democratic Party as he became the first Democratic presidential candidate of the twentieth century elected to office without bringing with him a Democratic House and Senate. During Bill Clinton's eight years in office the Democrats suffered their greatest losses in electoral politics since the 1920s. In 1994 Democrats lost control of both Houses of Congress for the first time since 1954; they would not recapture the House at least through 2004 and only regained control of the Senate briefly during 2001–2002. Republicans also won thirteen additional governorships during the Clinton years, holding thirty-one states in 2001, compared to eighteen in 1993.

Some analysts heralded Bill Clinton as a "new kind of Democrat" whose "middle way" philosophy melded traditional Democratic compassion for the have-nots with support for fiscal responsibility, market-driven programs, free trade, tough anti-crime initiatives, and efficiently run government. He stressed people's responsibility for their own destiny and promoted government programs that provided opportunities rather than guaranteeing outcomes. But the middle way politics failed to instill voters with the same passion as the revived Republican Right, led by Governor George W. Bush of Texas—a more dedicated conservative than his father, George H. W. Bush. After winning the disputed election of 2000, Bush carried a majority of both the popular vote and the Electoral College in 2004. With Republicans winning 55 percent of Senate seats and 53 percent of House seats, Bush became the first Republican president since Herbert Hoover in 1929 to command clear majorities in both chambers of Congress.

1996: Lonesome Victory
Incumbent-party nominee: President Bill Clinton (Democrat)
Challenging-party nominee: Bob Dole (Republican)
Negative Keys: 5
Result: Clinton, 49.2%; Dole, 40.7%; Ross Perot (Reform), 8.4%

Key:	1	2	3	4	5	6	7	8	9	10	11	12	13
Call:	X	O	O	X	O	O	X	O	O	O	X	X	O

In 1996, Bill Clinton became only the second elected Democratic president since Franklin Delano Roosevelt to seek a second term in office. Unlike Jimmy Carter in 1980, however, President Clinton presided over a robust economy, avoided major setbacks abroad, and faced an uninspiring challenger in the 73 year-old Senator Bob Dole of Kansas.

Real per-capita GDP grew by a mean of about 3 percent during the Clinton years, with growth never falling below 2.5 percent in a single year. The president attributed the nation's prosperity to his free trade initiatives and 1993 budget that brought the persistent federal deficit under control. Others pointed to the rise of the new information economy of the 1990s. No matter. The four-year record of prosperity secured for the incumbent Democrats both short-term economy Key 5 and long-term economy Key 6.

Despite the glowing economy, Clinton's Democrats suffered catastrophic losses in the midterm elections of 1994: fifty-four House and seven Senate seats, as Republicans recaptured both chambers and the Democrats lost Key 1. It was the worst drubbing suffered by a presidential party in midterm elections since 1958. Voters defeated not a single Republican incumbent in the House, while dismissing 34 Democratic incumbents. Reflecting an ongoing shift in the geographic basis of American politics, the GOP secured a majority of southern House seats for the first time in history. Democrats in Congress still held to former House Speaker Tip O'Neal's dictum that "all politics is local." The GOP, however, led by future House Speaker Newt Gingrich of Georgia, nationalized the election with its "Contract with America." The Contract promised, among other initiatives, to place Congress under the civil rights laws, amend the Constitution to balance the federal budget, cut taxes, tighten the criminal justice code, limit punitive damages in tort cases, impose term limits on members of Congress, and reform the welfare laws to reduce spending, discourage births out of wedlock, and encourage work. The Contract deliberately avoided explosive social issues like abortion, affirmative action, and school prayer.

Controversy over the administration's eased policy on excluding gays from the military and the failure of its signature policy initiative on health care reform contributed to the Democrats' midterm defeat. Clinton's middle way health care plan, developed by a task force that First Lady Hillary Clinton led, covered the uninsured through the private sector by requiring employers to provide health care insurance for their workers. But it also included new federal bureaucracies and cost control measures. The proposal satisfied neither liberals, who favored a single-payer system run by government, nor conservatives, who charged that the plan would kill freedom of medical choice, lead to the rationing of health care, crush small business, and establish a "medical police" to meddle in people's private lives. And critics derided Hillary Clinton for crafting a plan so complex that it covered more than a thousand pages of text. But the incoming Republican Congress found its agenda stymied by presidential opposition and an overreaching of the 1994 mandate. A budget standoff between Congress and the president in 1995 led to two embarrassing shutdowns of the government, which most Americans blamed on Congress. The following year, the Clinton administration and the Republican leadership compromised on increasing the minimum wage and ending federal welfare as an entitlement program and placing time limits on the receipt of benefits. But these late-breaking measures fell short of the high standard needed to win policy change Key 7 for the Clinton administration, especially with welfare reform largely reflecting the initiative of Republicans. In the House and Senate, 98 percent of Republicans voted for final passage of welfare reform, compared to just 3 percent of Democrats.

Charges of scandal swirled around Bill Clinton during his first term. Beyond outlandish speculation that the president or First Lady were implicated in the suicide of White House aide Vincent Foster, critics charged fraud in connection with the Clinton's investment in the Whitewater Development Corporation in Arkansas during the 1980s. In January of 1994, Attorney General Janet Reno appointed Republican Robert Fiske as a special prosecutor to investigate the Whitewater allegations. Later that year, a three-judge federal court, which supervises the office of Independent Counsel, replaced Fiske with Republican Kenneth Starr, Solicitor General in the Bush administration. Starr's investigation of Whitewater was still ongoing through the 1996 election. Starr was also investigating, without resolution, allegations that the White House had improperly dismissed travel office employees ("Travelgate") and acquired FBI files on political opponents ("Filegate"). In late 1996, a Justice Department task force began investigating charges of fundraising abuses by the Clinton re-election campaign. But no credible scandal touched the president by election day and his party retained Key 9. With the country generally calm domestically during this term, the Democrats also held Key 8.

President Clinton's administration presided over a relatively tranquil period in foreign and military affairs. Clinton surveyed the world from a greater position of strength than any prior president. America comprised 40 percent of the world economy and spent more on defense in the post–Cold War era than any five other countries combined. Ethnic conflict now seemed to pose a greater threat to American security than nuclear confrontation. The administration put a high priority on promoting a global, free-market economy. It rescued Mexico from a financial crisis and supported the North American Free Trade Agreement, the Uruguay Round of the General Agreement on Trade and Tariffs, and the World Trade Organization. In recognition of an interdependent world, the multilateral-minded president negotiated a new Comprehensive Test Ban Treaty and personally intervened in peace processes in the Middle East, although without final resolution.

While relations with Russia and China changed little during the Clinton term, the administration focused on trouble spots elsewhere, in several cases seeking to defuse crises through military intervention. Although its first venture in the African nation of Somalia went badly, the administration also intervened in Haiti in 1994 to restore its elected president to power. The following year, President Clinton, with NATO concurrence, launched a bombing campaign in Bosnia to halt the aggression of Bosnian Serbs against Muslims and Croats. He then arranged a settlement that partitioned Bosnia into separate ethnic regions. With neither a major setback nor a grand triumph abroad, the administration retained foreign/military failure Key 10, but forfeited foreign/military success Key 11.

In seeking a presidential candidate for 1996, most Republicans leaders agreed that the time had come for party stalwart Bob Dole, the majority leader of the Senate. But Dole faced challenges on his right from Pat Buchanan and wealthy publisher Steve Forbes, and on his own center turf from Lamar Alexander, the former governor of Tennessee. Buchanan stunned Dole by winning the New Hampshire primary, which historically was nearly tantamount to winning the GOP nomination. Buchanan, however, seemed unable or unwilling to turn this victory into a winning strategy for the flurry of upcoming primaries. Dole won a saving contest in South Carolina and proceeded to sweep the remaining primaries. The nomination of the earnest but lackluster senator secured for the party in power challenger charisma Key 13.

With President Clinton uncontested for re-election within his party, the Democrats secured party contest Key 2 and incumbency Key 3. However, despite President Clinton's considerable political talents, his questionable personal behavior, and his sometimes indecisive leadership kept him from capturing incumbent charisma Key 12. The Democrats lost an additional Key when Ross Perot launched a second insurgent presidential campaign, this time as the nominee of the newly formed Reform party. Although early polls suggested that Perot still enjoyed nearly 20 percent public support, he was no longer a new and exciting personality in 1996, and a falling federal budget deficit robbed him of a signature issue. Between 1992 and 1996, the deficit plunged from $290 billion to just $107 billion, as spending fell from 22.2 percent of GDP to 20.3 percent and receipts rose from 17.5 percent of GDP to 18.9 percent. The major parties also kept Perot out of the presidential debates in 1996, depriving him of a forum in which he had shined in 1992. Although Perot's share of the popular vote shrank to 8.4 percent in 1996, as expected, he exceeded the 5 percent threshold needed to topple third party Key 4.

Ultimately President Clinton faced the electorate with a final deficit of five Keys: mandate Key 1, third party Key 4, policy change Key 7, foreign policy success Key 11, and incumbent charisma Key 12, making him a predicted winner by the margin of but a single Key. Only once before in the twentieth century had the incumbent party prevailed by such a narrow margin on the Keys. That was in 1948 when Democratic president Harry Truman beat Republican challenger Tom Dewey in the so-called surprise election. Unlike Truman, however, Clinton led in the polls from start to finish in a low-key campaign, lacking in ideologically charged issues. Clinton finished with 49.2 percent of the popular vote—to 40.7 percent for Dole—under his poll margins, and nearly identical to Truman's 49.6 percent. Clinton won easily in the Electoral College with 379 votes to just 159 for Dole. But the president, like Eisenhower in 1956, Nixon in 1972, and Reagan in 1984, lacked coattails. With his lonely victory, the Democrats failed to recapture either chamber of Congress, winning just 9 seats in the House while losing 2 in the Senate.

2000: Showdown in Florida
Incumbent-party nominee: Al Gore (Democrat)
Challenging-party nominee: George W. Bush (Republican)
Negative Keys: 5
Result: Gore, 48.4%; Bush, 47.9%; Ralph Nader (Green), 2.7%

Key:	1	2	3	4	5	6	7	8	9	10	11	12	13
Call:	O	O	X	O	O	O	X	O	X	O	X	X	O

In 2000, the Democrats hoped to win the White House for a third consecutive term for the first time since the Roosevelt–Truman era. Much was hanging in the balance that year, with the parties competing for control of all three branches of government and of the legislative redistricting that would begin in 2001. Democrats hoped to retain the presidency, recapture at least the House of Representatives, reverse the conservative direction of the Supreme Court with new appointments, and hold their edge in the state legislative seats that were crucial for the redrawing of state and national legislative districts after the Census of 2000. Republicans, who already controlled governors' mansions in most big states and both houses of Congress, looked for a breakthrough election to restore their party to the dominance over American government that it had last achieved in the 1920s.

Ideologically, the election was significant as well. The centers of the Republican and Democratic parties had moved poles apart in the last decades of the twentieth century. In 1972, the year Republicans nominated Richard Nixon and Democrats George McGovern, House Republicans, on average, supported the conservative position on 64 percent of key roll calls identified by the American Conservative Union. House Democrats averaged 32 percent support for the conservative position, for a difference of 32 percent. In 1998, polarization between the parties more than doubled to 71 percent, as the Republican conservatism rating soared to 85 percent and the Democratic rating plummeted to 14 percent.

The day after Clinton defeated Dole in 1996—and years before the polls or other prediction systems were of any use—the Keys began defining the structure of the race for president in 2000. The early lineup of the thirteen Keys indicated that it would once again be difficult for the Democrats to keep control of the White House after the retirement of a sitting president. The party in power seemed almost certain to lose four Keys. Without President Clinton heading the ticket, his party would lose incumbency Key 3. Republican control of Congress would foreclose the achievement of major policy change by the administration, toppling Key 7. A foreign policy triumph would be difficult to achieve in the complex, post–Cold War world, likely toppling Key 11 and the Democrats lacked a potential nominee with the magic needed to win incumbent charisma Key 12. With a prospective deficit of at least four Keys, the Democrats could afford few setbacks during the four years of Bill Clinton's second term. Yet no less than seven other Keys were in severe jeopardy of turning against the party in power, including party mandate Key 1, nomination contest Key 2, third-party Key 4, economic Keys 5 and 6, scandal Key 9, and foreign failure Key 10.

A necessary, although insufficient condition for Democratic success in 2000, was continuation of the first-term economic expansion for another four years. No two-term president in the modern history of the United States had ever presided over eight full years of a growing economy. Yet the boom times of Clinton's first four years continued through his second term. The pace of economic growth actually accelerated after 1996, creating the longest economic expansion in the history of the country. After averaging a robust 3.2 percent during Bill Clinton's first term, growth in real Gross Domestic Product soared to an average of 4.2 percent from 1997 to 2000, one of the best four-year performances in American history. The growth of real mean per capita GDP during the second term was far above the mean for the previous eight years. Although the distribution of income remained heavily skewed in favor of the affluent, the economic expansion of the late 1990s still created bright economic prospects for a broad range of Americans. The party in power secured both short-term economy Key 5 and long-term economy Key 6 for 2000.

In domestic policy, a Republican House and Senate stymied most Clinton initiatives, turning policy change Key 7 against the Democrats for 2000. The main domestic policy accomplishment of President Clinton's second term was an agreement with the GOP Congress on a deficit-reduction package designed to achieve a balanced federal budget. Before any of the substantial budget cuts mandated by the agreement took effect, the federal budget registered a surplus of $79 billion in fiscal 1998. Budget surpluses continued to pile up in each year of the Clinton presidency. The transformation of federal budget deficits into surpluses was of historic importance for the country, but resulted primarily from the soaring economy rather than from the kind of major policy change needed to secure Key 7.

Shocking incidents of violence involving young Americans disrupted an otherwise tranquil nation during Clinton's second term. Between 1997 and 1999, student gunmen killed a score of fellow students and

teachers in West Paducah, Kentucky; Jonesboro, Arkansas; and Little-
ton, Colorado. But these were individual incidents rather than part of a
sustained breakdown of the social order in the United States. During
the late 1990s, crime, both overall and among juveniles, dramatically
declined. The party in power retained social unrest Key 8.

Domestic tranquillity and the buoyant economy helped President
Clinton withstand the impeachment crisis that engulfed his second term.
Since 1994, Independent Council Kenneth Starr had been investigating
matters relating to President Clinton's conduct in office and his earlier
activities as governor of Arkansas: the Whitewater land deal in Arkansas, the unauthorized appearance of confidential FBI files in the White
House, and the allegedly improper firing of White House travel office
workers. Allegations of illegal fundraising activities by President Clinton and Vice President Gore also led Republicans in Congress to futilely demand that Attorney General Janet Reno authorize another
Independent Counsel investigation.

It was none of these matters, however, that led to the impeachment
of President Clinton. In 1998, the Attorney General and the supervising
federal court expanded Starr's authority to include allegations of per-
jury and obstruction of justice in President Clinton's efforts to conceal
an affair with White House intern Monica Lewinsky. After adamantly
denying having sex with Ms. Lewinsky, President Clinton admitted in
August of 1998 that he had had a relationship with the former intern
that was "not appropriate." Less than a month later, Starr released a
report that included salacious details of the affair and charged the president with no less than eleven potentially impeachable offenses.

Starr's sensational charges and meticulous documentation had the potential to drive the president from office; many of the nation's leading
newspapers called for the president's resignation. Pundits also expected
the president's party to suffer at the polls during the midterm elections
of 1998, costing the Democrats Key 1.

Yet, even after the release of the Starr report, some two-thirds of
Americans approved of the president's performance in office and opposed either impeachment or resignation. The president's support reflected the booming economy, the lack of a foreign threat, and
tranquillity at home. Most Americans also believed that the president's
conduct, however deplorable, was a private matter and that politics, not
patriotism, motivated his Republican critics. A backlash against the Republican Congress contributed to surprising Democratic success in the
midterm elections of 1998. For the first time since 1934, the party controlling the White House won House seats during the midterm contests,
securing party mandate Key 1 for the 2000 election.

Undaunted by their setback at the polls, Republicans, who still controlled the House, impeached President Clinton on a nearly straight party-line vote. On December 19, 1998, a majority of the House ratified two articles of impeachment. The House charged that the president perjured himself in testimony before a federal grand jury investigating the Lewinsky scandal and that he obstructed justice by pressuring others to lie about and cover up his affair with Lewinsky. The impeachment of an incumbent president for only the second time in American history turned scandal Key 9 against the party in power, even though the Senate acquitted the president in February of 1999, after a one-month trial. Neither article gained a simple majority of Senators, falling far short of the two-thirds vote needed for conviction.

In foreign affairs, the Clinton administration largely continued the policies of the first term. The administration confronted so-called rogue states such as Iraq and North Korea. It attempted to bring peace to trouble spots such as Northern Ireland, the Middle East, and Kashmir. It promoted global cooperation on human rights, the environment, and arms control. The administration again used military force to promote humanitarian goals and regional stability, including negotiation of the Kyoto Accords to reduce the threat of global warming.

The Clinton administration achieved a mixed record of success internationally. Unable to maintain its weapons inspection program in Iraq, the administration resorted to air strikes designed to limit Iraq's capacity to produce highly destructive weapons and threaten its neighbors. Despite some progress, peace remained elusive in the unsettled regions of the world and the Republican Senate stymied efforts to achieve multilateral accords. In October of 1999 the administration suffered a setback when the Senate rejected the Comprehensive Test Ban Treaty that Clinton had signed in 1996.

The war over Kosovo in 1999 was the administration's most notable and perilous venture in foreign policy. In March of 1999, after failing to persuade Yugoslav President Slobodan Milosevic to cease his campaign against ethnic Albanians in the province of Kosovo, the North Atlantic Treaty Organization began U.S.-led air strikes against Yugoslavia. The air war dragged on for 11 weeks, remarkably without American casualties, until Milosevic finally capitulated and agreed to withdraw his forces from Kosovo and clear the way for the return of refugees and the presence of an international peacekeeping force. The administration averted a potential humiliation in Yugoslavia that would have toppled foreign failure Key 10. However, it failed to achieve the major triumph needed to secure foreign success Key 11. Even after the peace settlement, only a bare majority of Americans believed that it had been worthwhile for the United States to intervene in Kosovo. On balance, as in 1996, the administration split the two foreign policy Keys in its second term.

The 2000 campaign for president began in mid-1999 as candidates lined up to compete in presidential nomination contests. Already, Democrats faced a five-Key deficit, having almost certainly lost incumbency Key 3, policy change Key 7, scandal Key 9, foreign/military success Key 11, and incumbent charisma Key 12—with no inspiring Democratic candidate on the horizon. Still in potential jeopardy for the incumbent Democrats were contest Key 2, third party Key 4, and possibly challenger charisma Key 13. The loss of any one of these political Keys would have produced a six-Key deficit and a predicted general election defeat.

Among Democrats, potential challengers to Al Gore—the presumptive front-runner for the nomination—melted away. House Minority Leader Richard Gephardt decided to take his chances on becoming Speaker should the Democrats regain majority control of the House. Nebraska Senator Bob Kerrey, who had competed for the 1992 nomination, opted to retire from politics. Civil rights leader Jesse Jackson decided that he lacked the broad support needed to make a competitive race for the nomination. Ultimately, only former New Jersey Senator Bill Bradley challenged Gore, running to the Vice President's left on issues such as poverty and health care. Although Bradley trailed Gore by a wide margin in national polls of registered Democrats, he jumped ahead of the Vice President in the New Hampshire primary polls.

The Bradley campaign collapsed, however, after Gore trounced him in the first delegate selection contest, the Iowa Caucuses, and narrowly defeated him in New Hampshire. When he failed to win any of the numerous primaries held on March 7, 2000, so-called "Super Tuesday," Bradley ended his campaign and endorsed the Vice President. Bradley won only a small fraction of the delegates to the Democratic Convention and the Democrats secured contest Key 2.

Among Republicans, a crowded field narrowed to two serious contenders after the New Hampshire primary: Texas Governor George W. Bush, the early front-runner, and Arizona Senator John McCain, who stunned Bush with a 18 point win in New Hampshire. Governor Bush, like Senator Dole in 1996, recovered his momentum by winning the South Carolina primary a few weeks later. Although McCain would achieve another major victory in the Michigan primary, Bush won every major state primary on Super Tuesday and McCain suspended his campaign rather than compete against Bush in the Governor's southern stronghold the following week. Although McCain did not immediately endorse George W. Bush, he ruled out an independent or third party campaign for president. Instead, he would focus on assisting Republican candidates for Congress.

By nominating the safe and predictable Bush, the Republicans forfeited any chance of turning challenger charisma Key 13 against the incumbent Democrats. Ironically, the defeated John McCain may have developed the kind of inspirational appeal needed to topple challenger charisma Key 13 and turn the critical sixth Key against the administration.

Two potentially significant third-party candidates entered the lists in 2000. After Perot decided not to run again, erstwhile Republican Pat Buchanan won the Reform Party nomination, with its $13 million in federal funds available for the general election. But Buchanan squandered the money and disappeared in the fall campaign, ultimately garnering only .4 percent of the popular vote. Consumer advocate Ralph Nader proved to be a much more serious contender, surpassing the 5 percent threshold in some polls. However, third-party candidates tend to fade in the voting booth as voters focus on the major-party contenders and it appeared that the incumbent Democrats would retain their five-Key deficit by the narrowest possible margin.

Nader failed to match his top poll numbers and finished with 2.7 percent of the popular vote, just short of the threshold needed to topple Key 4. As predicted, Gore prevailed in the popular, vote winning 48.4 percent to Bush's 47.9 percent. However, the vote for Nader was sufficient to tip the critical state of Florida against the Vice President. Bush ultimately prevailed by 537 votes in Florida, whereas Nader won more than 97,000 votes in Florida, enough to cost Gore far more votes than necessary to change the outcome. The results in Florida, however, were inconclusive until December 12, when the U.S. Supreme Court halted a statewide hand recount (ordered by the Florida Supreme Court) of ballots where no vote for president was recorded by machine. In retrospect, it appears that Gore made a serious strategic error by not immediately seeking a statewide recount which could have proceeded in timely fashion. With Florida's 25 votes in his column, Bush garnered 271 Electoral College votes, compared to 266 for Gore. Final congressional tallies showed near equipoise in the House as the GOP lost a single seat. More significantly, the Republicans lost four Senate seats, bringing the Senate to a 50–50 tie, which became a 51-seat Democratic advantage during Bush's first year when Senator James Jeffords of Vermont switched from Republican to Independent and voted with the Democratic caucus.

Controversy over the vote in Florida, however, lingered long afterwards as critics charged that election officials had purged alleged disenfranchised felons from the rolls with a flawed list of felons that heavily overrepresented Democratic African-Americans and vastly underrepresented primarily Republican Hispanics. Critics further charged that a confusing "butterfly" ballot in Palm Beach County had led more than a thousand intended Gore voters mistakenly to vote for Buchanan, that Republican officials had tampered with absentee ballots in two counties, and that election officials had disqualified as invalid a vastly greater percentage of ballots cast by African-Americans than whites. Nonetheless, George Bush became president of the United States on January 6, 2001, when Al Gore, as president of the Senate, read the Electoral College votes before both Houses of Congress, with only five Democrat Senators in attendance.

2004: A Majority at Last
Incumbent-party nominee: President George W. Bush (Republican)
Challenging-party nominee: John F. Kerry (Democrat)
Negative Keys: 4
Result: Bush, 50.7%; Kerry, 48.3%

Key:	1	2	3	4	5	6	7	8	9	10	11	12	13
Call:	O	O	O	O	O	X	X	O	O	X	O	X	O

Despite losing the popular vote in a disputed election, George W. Bush declined to govern from the center or make concessions to Democrats. Instead, he pursued a conservative agenda, keynoted by an ambitious plan for deep cuts in federal income taxes. But the Bush presidency changed fundamentally on September 11, 2001, when Al Qaeda terrorists crashed hijacked airplanes into both towers of New York City's World Trade Center and the Pentagon in Arlington, Virginia, just outside of Washington, D.C. After 9/11, Bush found his historic mission: to protect the United States from future terrorist attack and pursue the forces of evil and terrorism worldwide. "America will do what is necessary to ensure our nation's security," President Bush told the world in his 2002 State of the Union Address. "History has called America and our allies to action, and it is both our responsibility and our privilege to fight freedom's fight."

During this first 100 days, President Bush succeeded, beyond expectations, in pushing his tax cut plans through Congress. The legislation that Bush signed on June 7, 2001, cut rates for every personal income tax bracket, reduced the marriage penalty and the alternative minimum tax, increased the child credit, expanded individual retirement accounts, and phased out the estate tax. The legislation was scheduled for expiration in 2010, but advocates expected that Congress would eventually make most provisions permanent. Although liberals charged that the tax cuts heavily favored the rich and threatened the budget surpluses built up during the Clinton years, twenty-eight Democrats in the House and twelve in the Senate voted with the administration. Two years later, Bush gained passage of new legislation that accelerated the 2001 tax cuts, slashed the long-term capital gains tax rate and the dividend tax rate to 15 percent, and expanded deductions for business equipment purchases. During his first year, Bush also succeeded in a second priority when Congress passed his No Child Left Behind Act to hold states and communities accountable for achievement in public education. Critics complained, however, that the Act lacked sufficient funding for its lofty goals.

Although the 9/11 attacks focused the administration on national security, the president won passage of additional significant domestic legislation. Congress overwhelmingly enacted the USA Patriot Act, which expanded the power of law enforcement agencies to combat terrorist threats to the American homeland. The Act, which produced much controversy among civil libertarians, loosened restrictions on domestic surveillance by federal authorities, facilitated information sharing by law enforcement and intelligence agencies, eased requirements for obtaining search warrants, prohibited the harboring of terrorists, and increased penalties for several categories of crime. Two years later, the administration narrowly steered through Congress a major rewriting of the Medicare program to provide a prescription drug benefit for seniors. Taken together, however, the Bush initiatives did not constitute a revolution in policy, leaving the Republicans just short of securing policy change Key 7.

The economy proved to be a sore spot for the Bush administration as the ten-year expansion—the longest in history—finally lost steam at the beginning of his term. According to the National Bureau of Economic Research, the economy descended into recession in March of 2001. Although the recession was relatively shallow and short—lasting only eight months—the subsequent recovery failed to produce the usual growth in jobs. Also, the 2001 tax cuts and economic slowdown transformed a budget surplus of $127 billion during Bush's first year into a record $412 billion deficit for 2004. However, the economy continued expanding through the election year, with annual real GDP rising by a robust 4.4 percent. And growth finally translated into jobs: a net gain of nearly 2 million new jobs in the first eleven months of 2004. The strong election year economy salvaged short-term economy Key 5 for the Republicans. But the lagging four-year economy under Bush, as compared to the eight Clinton years, cost the incumbent party long-term economy Key 6.

The president's response to 9/11 extended far beyond the Patriot Act. The administration established a policy of indefinitely detaining foreign terror suspects, their fates ultimately decided by secret military tribunals under limited due process rights. By March 2002, the military was holding some 300 terror suspects at Camp X-Ray at the American base of Guantanamo Bay, Cuba. Although the 9/11 attacks came from Al Qaeda, an entity that transcended national boundaries and loyalties, the administration mainly responded by invading two nation states— Afghanistan and Iraq. The attack on Afghanistan in October 2001 generated little controversy given that its Taliban government trained and harbored Al Qaeda operatives, including Osama bin Laden, the strategist behind the 9/11 atrocity. American troops, aided by a British contingent, quickly captured the capital of Kabul by early November, precipitating the collapse of the Taliban across the country. But American forces and their local anti-Taliban allies failed to capture bin Laden and other Al Qaeda leaders who had taken refuge in the Tora Bora cave complex near the Pakistan border. The public overwhelmingly approved of the war in Afghanistan, which resulted in fewer than 200 American casualties through 2004 and led to the country's first nationwide free elections in October 2004.

Far more controversial was the decision to invade Iraq in March of 2003, based on much murkier justifications than the war in Afghanistan. Military action in Iraq, the administration suggested during the year before the invasion, was required by its complicity in the 9/11 attack, its ties to Al Qaeda terrorists, and its rule by the brutal dictator Saddam Hussein, a repressive and destabilizing force in the Middle East. But the administration argued for war primarily on the basis of the threat to American security posed by Saddam's alleged nuclear weapons program and purported stockpiles of biological and chemical weapons of mass destruction. In October 2002, the Bush administration won authorization from Congress for the use of force in Iraq. Many, however, argued that given the lack of Iraq's connection to 9/11, the thin case for an Iraqi threat to the U.S., and the lack of unified international support, George W. Bush was rejecting the multilateralism of his predecessors—

including George H. W. Bush—and setting a new precedent for "pre-emptive war." As a further indication of the president's unilateral approach to foreign affairs, he rejected the Kyoto Accords and American participation in the International Criminal Court.

The war against Iraq, begun in March 2003, was a short-term military success. American troops quickly swept aside Saddam's military and overthrew his government with far fewer American casualties than anticipated. On May 1, 2003, aboard the aircraft carrier Abraham Lincoln, President Bush declared "mission accomplished" in Iraq, with major combat operations at an end. But the mission was far from accomplished since American occupying troops and their Iraqi allies had grave difficulties securing Iraq, even after the capture of Saddam Hussein on December 13, 2003. From May of 2003 through the end of 2004, more than 1,200 American troops died in Iraq, compared to fewer than 150 before the president had declared the end of major combat. Moreover, American weapons inspectors found no weapons of mass destruction or any evidence of an Iraqi nuclear bomb program.

The Bush administration had several notable achievements in foreign policy: keeping America secure from homeland attacks after 9/11, driving the Taliban from power in Afghanistan, toppling the Iraqi government, and capturing Saddam Hussein. Thus, it secured foreign/military success Key 11. But it had its share of failures as well: the 9/11 attack (comparable to Pearl Harbor in 1941), rising casualties in Iraq, and the failure to secure the peace in that strife-ridden country. Thus, it lost foreign/military failure Key 10. Polls taken on the eve of the election, which showed the country evenly divided on the president's stewardship of foreign affairs, reflected this split verdict of the Keys.

As in Clinton's first term, allegations of scandal swirled around the White House during the Bush administration. These included charges of presidential negligence—or worse—in failing to prevent the 9/11 attacks, complicity in the abuse of prisoners in American custody, and the manipulation or misreading of intelligence data to justify the invasion of Iraq. The Attorney General also appointed a special prosecutor to investigate the disclosure of the identity of CIA undercover agent Valerie Plame, possibly by high White House officials. Plame was married to former ambassador Joseph Wilson, whose on-site investigations cast doubt on administration claims that Iraq was purchasing uranium in Africa. But none of the charges or innuendoes struck home against the president by Election Day. The commission investigating the 9/11 attacks did not blame the president. The prisoner abuse scandals never reached the Oval Office and the president attributed misleading information on weapons of mass destruction in Iraq to flawed information that he received from the CIA. The Special Prosecutor's investigation remained ongoing and inconclusive. Thus, the administration retained scandal Key 9. It also held on to social unrest Key 8, given the lack of domestic upheavals during the term as anti-war protests never approached the levels of the Vietnam era.

The political Keys 1 through 4 also aligned perfectly for the incumbent Republicans in 2004. The surge of patriotism during the prelude to the war in Iraq led to Republican victories in the midterm elections of 2002. The GOP picked up two seats in the U.S. Senate and six in the House, recapturing the Senate, strengthening their narrow hold on the House, and securing mandate Key 1. For the first time since 1994, Republicans won a majority of the nationwide vote for the House. President Bush's uncontested nomination secured Keys 2 and 3 for the incumbent party and the lack of a third-party challenger with prospects of securing 5 percent or more of the popular vote. Bush's nomination, however, cost the GOP incumbent charisma Key 12.

Numerous Democratic hopefuls sought their party's nomination in 2004, but the field lacked its two strongest contenders, former Vice President and presidential candidate Al Gore and former First Lady and New York Senator Hillary Clinton. One of the least known candidates, former Vermont Governor Howard Dean, jumped to a surprising early lead in fundraising and public esteem, primarily through his staunch anti-war position and his innovative use of the Internet for fundraising and organizing. But Dean failed to sustain his momentum as voters in the Iowa caucuses and the New Hampshire primary turned to a steadier and more experienced candidate, Vietnam war medal winner and five-term senator from Massachusetts John F. Kerry. Senator Kerry overwhelmed Senator John Edwards of North Carolina—his major rival after Dean's collapse—in subsequent primaries and wrapped up the nomination many months before the Democratic convention in July. For his running-mate, Kerry opted for geographic balance by choosing Edwards, who had also emerged as an effective speaker during the primary campaigns.

The selection of the solid but uninspiring Kerry, secured challenger charisma Key 13 for the party in power. This left the Republicans with a deficit of just four Keys: long-term economy Key 6, policy change Key 7, foreign/military failure Key 10, and incumbent charisma Key 12. With a two-Key cushion, the administration could even withstand another setback such as the improbable loss of the scandal Key and still hold enough Keys for victory in the fall. As in every election since

1864, however, no Keys turned during the period from the nominating convention through Election Day.

By conventional measures, challenger Kerry performed well in the campaign. According to most polls he won each of the three supposedly crucial presidential debates, although his advantage in the second debate fell within the margin of error. Yet, ignoring the verdict of the Keys, Kerry and his advisers made the strategic error of thinking they could back into the White House against an unpopular president by running a competent, mistake-free campaign—shades of Mike Dukakis in 1988. Thus, despite outside suggestions to the contrary, the Kerry campaign failed to depart from politics as usual with creative efforts to turn back the tide of history that pushed against his election. Predictably, the Democratic effort failed. In the highest turnout election in a generation, Bush won with 50.7 percent of the popular vote and 286 Electoral College votes to 48.3 percent and 251 for Kerry. Bush became the first presidential candidate since his father in 1988 to secure a majority of the national popular vote. Although Bush's Electoral College victory depended on winning the swing state of Ohio, the outcome there was not close, as Bush prevailed by 119,000 votes. Allegations of electoral irregularities in Ohio lacked the substance of the charges made against Florida officials in 2000.

Bush's victory advanced Republican control of the Senate, expanding the GOP's majority from 51 to 55 seats. The party only picked up three House seats, with five gained in Texas through an unprecedented redrawing of previously established congressional district lines. Still, the minimum Republican net gains nationwide placed mandate Key 1 in jeopardy for 2008.

Chapter 10

The Winds of Political Change: 2008

2008: The Bush Dynasty Ends
Incumbent-party nominee: John McCain (Republican)
Challenging-party nominee: Barack Obama (Democrat)
Negative keys: 9
Result: Obama, 52.9%; McCain, 45.7%

Key:	1	2	3	4	5	6	7	8	9	10	11	12	13
Call:	X	0	X	0	X	X	X	0	0	X	X	X	X

The winds of political change began blowing through the nation soon after George W. Bush took his oath of office for a second term. In a paper delivered in June 2005 and published in early 2006, I noted, "Already the Keys are lining up for 2008, demonstrating surprisingly bright prospects for Democrats to recapture the White House." Well before Election Day, additional keys fell into place, reinforcing the original forecast of a Democratic victory in 2008 and reversing the Republican Party's eight-year hold on the White House. Even the unprecedented nomination of an African-American presidential candidate by the Democratic Party did not shake the verdict of the Keys. With nine discrepant keys lined up against them, the Republicans clearly had the burden of history against them in 2008. The incumbent party's problems included a sour economy at home and disappointing events abroad.[1]

President Bush continued to build a version of conservative big government during his second term. The president continued the trend of substantially increasing government spending. During Bush's eight years in office federal spending as a percentage of Gross Domestic Product rose from 18.2 percent to 20.7 percent, compared to a substantial net decline during President Bill Clinton's two terms. In late 2005, the administration confirmed that the president authorized the National Security Agency to wiretap Americans without warrants, bypassing requirements of the Foreign Intelligence Surveillance Act of 1978. In July 2005, the administration won passage of an energy bill that subsidized big energy companies. Members of Congress, both Republicans and Democrats, seized their opportunities to benefit from big government through the record $286 billion transportation bill of 2005 that earmarked more than six thousand special projects for nearly every member's state or district. The administration gained a renewed Patriot Act and the Military Commissions Act of 2006 that gave the executive authority to define persons, including U. S. citizens as "unlawful enemy combatants" who could potentially be detained indefinitely. Aliens, including legal residents of the U. S., tried by military tribunals would be denied protections of the Geneva Convention against torture, habeas corpus rights to challenge their imprisonment, and constitutional safeguards against the use of coerced and secret testimony. The Act sought to block the Courts from reviewing its procedures, with the exception of verdicts rendered by military tribunals.

In the midst of these controversies, in March 2005, President Bush and Republican Congressional leader Tom DeLay pushed Congress to intervene in the case of Terri Schiavo, a brain-damaged patient in Florida who had existed in a vegetative state for fifteen years. State courts had sanctioned a decision by Schiavo's husband to remove her feeding tube and stop prolonging her life, but right-to-life conservatives had made her plight a national issue. This federal intrusion into a state and family matter contradicted many of conservatism's self-professed principles, including judicial restraint, the sanctity of the family, the sacred bond between husband and wife, private decision-making, and deference to states and localities. Prominent conservatives criticized the intervention and three-quarters of Americans registered their disapproval in opinion polls. The conservative movement seemed to be fragmenting in full public view. In late August 2005, Hurricane Katrina struck New Orleans with devastating effect in late August 2005. The administration's failed response to this natural disaster seemed to demonstrate a lack of competency, caring, and strong leadership at the top.

Still, the war in Iraq weighed most heavily on President Bush and his party. By the midterm election year of 2006, Iraq appeared to be descending into civil war and a leaked National Intelligence Estimate concluded, "The Iraq war has made the overall terrorism problem worse." The American death toll approached 3,000 on election eve,

Iraq deaths numbered in the scores to hundreds of thousands, and America lost world esteem. A consensus of polls released in early November showed that Bush's approval ratings had fallen below forty percent and that only a third of Americans approved his handling of the Iraq war. Democrats cut in half the Republicans fund-raising lead of 2002 and won control over Congress by picking up 6 Senate and 31 House seats, thereby forfeiting mandate Key 1 for the incumbent Republicans.

In 2007, Bush took a dramatic gamble on improving the situation in Iraq by ordering a "surge" of some 28,000 additional American troops. The surge worked in improving conditions on the ground in Iraq, including a significant decline in American deaths. The surge did not reverse the public's negative view of the war. According to an analysis by Gary C. Jacobson of the post-election American National Election Study, consistent supporters of the war in Iraq comprised 25 percent of the electorate, consistent opponents 54 percent, and those with mixed opinions 21 percent. Most Americans at the time of the election still supported the war in Afghanistan, but were unhappy with Bush's handling of the war. Given the long-term public opposition to the war in Iraq, and no foreign or military triumphs elsewhere, the incumbent Republicans lost both the foreign/military failure Key 10 and the foreign/military success Key 11.[2]

At home, the policy initiatives of the Bush administration through the midterm contests largely extended programs of the first term. With the Democrats controlling Congress for Bush's last two years in office, his administration achieved no major breakthroughs on Republican priorities, resulting in the loss of policy change Key 7. A severe economic recession began in the United States at the end of 2007, which quickly spread worldwide. Inflated commodity prices and the bursting of a global speculative bubble in real estate and equities contributed to the sharp economic decline. Real per-capita Gross Domestic Product declined in the both the third and fourth quarters of 2008. The fall of Lehman Brothers, the fourth largest investment house in the United States, on September 15, 2008—the largest bankruptcy in U. S. history, led to a financial panic.

Economists and political leaders feared that other major financial institutions could collapse, perhaps plunging America and the world into another Great Depression. To avert a potential economic meltdown, the Bush administration and congressional Democrats negotiated proposals to rescue the financial system, at least short term. Still, the economic crisis took a toll on the public standing of the already unpopular President Bush. In October 2008, his mean approval rating crashed to a record low for presidents of 24 percent in the polls. The election year recession cost the incumbent Republicans short-term economy 5 and lagging growth cost it long-term economy Key 6.

Charges of scandal over the recent firing of seven United States Attorneys, allegedly for political reasons, struck the Bush administration in early 2007. Allegations broadened to include improper political influence on decisions at the United States Department of Justice. After a miserable performance in congressional hearings, Attorney General Alberto Gonzalez resigned in August 2007. Neither scandal directly implicated President Bush, and he narrowly retained scandal Key 9. The lack of major social disturbances during Bush's second term also kept social unrest key 8 in line for the GOP.

The Republican nomination campaign for 2008 began with a host of candidates, but no clear frontrunner. Each of the four leading contenders had significant handicaps. George Romney was a superb businessman with a mastery of economic issues. Still, he had been a moderate governor of Massachusetts who had signed into law a bill for mandatory health care coverage that most Republicans opposed. Many within the GOP's Protestant evangelical base also hesitated for vote for a Mormon, a member of the Church of Latter Day Saints. Rudy Giuliani, the former mayor of New York City, had become something of a national hero in the wake of the 9/11 attacks on the World Trade Center. However, he had been twice divorced and had liberal positions on social issues, not good calling cards for the conservative Republican primary electorate. Mike Huckabee, the former governor of Arkansas appealed to Republican voters on social issues, but lacked a firm grasp of economics or foreign affairs. Senator John McClain was a long-time officeholder and the only contender with previous national campaign experience. Yet he was seventy-two years old and lacked the charisma that he had displayed when almost defeating George W. Bush for the Republican presidential nomination in 2000.

It appeared that the GOP would undergo a major nomination contest and forfeit contest Key 2. However, it did not work out that way. Mike Huckabee gained some momentum when he won the Iowa caucuses. However, John McCain repeated his triumph of 2000 in the New Hampshire primaries. Giuliani faded as he failed to win any of the early primaries. McCain then gained an insurmountable edge when he won most of the primaries against Romney and Huckabee on Super Tuesday, February 5, 2008. Romney dropped out of the race on February 14 and McCain then swept the great majority of the remaining primaries against Huckabee, who exited the race on March 14. McCain entered the GOP Convention with far more than the two-thirds of the delegate votes needed to avoid the loss of contest Key 2. However, McCain's lack of charisma cost the White House party incumbent charisma/hero Key 12. Although many Americans admired his service during the Vietnam War, including his imprisonment by the North Vietnamese for five and a half years, he had not led the nation through war like Ulysses S. Grant or Dwight D. Eisenhower.

McCain shocked the nation when he named the nearly unknown governor of Alaska, Sarah Palin, as his running mate. Palin gave a jolt of momentum to the ticket with a stirring convention speech. However, she quickly became an embarrassment to McCain when she failed to demonstrate the basic knowledge and sophistication that Americans expect of a vice president who would be just a heartbeat away from the presidency. A CNN/Opinion Research Corporation Poll taken a few days before the election found that 63 percent of respondents did not believe that Palin had "the personality and leadership qualities a president should have."

Among Democrats, the race quickly boiled down to a heavyweight fight between former first lady and New York Senator Hillary Clinton and Senator Barack Obama of Illinois. Regardless of the outcome, the Democrats would choose a path-breaking candidate, either the first woman or the first African-American nominated on a major-party ticket. Both Clinton and Obama scored important primary victories. However, Clinton made a major strategic blunder by failing to contest strongly the states selecting delegates by caucuses rather than primary elections. Obama's significant edge in the caucus states gave him a small but insurmountable lead in the delegate count. On Saturday June 7, after an unusually protracted nomination struggle, Clinton endorsed Obama. The Democratic nominee resisted calls to put Clinton on his ticket, and instead choose for his running mate, veteran Delaware Senator Joe Biden, who had weakly contested for the presidential nomination. Biden proved to be rather gaffe prone during the campaign, but the great majority of voters believed that he was qualified to assume the presidency.

The selection by Democrats of an African-American nominee introduced a new element into a presidential campaign. However, as I wrote in the pre-2008 edition of this book, "The Keys, however, are a robust system that has endured through vast changes in the electorate, the economy, the society, and the technology of elections. It is unlikely that any of these contingencies [the nomination of a woman or an African-American] will alter the negative verdict on the party in power."[3]

In 2008, for the first time in the history of the United States two sitting Senators competed for the presidency. It was also the first time since 1952 that neither a sitting president nor vice president was running for the presidency. Obama emerged as a charismatic campaigner in both the primary and general election contests, especially after a brilliant March 18, 2008 speech on race relations in America defused criticism of his association with radical black pastor Reverend Jeremiah Wright. Thus, the incumbent Republicans lost challenger charisma/hero Key 13. Although McCain gained a significant, but short-lived bounce in the polls after the Republican Convention, Obama otherwise led consistently in virtually all the pre-election polls. Obama won all three presidential debates, according to the polls, and cooperated with the Bush administration in forging a response to the economic crisis of September 2008. McCain's response, in contrast, appeared erratic and uninformed. Obama won a convincing victory on Election Day, with 53.7 percent of the two-party popular vote and 68 percent of the Electoral College vote. He made inroads into the previously solid Republican South, winning the states of Virginia, Florida, and North Carolina. Al Gore in 2000 and John Kerry in 2004 had won not a single southern state between them. Obama's victory had coattails, the Democrats picked up 8 Senate seats and 21 in the House, strengthening their hold on Congress.

Chapter 11

Stability in the White House: Forecast for 2012

2012: Obama Emdures
Incumbent-party nominee: Presumptive: Barack Obama (Democrat)
Challenging-party nominee: Unknown (Republican)
Predicted negative keys: 3–4
Predicted result: Incumbent party victory

Key:	1	2	3	4	5	6	7	8	9	10	11	12	13
Call:	X	0	0	0	?	X	0	0	0	0	0	0	X

The 2008 contest was the seventh consecutive election in which the Keys to the White House correctly forecast the popular-vote outcome of an American presidential election, beating odds of more than a hundred to one against such consistently accurate results. No other prediction system has matched this record. In recent years, the Keys to the White has House gained new prominence among professional forecasters. I twice keynoted the International Symposium on Forecasting, and published several articles on the Keys in *Foresight: The International Journal of Applied Forecasting*, an article in *The International Journal of Forecasting* and one in the *International Journal Of Information Systems & Social Change*.[1]

After his convincing election victory in 2008, Obama's supporters had high expectations of America's first African-American president and arguably the first liberal Democratic president since Lyndon Johnson. They believed that he had the potential to become a transformational president on the model of Franklin Delano Roosevelt. Under their most optimistic scenario, Obama would end the era of conservative politics that had begun with the election of Ronald Reagan. He would re-

store the Democrats as the dominant political party in the United States
and enact a roster of progressive reforms. The first three and a half
years of Obama's presidency did not work out as his backers had hoped.
Nonetheless, Obama now has enough favorable Keys to win reelection
in 2012, no matter whom the Republicans nominate as his opponent.
Only major, unlikely setbacks in the year prior to the election could
derail Obama's journey to a second term in office.

Just over a year into Obama's presidency, the Keys already indicated
his positive prospects for reelection. In the May 2010 edition of the
journal *Foresight*, I wrote, "The early verdict of the Keys is that President Barack Obama will secure re-election in 2012, regardless of the
identity of the Republican nominee." Although Obama has had a most
eventful presidency, nothing has happened since the spring of 2010 to
alter the initial verdict of the Keys.[2]

The first four keys—the political keys—clearly indicate the positive
reelection prospects for Obama. In 2010, Obama's Democratic Party
suffered midterm losses of historic dimensions. The Democrats barely
retained their Senate majority, losing eight seats. The party, however,
decisively lost control of the U. S. House of Representatives, dropping
63 seats, including 52 held by incumbents. The spring 2010 forecast
already anticipated that Democratic losses in the 2010 House elections
would topple mandate Key 1. The remaining three political keys all still
seem solidly in line for the party holding the White House. No prominent Democrat is likely to challenge Obama for the 2012 nomination,
securing contest Key 2 for the incumbent party. Obama, of course, is
the sitting president, which locks in incumbency Key 3 for the Democrats. No third party is on the horizon with prospects of winning at least
5 percent of the popular vote, which gains third party Key 4 for the
Democrats. The White House party can with confidence count on winning three of the four political keys.

The Obama presidency began during a deep recession, but with high
and approval ratings for the path-breaking African-American president.
The president achieved some notable accomplishments during his first
six months in office and consistently sustained approval ratings above
60 percent, according to the Gallup Poll. In February 2009, Obama
steered through Congress an economic stimulus package worth some
$787 billion, the largest in the history of the United States. Other early
domestic initiatives included executive orders that allowed states to
raise emission standards above national benchmarks, lifting prior restriction on stem cell research; and legislation that facilitates lawsuits
by women challenging discrimination in pay and expands coverage

under the children's health care program from 7 million to 11 million children. He also successfully backed credit card reform laws, and legislation to help borrowers avoid the foreclosure of their homes.

In foreign affairs, Obama promised to shift from what he saw as George W. Bush's unilateral, military-oriented approach to multilateral, diplomatically based policies. A major goal of his new approach was to improve America's tarnished image in the world. He ordered federal officials to close the controversial prison at Guantanamo Bay in Cuba and to review America's detention and interrogation policies. He also prohibited the use of torture as an interrogation technique. He announced a plan to end America's combat role in Iraq, to begin negotiating a new treaty with Russian for reducing strategic nuclear arms, and to limit the proliferation of nuclear weapons. However, Obama disappointed his liberal base by escalating the war in Afghanistan, which America had been waging since 2001. He also seemed to downplay issues of human rights and the promotion of democracy abroad. However, Obama eventually achieved a major success in foreign policy with the commando raid by Navy SEALS that killed Osama Bin Laden in early May 2011, without any American casualties. Although the elimination of Bin Laden produced only a temporary bump in Obama's approval rating, it undoubtedly helped his rating from collapsing into heavily negative territory as Americans continued their pessimism about the economy.

Obama's presidency first ran into difficulty at home during the second six months of his first year. Obama's most serious problem was the sour economy. Despite optimistic forecasts by the Congressional Budget Office and the Council of Economic Advisors that the stimulus package would save jobs and promote growth, the American unemployment rate soared from about 8 percent when Obama took office to 10 percent in the fall of 2009. This was only the second time since the Great Depression that unemployment in America had reached double digits. Federal legislation had failed to stem the foreclosure crisis and housing prices continued to fall across the nation.

Other problems afflicted the Obama administration as well. The president had not yet fulfilled his pledge to close the prison at Guantanamo Bay. An administration-backed bill to control greenhouse gas emissions through a cap and trade program similar to plan adopted by the European Union passed the House of Representatives on June 26, 2009, but stalled in the Senate. Most controversial was Obama's plan for comprehensive health care reform designed to cover most of the nearly 50 million Americans lacking medical insurance. Rather than defining and selling health care reform to the American people, Obama largely deferred to lawmakers in Congress. As a result, opponents of the bill leaped into the breach with their own construction of the legislation. Critics captured public attention by charging, for example, the proposed legislation included "death panels" that would ration health care, in effect deciding who would live and who would die. They also charged that the bill amounted to a federal takeover of the health care industry, cost hundreds of billions of dollars, and killed jobs by imposing heavy costs on business. In January 2010, a Gallup Poll found that only 37 percent of Americans approved the way in which President Obama was handling the health care issue.

Two other indicators also documented the diminished standing of the Obama administration at the beginning of his second year in office. The Gallup Poll for January 2010 found that the president's approval rating had slipped to 50 percent, an 18-point descent in just one year. In a special U. S. Senate election in January, Republican Scott Brown stunningly captured the seat previously held by the late Ted Kennedy, the Senate's liberal icon. A new grassroots uprising dubbed the "Tea Party" also energized the Republican Party and the conservative movement in the United States.

President Obama proved his resiliency by achieving two major legislative triumphs in 2010, despite approval numbers that remained generally below the 50 percent mark. In July, Congress passed regulations designed to avoid the financial mess that scuttled the economy in 2008. More significantly, however, Congress enacted a version of Obama's plan for comprehensive health care reform in March. Among many other provisions, the bill would expand coverage to most of those currently uninsured. It increased Medicaid coverage for the poor. It would eventually prohibit insurance companies from denying coverage to people with preexisting conditions and allow children to stay on their parent's insurance plans until age 26. By 2014, people must have adequate insurance coverage or else pay a fine.

The passage of this health care bill was an historic achievement for President Obama, which had eluded presidents since Theodore Roosevelt. It was sufficient to secure policy change Key 7 for the Democratic Party in 2012. However, the bill's passage did not improve Obama's standing with the American people. Although responses varied considerably according to the wording of questions, most polls taken in the summer and fall of 2010 showed that a plurality majority of Americans disapproved of the health care bill, which gave Republicans a powerful issue for the midterm elections. The president also had dismal ratings on his handling of the economy. Although the public generally approved of his handling of foreign policy, domestic issues triumphed. On the eve of the midterms, the Gallup Poll pegged Obama's approval rating at just 43 percent.

Although the Republicans trounced Obama's Democrats in the midterm elections, perhaps never before in the history of the United States has such a sweeping victory by one political party elicited so little joy and such minimal expectations. The American voters rejected the leadership of the Democratic Party that controlled the presidency and both houses of Congress. However, the voters did not deliver a mandate to the Republican Party or its leaders. Exit polls showed that just over half of all voters gave negative grades to both the Republican and the Democratic parties.

The elections only cost the incumbent party, one key, mandate key 1. Three times since World War II, a first-term president has seen his party lose control of not just one, but both houses of Congress: Democrat Harry Truman in 1946, Republican Dwight Eisenhower in 1954 and Democratic Bill Clinton in 1994. All three won election to a second term in office.

President Obama recovered quickly from his midterm setback. Lame duck sessions of Congress usually are limited to posing and posturing. The lame duck session that following the 2010 elections, however, was remarkably productive. Democrats and Republicans forged a compromise on extending both tax cuts and unemployment benefits. The Senate ratified the START treaty with the Russians. Congress repealed the ban on gays serving in the military and enacted a new food safety law.

Relations between the President and Congress deteriorated in January 2011, after Republicans took control of the House and seated seven new senators. The House leadership, prompted by Tea Party activists sought to repeal or cripple the new health care law, reign in the Environmental Protection Agency, and cut the funding such left-oriented groups as Planned Parenthood. Although these initiatives had little chance of enactment, they tied up business in Congress, despite a last-minute agreement to avert a government shutdown in 2011.

The conflict between the president and Republicans in Congress was on open display in the imbroglio over raising the debt ceiling in the summer of 2011. In seeking a deal with House Republicans over deficit-reduction plans as part of a vote to raise the debt ceiling, the president and Democrats in Congress pushed for a package of spending cuts and revenue enhancements. Conservatives in the House refused to agree to any tax increases or the closing of tax loopholes for corporations or wealthy Americans. Liberal Democrats balked at considering any cuts in the major entitlement programs of Medicare and Social Security.

The final deal, reached on July 31, 2011, satisfied neither side. It postponed another battle over the national debt ceiling until after the 2012 elections. The deal will supposedly reduce the deficit by $917 through 10-year spending reductions. Most of the cuts, however, are back-loaded into the last five years and may never be realized. A special congressional panel is mandated to find another $1.2 trillion to $1.5 trillion in savings over decade, through some unspecified combination of budget cuts and increases in revenue. If the panel fails in its task, automatic budget cuts are supposed to kick in, equally divided between defense and discretionary domestic programs. Still, the equal partisan composition of the panel will make it difficult to reach agreement. Overall, the deal did little to bring the nation's finances into order or meet other pressing needs. In its aftermath, Standard and Poor's downgraded America's AAA credit rating for the first time in history. The economy remains in peril going into the election year, which topples long-term economy Key 6 and threatens the possible loss of short-term economy key 5.

A populist revolt that spread across nations in the Middle East in early 2011 posed significant challenges for the Obama administration. After exercising restraint in the wake of uprisings against authoritarian regimes in Tunisia, Egypt, and other nations, Obama intervened in Libya in March 2011. In conjunction with NATO allies, but without consulting Congress, Obama deployed American air power to limit the killing of dissidents and to help remove the dictator Muammar Khadaffi from power.

The Libya incursion provoked criticism that crossed partisan and ideological lines. From the left, Democratic Representative Dennis Kucinich of Ohio said, "The war in Libya is one of a series of dangerous missteps by U.S. administrations in a march of folly toward economic, diplomatic and spiritual disaster." From the right, former Republican Speaker of the U. S. House Newt Gingrich said that Obama had relied on a misguided standard of "humanitarian intervention" and America's military intervention in Libya was "nonsense" and a "mess." Ironically, before Obama had intervened in Libya, Gingrich had called for America to act, saying, "All we have to say is that we think that slaughtering your own citizens is unacceptable and that we're intervening." Other conservative critics took an opposite stance, charging that Obama failed to act promptly or decisively in Libya. "It's too little too late," said conservative talk show host Sean Hannity. "We telegraph no boots on the ground. That means we are not committed to victory.'' The American people, however, cautiously backed Obama's policy, if the intervention remained limited.[3]

In October 2011, the intervention helped rebels topple the Khadaffi regime, despite the uncertain circumstances of the dictator's death. At about the same time the president announced the withdrawal of American troops from Iraq. The elimination of Bin Laden and Khadaffi secured foreign/military success key 11, while the president narrowly retains foreign/military failure Key 10 despite the continuation of the generally unpopular war in Afghanistan. Two other keys, however, lined up solidly for the White House party. The lack of significant social upheaval comparable to the 1960s, secures social unrest Key 8 and the lack of a major scandal touching on the presidency locks in scandal key 9.

The results of the Republican Party nomination contest are highly uncertain. Early polls show a wide-open race, with all potential candidates scoring below 30 percent among Republicans. Former governor Mitt Romney of Massachusetts has consistently maintained a position at or near the top of the polls, while several other candidates have challenged his front-running status. A long list of secondary candidates trails. The GOP might see a replay of the 1964 nomination contest that pitted a northeastern moderate, Governor Nelson Rockefeller of New York against a southwestern conservative, Senator Barry Goldwater of Arizona. None of the potential challengers to Barack Obama has the broad star power needed to topple challenger charisma/hero Key 12, which is in line for the party in power. In the most difficult call for 2012, Barack Obama as of August 2011 does not secure the incumbent charisma/hero Key 12. Much of the charisma emerged during the 2008 campaign has been lost during a difficult and for many observers a presidency that failed to realize its expectations.

Thus, only three to four keys have fallen or are likely to fall against the party holding the White House in 2012. These include mandate Key 1, short-term economy key 5 (a question mark), long-term economy Key 6, and incumbent charisma/hero Key 12. Obama thus has a one to two key cushion. Depending on the state of the election year economy, one or two additional keys could topple and he still would be a predicted winner for 2012.

Even further major setbacks in the economy at home and events abroad are unlikely to turn enough keys against the incumbent Democrats to predict their defeat in 2012. On the negative side for President Obama, the economy could slide into recession again during the election year (turning Key 5 from a question mark to a negative) or he could face a scandal or a disaster in Libya. It would be necessary, however, for all of these events to occur to threaten Obama's reelection. Obama could also conceivably regain his tarnished charisma. It is a close call now on charisma, but in the interest of caution, I have not yet turned the Key for Obama. Keys do not readily change; nothing has occurred to alter my initial early 2010 analysis, predicting Obama's reelection.

Chapter 12

Lessons of the Keys: Toward a New Presidential Politics

.

The Keys that anticipate the outcome of the popular vote in every election since 1860 close the chasm opened by conventional political commentary between the selection of a president and the governing of the country. Horse race commentary purports to tell us who is surging ahead or falling behind in a campaign. The record of the incumbent administration in governing America becomes little more than a backdrop for the real action of debates, speeches, ads, rallies, events, endorsements, and so on. The Keys, however, show that what counts in presidential elections is governing, as measured by the consequential events of a presidential term, not packaging, image-making, or campaigning. Effective governing keeps incumbent parties in office and renders conventional campaigning by challengers futile.

This relationship between governing and politics has held true across nearly 150 years of American history and vast changes in our economy, society, and politics: suffrage for women and blacks; new immigrants from Eastern Europe, Asia, and Latin America; the rise of the corporation; and the advent of polling, television, and the Internet. The same thirteen Keys that diagnosed the winner in 1860 predicted the outcome in 2004, according to the logic followed by a pragmatic electorate that considers not just the economy, but such vital matters as foreign policy successes and failures, policy change, social unrest, and scandal. Throughout this period of our history, the presidency has been up for grabs each four years; no party has an enduring hold on the White House. Neither liberal nor conservative ideology is permanently excluded from power and "centrist" ideology is no advantage in presidential politics. Compare, for example, the political success of the staunchly conservative George W. Bush with the failure of his more centrist father.

The question sometimes arises, however, whether simply knowing the Keys presents the temptation to try to manipulate them. It might seem, for example, that the challenging party's best strategy is to obstruct an administration's key initiatives in order to block policy change and triumphs in foreign policy. But such a strategy carries heavy political risks. Obstructing popular measures, particularly those that appear to be in the national interest, clearly could create a backlash, hurting the re-election prospects of opposition legislators and increasing chances that the executive party will secure the mandate Key, thereby improving its prospects for legislative success. Administrations already manage what they can—doing their best to stimulate the election-year economy, effect policy change, and realize achievements abroad, for example. But the party in power is judged according to its genuine successes and failures—a record that cannot be manufactured or dispelled by either party.

By explaining how elections really work, the Keys do suggest practical lessons for parties and their candidates, as well as for the public. The major lesson is that we do not have to settle for presidential politics as usual. Certainly today's shallow, sound-bite driven politics do not benefit the parties, the candidates, or the country. In July 2004, for example, Keilis-Borok and I warned Democratic nominee Kerry that given the lineup of the Keys against him, he had "a choice between following the usual meaningless routine in the hope that setbacks to the administration and the country will elect him in November or take a chance on running a new kind of daring, innovative, and programmatic campaign. With the right choice, Kerry can achieve an historical breakthrough that would establish the basis for a principled choice of our national leader and a grassroots mobilization on issues that matter to America's future." Kerry made the wrong choice of sticking with conventional advisers and strategies and suffered the same fate as Michael Dukakis in 1988, becoming a derided losing candidate. Presidential politics, the Keys teach us, can be different.[1]

If campaigns have always been with us, they have not always been what they are today, and they do not have to be so in the future. Not just campaigns, but the practice of presidential politics throughout the course of a term can be changed without risk to the parties, the candidates, or the public interest—and to the advantage of all.

Fire the hucksters. The only people who benefit from the way presidential campaigns are currently conducted are the political consultants, pollsters, advertising and media strategists, and others who make their livings conducting them. Because the public is not duped about the factors critical to elections, efforts at spin control, media manipulation, and measuring every purported blip in public sentiment are largely wasted, both throughout the term and in the fall campaign. Political hucksters and hype artists have always been around, but they have never been so highly regarded or richly rewarded as they are today—and they have never made a difference in the outcome of an election, except to discourage candidates from embracing new ideas and bold initiatives. Candidates should fire the hucksters, tear up their scripts, and speak directly from the heart to the American people, articulating clearly and forthrightly their ideas for governing the country. Al Gore said in 2001—perhaps a year too late—that what he had learned from the 2000 election was the need to "speak from the heart and let the chips fall where they may."[2]

Concentrate on substance. From a strictly pragmatic perspective, an administration's time and talents are best devoted to dealing with the exigencies of government and formulating, enacting, and implementing new policies. This is not to say that presidents don't have to "sell" their ideas, at least to the Congress and, if necessary, to the public as well. But salesmanship alone is not enough; if it is to help an administration secure the Keys that turn elections it must be tied to a driving idea, a real accomplishment, or a perceived need. Bill Clinton, for all the magic of his rhetoric, could not talk his way into winning the policy change Key for Democrats either in 1996 or in 2000. Likewise, challenging candidates regardless of where they stand on the Keys, have an incentive to focus on the substance of issues and build grassroots support—either for governing or developing an effective opposition during the next four years.

Don't play it safe. Political leaders have a much freer hand both in proposing ideas and in governing America than is generally thought. Modern politics is often directed at the lowest common denominator because politicians worry that confronting hard issues or proposing new ideas risks antagonizing some interest group supposedly needed for a winning coalition. But coalition politics does not work in presidential elections. Rather, the Keys demonstrate that elections turn on enduring, across-the-board factors that transcend demographic, ideological, class, and other differences. Freed from the dictates of coalition-building, candidates of both the executive and opposition parties are free to tackle difficult issues and craft serious proposals in the midst of a campaign.

Don't hide from ideology. Not only are parties and presidential candidates not punished for their philosophies, but ideology can be the driving force behind the initiatives that contribute to the reelection of an executive party. In 1980, Ronald Reagan presented a bold conservative message—government is the problem, not the solution—that many analysts warned was too narrowly pitched to win over the electorate. This message did not produce Reagan's landslide victory—the dismal record of the Carter administration did that—but it did the next best thing: It enabled Reagan to enter the White House with a powerful mandate for setting government on a new course.

Take the high road. In 1988, George Bush should have followed Reagan's example. With no risk of losing the election, he had no reason to attack his opponent—a useless tactic in any event—and plenty of reason for taking the high road to the White House. By setting out a substantive agenda of his own—not repudiating Reaganism but proposing new initiatives for dealing with the problems of the 1990s—he could have won a mandate for policy-making during his own presidency. Having forgone this opportunity in favor of Dukakis-bashing, Bush hurt his ability to perform effectively in the Oval Office, thereby contributing to his defeat in 1992.

Pick the best candidate available for the number-two slot. The usual "ticket-balancing" strategy of choosing a vice-presidential candidate to appeal to a particular region, state, or demographic group adds nothing to a party's prospects for electoral success. The last two Democratic presidential candidates from a northern state, Dukakis in 1988 and Kerry in 2004—both from Massachusetts—chose southern running mates to no political avail. Each Democrat lost the home state of their number two pick and every other southern state as well. The best strategy is to choose the party's ablest available leader for the number-two slot. Thus, if the vice president were to succeed to the White House the party would increase its chances of securing the political and performance Keys and of capturing the charisma Key in an upcoming campaign. Inadvertently, an executive party actually did this once—in 1900 when the Republicans chose New York Governor Theodore Roosevelt as William McKinley's running mate, primarily to keep the ambitious, progressively oriented governor out of the political fray. The strategy failed—and in failing worked spectacularly for the GOP. After becoming president upon McKinley's death in 1901, the charismatic Roosevelt completed a perfect term (as judged by the Keys), swept to a landslide victory in 1904, and then passed on the presidency to William Howard Taft in 1908.

Get off the merry-go-round. Until the early twentieth century, most presidential candidates did not even personally campaign, leaving the touring and speechmaking to party professionals. (In fact, every nominee who took to the hustings himself prior to 1908—Stephen Douglas, Horace Greeley, James G. Blaine, and William Jennings Bryan—lost the election.) Contemporary candidates are hardly likely to revert to that practice, but the exhausting cross-country schedules and mind-numbing photo opportunities of today's general-election campaigns are pointless—particularly in the age of instant communications. Contrary to the contention that candidates "prove" themselves in the marathon of a campaign, elections are not endurance tests. Without ceasing to campaign entirely, parties can substantially reduce both the frenzy and the exorbitant expense of running for the White House, creating presidential campaigns that are both more humane to the candidates and more sensible to the public.

Campaigning by the Keys

Ideally, general election campaigns should be two things: a continuation of what the parties have been doing throughout the term, and the occasion for developing agendas for the future. The party favored by electoral circumstances has reason only to articulate, both thematically and programmatically, its ideas on what America should be accomplishing in the years to come. This is true even if the favored party already controls the White House; a separate mandate may be required for effecting policy change and, to some extent, for dealing with the exigencies of government in each presidential term. The main focus of the party in power, of course, should be on continuing to govern as effectively as possible in order to prevent the toppling of any additional Keys. This does not mean adopting a defensive, hold-the-line strategy, but rather that the administration should continue the method of governing that put it ahead in the first place and be prepared to deal with challenges as they arise.

An incumbent administration facing prospective defeat according to the Keys has an incentive to change course, to take bold action in an effort to alter circumstances sufficiently to reverse one or more Keys. It could attempt to jump-start a stalled economy (Key 5); initiate a major change in national policy (Key 7); rectify, if possible, a failing foreign or military situation (Key 10); or push for a triumph abroad (Key 11). Achieving such changes would be extremely difficult given the limited time-span and the partisan, highly charged context of a campaign, and failure in any perilous venture could harm both the national interest and the standing of the incumbent party. Although Keys have changed during the fall campaign, they have done so very rarely, and never have they changed enough to reverse a prior verdict. Still, a losing incumbent party stands only to gain by adopting a creative approach to governing during the campaign.

A challenging party faced with a losing situation is even more restricted because it cannot directly affect the political or performance Keys. It should, of course, call attention to failures and scandals, understanding that doing so is unlikely to change public perceptions in a way that would change the call on any Key. Presuming that the verdict of the Keys stays the same during the campaign, the out-party's only hope would be somehow to alter the basis on which the electorate makes its decision, breaking the pattern of electoral history that has prevailed since 1860. Whether this could be done, or how, is impossible to say. What is clear is that the kind of safety-first, "me-too" campaign that challengers so often conduct—not wanting to risk the appearance of being outside the "mainstream"—does not improve the party's chances of gaining the presidency. Keilis-Borok and I suggested (futilely) to Kerry in 2004, for instance, that he "lead a debate on critical neglected issues . . . break precedent and set up a shadow government" and "submit an alternative budget and drafts of international agreements and major legislation." Even if Kerry had still failed to win the election, he would have set himself up as a principled opponent to the Bush administration and positioned himself for another presidential run in 2008.[3]

Any challenger—no matter what the verdict of the Keys—should run as though he is going to win, articulating honestly and forthrightly the policies and programs that the nominee believes should carry the nation through the next four years. This is not a Pollyanna-ish prescription: Keys have turned during campaigns, and though it has never happened in the past, lightning could strike and enough Keys fall to lift a challenger to victory; in a five-Key election, the toppling of a single Key would suffice. In this event, however unlikely, the winning challenger would have established a solid foundation for governing.

An opposition party that hopes to influence electoral circumstances must start well before the campaign. Throughout the term it should exercise its political and legislative skills to maintain or increase its numbers in Congress, thereby denying the executive party mandate Key 1. It should press to achieve bipartisan acknowledgement of administration scandals and failures, recognizing that charges perceived as purely partisan will be lightly regarded by the public; for this reason, conditions that would turn scandal Key 9 and foreign-failure Key 10 against the executive party should be established well before the general-election campaign, when everything is interpreted in partisan terms. The out-party also should press its own agenda both inside and outside of government to expand its intellectual and organizational base, much as conservative Republicans did in the late 1970s, when think tanks such as the Heritage Foundation; books such as Jude Wanniski's supply-side primer, *How the World Really Works*; and journals such as *The Public Interest* and *Commentary* helped pave the way for the Reagan revolution once the Republicans attained the White House. Finally, during the election year itself, the opposition should nominate its most passionate and effective leader in hopes of turning charisma Key 13 against the party in power.

What the out-party need not do is bother with the generally prescribed nostrums for regaining the presidency: improving the technology of campaigning, shifting its policy agenda toward the perceived ideological "center," or nominating candidates that supposedly appeal to voters of a particular region. Such tactics are futile, because they do not influence the fundamental factors upon which elections turn. All such tactics were used without success by the Republican Party during the Roosevelt-Truman years, when the Democrats won five consecutive terms in the White House. During this period the GOP strengthened its national organization, moderated its conservative image, and twice (1944 and 1948) chose as its nominee a centrist governor of New York, Thomas Dewey, who was considered best able to capture the electoral votes of crucial states in the Democrats' northeastern bastion. In 1948 the Republicans even created a "dream ticket" by pairing Dewey with Earl Warren, the popular centrist governor of California, but the party still lost California—and the election.

In the final analysis, neither party has anything to lose by forthrightly advancing its own ideas, by actively trying to lead the public rather than following the polls, and by tying issues together in a unifying theme that goes beyond "I'll do better than he will" to express a compelling and activist vision of the nation's future. At the very least, a new style of campaign would significantly advance the development of policy initiatives that serve the people's interests.

Notes

Introduction

1. Allan J. Lichtman, "The Keys to the White House: Forecast for 2008," *Foresight: The International Journal of Applied Forecasting* 3 (February 2006): 5–9.

2. "Carter to Head Elections Panel," *Washington Post*, 25 March 2005, A11.

3. Lichtman, "The Keys to the White House: A Preliminary Forecast for 2012," *International Journal of Information Systems and Social Change* 1 (January–March 2010).

4. Lichtman, "The Keys to the White House: Forecast for 2008," 5–9; Lichtman, "The Keys to the White House: A Preliminary Forecast for 2012," 31–43.

Chapter 1

1. Lichtman, "How to Bet in '84," *Washingtonian* (April 1982) 147; Lichtman, "President Bill?," *Washingtonian* (October 1992) 45; Allan J. Lichtman and Ken DeCell, *The Thirteen Keys to the Presidency* (Lanham, Md.: Madison Books, 1990), 419.

2. Jack W. Germond and Jules Witcover, *Blue Smoke and Mirrors: How Reagan Won and Why Carter Lost the Election of 1980* (New York: Viking, 1981), 318–19.

3. *Washington Post,* 9 Nov. 1980, 2.

4. The classic statement of party voting is Angus Campbell et al., *The American Voter* (New York: John Wiley, 1960); Morris P. Fiorina, *Retrospective Voting in American National Elections* (New Haven: Yale University Press, 1981) provides an updated and critical viewpoint. Classic works on realignment election theory include V. O. Key, Jr., "A Theory of Critical Elections," *Journal of Politics* 17 (1955): 3–18; and Walter Dean Burnham, *Critical Elections and the Mainsprings of American Politics* (New York: W. W. Norton, 1970). Allan

J. Lichtman, "The End of Realignment Theory? Toward a New Research Program for American Political History," *Historical Methods* 15 (1982): 170–88, offers a critical perspective. See also *The End of Realignment? Interpreting American Electoral Eras,* ed. Byron Shafer (Madison: University of Wisconsin Press, 1991).

5. For examples of the long-running debate on issue voting, see Anthony Downs, *An Economic Theory of Democracy* (New York: Harper and Row, 1957); Philip E. Converse, "The Nature of Belief Systems in Mass Publics," in *Ideology and Discontent,* ed. David E. Apter (London: Free Press, 1964), 202–61; David E. RePass, "Issue Salience and Party Choice," *American Political Science Review* 65 (1971): 389–400; George Rabinowitz and Stuart Elaine MacDonald, "A Directional Theory of Issue Voting," *American Political Science Review* 83 (1989): 93–121; Michael S. Lewis-Beck and Tom W. Rice, *Forecasting Elections* (Washington, D.C.: Congressional Quarterly, 1992), 45–56.

6. George Gallup, Jr., *The Gallup Poll: Public Opinion 1984* (Wilmington: Scholarly Resources, 1985), 234–50; *New York Times,* 17 July 1988, 16; George Gallup, Jr., *The Gallup Poll: Public Opinion 1992* (Wilmington: Scholarly Resources, 1993), 129.

7. This thesis is stated most forcefully in Richard M. Scammon and Ben J. Wattenberg, *The Real Majority* (New York: Coward-McCann, 1970); for a critical view of "centrist" theory, see Rabinowitz and MacDonald, "A Directional Theory."

8. See, for example, William A. Niskanen, "Economic and Fiscal Effects on the Popular Vote for President," Working Paper no. 25, Graduate School of Public Policy, University of California, Berkeley, 1975; Edward R. Tufte, *Political Control of the Economy* (Princeton: Princeton University Press, 1978); Ray C. Fair, "The Effect of Economic Events on Votes for President," *Review of Economics and Statistics* 60 (1978): 159–73, "The Effect of Economic Events on Votes for President: 1980 Results," *Review of Economics and Statistics* 64 (1982): 322–25, and "The Effect of Economic Events on Votes for President: 1984 Update," *Political Behavior* 10 (1988): 168–79; Gregory B. Markus, "The Impact of Personal and National Economic Conditions on the Presidential Vote: A Pooled Cross-sectional Analysis," *American Journal of Political Science* 32 (1988): 137–54; Alan I. Abramowitz, "An Improved Model for Predicting Presidential Election Outcomes," *PS: Political Science and Politics* 34 (1988): 843–47; Robert S. Erickson, "Economic Conditions and the Presidential Vote," *American Political Science Review* 83 (1989): 567–73.

9. Fair, "The Effect of Economic Events," 165.

10. Fair, "The Effect of Economic Events, 1980 Results," 324.

11. Lewis-Beck and Rice, *Forecasting Elections* 91–96; Jay P. Greene, "Forewarned before Forecast: Presidential Election Forecasting and the 1992 Election," *PS: Political Science and Politics* 39 (1993): 17–21.

12. Lawrence R. Klein, "Past, Present, and Possible Future Use of Macroe-

conometric Models and Their Uses," in *Comparative Performance of U.S. Econometric Models,* ed. Klein (New York: Oxford University Press, 1991), 8.

13. Ken DeCell, "A Bush Victory," *Washingtonian,* Sept. 1992, 123–26; Lichtman, "President Bill."

Chapter 2

1. See, for example, Clifford Cobb, Ted Halstead, and Jonathan Rowe, "If the Economy Is Up, Why Is America Down?," *The Atlantic Monthly,* October 1995: 59–78.

2. For statistics on manufacturing production, see U.S. Department of Commerce, *Longterm Economic Growth: 1860–1970* (Washington, D.C.: U.S. Government Printing Office, 1977), 168. Prior to 1960, statistics on per-capita income are obtained from U.S. Department of Commerce, *Historical Statistics of the United States: Colonial Times to 1970* (Washington, D.C.: U.S. Government Printing Office, 1975).

3. For further evidence that the four-year economy correlates with presidential-election results, see Erickson, "Economic Conditions."

Chapter 3

1. William E. Giennap, *The Origins of the Republican Party, 1852–1856* (New York: Oxford University Press, 1987); Michael F. Holt, *The Political Crisis of the 1850s* (New York: Wiley, 1978).

2. Stephen B. Oates, *To Purge This Land with Blood: A Biography of John Brown* (New York: Harper and Row, 1970), esp. 310–12, 320–24, 353–61.

3. Elbert B. Smith, *The Presidency of James Buchanan* (Lawrence: University of Kansas Press, 1975), 98–99; Mark W. Summers, *The Plundering Generation: Corruption and the Crisis of the Union, 1849–1861* (New York: Oxford University Press, 1987), 239–60.

4. Isaac Selley to William E. Chandler, 26 March 1872, William E. Chandler Papers, Box 20, Library of Congress, Washington, D.C.

5. This was not, perhaps, as unjust as it might seem; for several years the Democrats had used violence and fraud to intimidate Blacks and recapture state governments in the South. By 1876, these tactics might have had the cumulative effect of turning several southern states in the Democrats' favor. "A fair election," Hayes claimed on 27 November 1876, "would have given us about forty electoral votes in the South." Keith Ian Polakoff, *The Politics of Inertia: The Election of 1876 and the End of Reconstruction* (Baton Rouge: Louisiana State University Press, 1973), 242.

Chapter 4

1. Vincent P. DeSantis, "Rutherford B. Hayes and the Removal of the Troops and the End of Reconstruction," in *Region, Race, and Reconstruction: Essays in Honor of C. Vann Woodward,* ed. J. Morgan Kousser and James M. McPherson (New York: Oxford University Press, 1982), 417.

2. Michael E. McGerr, *The Decline of Popular Politics: The American North, 1865–1928* (New York: Oxford University Press, 1986), 90–137.

3. William Jennings Bryan, *Speeches of William Jennings Bryan* (New York: Funk & Wagnalls, 1911), 249.

Chapter 5

1. *New York Times,* 9 Nov. 1904, 1.

2. Allan J. Lichtman, *Prejudice and the Old Politics: The Presidential Election of 1928* (Chapel Hill: University of North Carolina Press, 1979), 159–65.

Chapter 6

1. Albert U. Romasco, *The Poverty of Abundance: Hoover, the Nation, the Depression* (New York: Oxford University Press, 1965); Joan Hoff Wilson, *Herbert Hoover: Forgotten Progressive* (Boston: Little, Brown, 1975).

2. Secret polls commissioned by FDR (he was the first president to use modern polling techniques) also showed him to be potentially vulnerable to opposition from the Left: "City Data: Polls," Emil Hurja Papers, Box 69, Franklin D. Roosevelt Presidential Library, Hyde Park, New York.

3. *New York Times,* 10 Sept. 1948, 17.

4. "The Campaign," *Life,* 1 Nov. 1948, 36.

5. George H. Gallup, *The Gallup Poll: Public Opinion, 1935–1971,* Vol. 1 (New York: Random House, 1972), 232.

6. "Wrong Again," *Time,* 10 Nov. 1952, 26.

Chapter 7

1. Theodore H. White, *The Making of the President, 1960* (New York: Mentor, 1967), 393.

2. Kevin P. Phillips, *The Emerging Republican Majority* (New Rochelle, N.Y.: Arlington House, 1969).

Chapter 8

1. *New York Times,* 27 July 1979, 1.
2. Jane Mayer and Doyle McManus, *Landslide: The Unmaking of the President, 1984–88* (Boston: Houghton Mifflin, 1988), 139–57.
3. *Ibid.,* 192.
4. *New York Times,* 23 December 1992, D1.
5. George H. Gallup, *The Gallup Poll: Public Opinion, 1993* (Wilmington: Scholarly Resources, 1994), 209. *Los Angeles Times,* 28 Oct. 1992, 11.

Chapter 9

1. *Bush v. Gore,* 531 US 98 (2000).
2. "President Delivers State of the Union Address," January 2002, http://www.whitehouse.gov.

Chapter 10

1. Allan J. Lichtman, "The Keys to the White House: Forecast for 2008," *Foresight: The International Journal of Applied Forecasting* 3 (Feb. 2006), 5–9.
2. Gary C. Jacobson, "George W. Bush, the Iraq War, and the Election of Barack Obama," *Presidential Studies Quarterly* 40 (June 2010), 217.
3. Allan J. Lichtman, *The Keys to the White House: pre-2008 Edition* (Lanham, MD: Rowman & Littlefied, 2008), 180.

Chapter 11

1. Allan J. Lichtman "The Keys to the White House: Forecast for 2008," *Special Feature, Foresight: The International Journal of Applied Forecasting* 3 (February 2006), 5–9; Lichtman, "The Keys to the White House: Updated Forecast for 2008," *Foresight: The International Journal of Applied Forecasting* 8 (Fall 2007); 36–40; Lichtman, "The Keys to the White House: Forecast for 2012," *Foresight: The International Journal of Applied Forecasting* 18 (Summer 2010), 33–37; Lichtman, "The Keys to the White House: An Index Forecast for 2008," *International Journal Of Forecasting* 4 (April–June 2008), 301–9; Lichtman, "The Keys to the White House: A Preliminary Forecast for 2012" *International Journal Of Information Systems & Social Change* 1 (Jan.–March 2010), 31–43.
2. Lichtman, "The Keys to the White House: Forecast for 2012," *Foresight,* 34.

3. Dennis Kucinich, "Opposing Views: Another Unnecessary War," *USA Today*, 24 March 2011;" Air Strikes in Libya: Questions Back Home," *New York Times,* 21 March 2011, p. 12; "New Gingrich Accused of Flip-Flopping," *St. Petersburg Times*, 24 March 2011; www.foxnews.com/on-air/hannity/transcript/mccain-039we-need-finis h-job039-libya.

Index

About the Author

Allan J. Lichtman received his Ph.D. from Harvard University and is Distinguished Professor of History at The American University in Washington, D.C. He is the author of seven books, including *Prejudice and the Old Politics: The Presidential Election of 1928* and *White Protestant Nation: The Rise of the American Conservative Movement*, which was a finalist for the National Book Critics Circle Award in non-fiction.

Dr. Lichtman has provided political commentary for all major U.S. television and radio networks, the Voice of America, and numerous broadcast companies throughout the world. He has published more than one hundred scholarly and popular articles that have appeared in such journals and newspapers as the *American Historical Review*, *Proceedings of the National Academy of Sciences*, *New Republic*, *Washington Monthly*, *New York Times*, *Washington Post*, *Christian Science Monitor*, and *Los Angeles Times*. He lectures frequently on political issues in the United States and abroad.

Dr. Lichtman has been a Sherman Fairchild Distinguished Visiting Scholar at the California Institute of Technology, an adviser to several political candidates, and a consultant to Vice President Albert Gore. He has been an expert witness or consultant in more than seventy-five federal voting rights and redistricting cases, and he was the recipient of the 1992-93 Scholar/Teacher Award (the university's highest faculty award) at The American University.

3rd Party Showings (20

1912 T Roosevelt 27.4
1992 R Perot   19.0%
1924 R LaFollette 16.6
1968 G Wallace   13.5%